REVISED AND EXPANDED 2ND EDITION

THE COMPLETE & UNAUTHORIZED GUIDE TO

Vintage Barbie Dolls

WITH BARBIE® & SKIPPER® FASHIONS
AND THE WHOLE FAMILY OF BARBIE DOLLS®

Hillary Shilkitus James

Schiffer Publishing Ltd

4880 Lower Valley Road, Atglen, Pennsylvania 19310

Schiffer Books are available at special discounts for bulk purchases for sales promotions or premiums. Special editions, including personalized covers, corporate imprints, and excerpts can be created in large quantities for special needs. For more information contact the publisher:

Published by Schiffer Publishing Ltd.
4880 Lower Valley Road
Atglen, PA 19310
Phone: (610) 593-1777; Fax: (610) 593-2002
E-mail: Info@schifferbooks.com

For the largest selection of fine reference books on this and related subjects, please visit our website at
www.schifferbooks.com
We are always looking for people to write books on new and related subjects. If you have an idea for a book please contact us at the above address.

This book may be purchased from the publisher.
Include $5.00 for shipping.
Please try your bookstore first.
You may write for a free catalog.

In Europe, Schiffer books are distributed by
Bushwood Books
6 Marksbury Ave.
Kew Gardens
Surrey TW9 4JF England
Phone: 44 (0) 20 8392-8585; Fax: 44 (0) 20 8392-9876
E-mail: info@bushwoodbooks.co.uk
Website: www.bushwoodbooks.co.uk
Free postage in the U.K., Europe; air mail at cost.

Contents

Acknowledgments.................................4
Introduction.......................................5
   How the Book is Organized.............5

Part 1: Dolls
Barbie®...8
   Barbie Ponytail...................................8
   Barbie Bubble Cut.............................9
   Barbie Fashion Queen....................10
   Barbie Swirl Ponytail......................11
   Miss Barbie.....................................11
   American Girl Barbie......................11
   Color Magic Barbie........................13
   Standard Barbie.............................14
   Hair Fair Barbie.............................14
   Twist 'n Turn Barbie.......................15
   Talking Barbie................................16
   Dramatic New Living Barbie...........18
   Living Barbie.................................18
   Live Action Barbie.........................18
   Barbie Hair Happenin's...................19
   Barbie with Growin' Pretty Hair.....19
   Busy Barbie...................................20
   Walk Lively Barbie.........................20
   Montgomery Ward
      Commemorative.........................20
   Malibu Barbie................................20
   Quick Curl Barbie.........................21
   Store Display Dressed Box Doll......21
Ken®...23
   Ken...23
   Ken Bendable Leg...........................24
   Talking Ken....................................24
   Live Action Ken.............................24
   Sun Set Malibu Ken........................25
   Busy Ken.......................................25
   Walk Lively Ken.............................25
   Mod Hair Ken................................26
   Store Display Dressed Box
      Ken Dolls..................................26
Midge®..27
   Midge..27

Wig Wardrobe Midge.....................27
Bendable Leg Midge.......................27
Store Display Dressed Box
   Midge Dolls.................................27
Skipper®...28
   Skipper..28
   Skipper Bendable Leg.....................29
   Skipper Twist 'n Turn.....................29
   Dramatic New Living Skipper.........30
   Skipper Re-Issue............................30
   Malibu Skipper..............................31
   Skipper Quick Curl........................31
   Skipper Pose 'n Play......................31
   Growing Up Skipper......................32
   Store Display Dressed Box
      Skipper Dolls.............................32
Allan®...32
   Allan...32
   Store Display Dressed Box
      Allan Doll..................................33
Francie®...33
   Francie..33
   Francie Hair Happenin's..................35
   Francie No Bangs...........................35
   Francie Twist 'n Turn Short Flip.......35
   Francie with Growin' Pretty Hair....36
   Busy Francie..................................36
   Francie Sun Set Malibu...................36
   Francie Quick Curl.........................37
Scooter®...37
   Scooter...37
   Scooter Bendable Legs...................37
   Store Display Dressed Box
      Scooter Doll..............................37
Fluff®..38
Tiff®...38
Ginger®..38
Ricky®...39
Casey®...39
Twiggy®..39
P. J.®...40

P. J...40
Live Action P. J. 40
P. J. Sun Set Malibu.......................41
Stacey...41
Christie®...42
   Christie...42
   Christie Talking..............................42
   Live Action Christie.......................43
   Christie Sun Set Malibu..................43
Brad®...43
Tutti®...44
Todd®...45
Chris®...46
Jamie®..46
Steffie®...46
   Steffie...46
   Steffie Busy Talkin'........................47
   Steffie Busy...................................47
Kelley®..47
   Kelley..47
   Kelley Yellowstone........................48
Julia®..48
   Julia Talking...................................48
   Truly Scrumptuous Talking..............48
   Truly Scrumptuous.........................49
Miss America®....................................49
Buffy & Mrs. Beasley®.........................50
Pretty Pairs®......................................50

Part II: Outfits & Accessories
Barbie Fashions..................................54
   900 Series......................................54
Skipper Fashions.................................132
   Skipper Gift Set.............................154
   Skipper Pak....................................155
   Japanese Skipper............................157
Scooter Gift Set.................................157
Fluff Gift Set......................................157

Index...158

Acknowledgments

This book would not have been possible if it weren't for the help and support of many special friends. These people selflessly welcomed me into their homes and hearts. They let me mess up their dolls, provided me with nourishment, and allowed me to photograph their beloved treasures.

I thank Anthony Alcaide, Susan Anderson of Desperately Seeking Vintage, Sherry Baloun of Gigi's Dolls and Sherry's Teddy Bears, Karen and Mark Bindelglass, Richard Chapman and Glenn Mandeville, Sandi Holder, Lisa and Tony Varuolo.

Introduction

In 1959 a special new doll came on the scene. She was a tall, shapely woman with a beautiful face. A hit among young girls almost from the beginning, over the years Barbie has become the most famous doll ever. The Barbie® doll is still the most collected item in the United States today, and she is loved all over the world, by the young, the old, and everyone in between.

Skipper® was introduced in 1964, and was a success. She had similar clothes as her older sister and you could tell she wanted to be just like her! Some of her fashions, though, were unique to her...she was special after all.

The Barbie doll and her little sister Skipper were created for children to play with, but as these same children grew up, they started to collect these childhood friends that had given them so many hours of joy. This book is intended to give these collectors an idea of what Barbie doll and Skipper dolls, their fashions, and their friends and family are worth in today's marketplace.

How the Book Is Organized

This book is a complete guide to all the vintage Barbie dolls, friends, and family from 1959 to 1972, the vintage years. It contains all the Barbie dolls, friends, and family that were offered during those years.

Organized with the various dolls first, followed by the outfits and accessories that were available for them, each entry includes the name of the item, a stock number, and a date, along with other identifying information.

This is followed by the value of the complete package, giving the Never Removed From Box (NRFB) value and, for the dolls, the Mint/No Box value, and the Average value. For the outfits and accessories a value for the Mint/Complete outfit is given in addition to the NRFB value.

Finally, with each entry, I have provided a detailed list of all the items that originally came in the package, included variations. A value is given for each piece.

Having all these items to make a doll or outfit complete is necessary if the doll is to attain its highest value.

A mint condition doll will be at the top of the value range, and a poor condition doll can sometimes be worth only a fraction of that. This book will give you the prices in today's market for each item, the doll, and fashion. It will assist you in determining how much it will cost to complete an outfit and how much that will add to your collection's value. Sometimes replacing one missing item to make an outfit complete can add as much as 50% to the value of the outfit.

The book has many photographs to illustrate what a mint in-box doll or outfit should look like, so you can see how the value is obtained.

With values, dates, and stock numbers, this guide can also be used to keep track of the many items a collector has and needs. A collector can mark the dolls and outfits along with missing items that are being sought after. The values will help determine what a collector can expect to pay for these items.

I have come to the prices in this guide based on values that I have researched from several areas. I have sold Barbie dolls, bought them, and seen thousands of them at shows around the country. I have searched the prices that these items have sold for at an on-site auction and on eBay and other Internet sites. The current values in this book should be used as a guide only and the prices do vary from country to country and state to state as demand and supply change. The prices will also vary based on condition.

PART I: Dolls

BARBIE PONYTAIL

Barbie #1
Ponytail
Stock # 850
Date 1959

	NRFB	Mint/ No Box	Avg
Blonde	6500-7200	4900-5500	2500-4000
Brunette	7400-8200	5500-6200	3000-4500

	Mint	Avg
#1 TM box	150-200	100-150
box liner	150-200	100-150
#1 TM stand	850-1000	650-850
#1 TM booklet	75-100	50-75
white rimmed sunglasses	15-20	10-15
hoop earrings	25-35	15-25
swimsuit: black & white	50-75	25-50
shoes: #1 black open toe	50-75	25-50

Barbie #2
Ponytail
Stock # 850
Date 1959-1960

	NRFB	Mint/ No Box	Avg
Blonde	6700-7500	4200-5800	3000-4000
Brunette	7900-8600	4400-6000	3000-4000

	Mint	Avg
#2 TM box	150-200	100-150
box liner	150-200	100-150
#2 TM stand	150-200	100-150
#1 TM booklet	75-100	50-75
white rimmed sunglasses	15-20	10-15
hoop earrings	25-35	15-25
swimsuit: black & white	50-75	25-50
shoes: #1 black open toe	50-75	25-50

Barbie #3
Ponytail
Stock # 850
Date 1960

	NRFB	Mint/ No Box	Avg
Blonde	1200-1700	600-800	300-500
Brunette	1300-1900	700-900	350-525

Note: either doll can be found with blue or brown eyeshadow equally

	Mint	Avg
#3 box	150-200	75-150
box liner	150-200	75-150
stand: wire	25-35	15-25
or stand pedestal R	50-75	25-50
booklet in cellophane	20-30	15-20
white rimmed sunglasses	15-20	10-15
hoop earrings	25-35	15-25
or pearl earrings	15-20	10-15
swimsuit: black & white	50-75	25-50
shoes: black open toe	15-20	10-15

#1 Barbie. Brunette.
Courtesy of Sandi Holder

#2 Barbie. Blonde. Never removed from box.
Author's Collection

#3 Barbie. Blonde.
Never removed from box.
Courtesy of Sherry Baloun

Barbie #4
Ponytail
Stock # 850
Date 1960-1961

	NRFB	Mint/ No Box	Avg
Blonde	650-850	300-450	175-275
Brunette	675-900	325-475	200-300

	Mint	Avg
box	100-125	75-100
box liner	75-100	50-75
stand: wire	25-35	15-25
booklet in cellophane	20-30	15-20
white rimmed sunglasses	15-20	10-15
pearl earrings	15-20	10-15
swimsuit: black & white	50-75	25-50
shoes: black open toe	15-20	10-15

#4 Barbie. Blonde. Never removed from box.
Author's Collection

Barbie #5
Ponytail
Stock # 850
Date 1961

	NRFB	Mint/ No Box	Avg
Blonde	600-825	275-350	175-275
Brunette	650-875	285-375	175-275
Redhead	675-900	325-450	250-325

	Mint	Avg
box	75-100	50-75
box liner	75-100	50-75
stand: wire	25-35	15-25
booklet in cellophane	20-30	15-20
white rimmed sunglasses	15-20	10-15
pearl earrings	15-20	10-15
swimsuit: red	20-30	15-20
wrist tag	75-100	50-75
shoes: red open toe	15-20	10-15

Barbie #6
Ponytail
Stock # 850
Date 1962

	NRFB	Mint/ No Box	Avg
Blonde	600-825	275-350	200-275
Brunette	650-875	300-375	225-300
Redhead	675-900	325-450	250-325

	Mint	Avg
box	75-100	50-75
box liner	75-100	50-75
stand: wire	25-35	15-25
booklet in cellophane	15-20	10-15
white rimmed sunglasses	15-20	10-15
pearl earrings	15-20	10-15
swimsuit: red	20-30	15-20
wrist tag	75-100	50-75
shoes: red open toe	15-20	10-15

BARBIE BUBBLE CUT

Barbie
Bubble cut
Stock # 850
Date 1961

	NRFB	Mint/ No Box	Avg
Blonde	350-425	75-150	50-75
Brunette	350-425	75-150	50-75
Redhead (Titian)	350-425	75-150	50-75
Brownette	950-1150	650-950	450-650
White Ginger	425-500	175-225	100-175

#5 Barbie. Blonde.
Never removed from box.
Courtesy of Anthony Alcaide

#5 Barbie. Titian. Never removed
from box, with early box.
Courtesy of Sherry Baloun

Bubble Cut. Titian.
Never removed from box.
Author's Collection

	Mint	Avg
box	75-100	50-75
box liner	75-100	50-75
stand: wire	25-35	15-25
or stand pedestal	50-75	25-50
booklet in cellophane	20-25	15-20
white rimmed sunglasses	15-20	10-15
pearl earrings	15-20	10-15
swimsuit: black & white	50-75	25-50
wrist tag	75-100	50-75
shoes: black open toe	15-20	10-15

Bubble Cut. Brownette. Rare.
Courtesy of Anthony Alcaide

Barbie
Bubble cut
Stock # 850
Date 1962

	NRFB	Mint/ No Box	Avg
Blonde	350-425	75-150	50-75
Brunette	350-425	75-150	50-75
Redhead (Titian)	350-425	75-150	50-75

Note: Carnation Mail-away: NRFB $1350

	Mint	Avg
box	75-100	50-75
box liner	75-100	50-75
stand: wire	25-35	15-25
booklet in cellophane	15-20	10-15
white rimmed sunglasses	15-20	10-15
pearl earrings	15-20	10-15
swimsuit: red	20-30	15-20
wrist tag	75-100	50-75
shoes: red open toe	15-20	10-15

BARBIE FASHION QUEEN

Barbie
Fashion Queen
Stock # 870
Date 1963

	NRFB	Mint/ No Box	Avg
	375-525	150-225	75-100

	Mint	Avg
box	75-100	50-75
stand: wire	25-35	15-25
booklet in cellophane	15-20	10-15
white rimmed sunglasses	15-20	10-15
pearl earrings	15-20	10-15
swimsuit: gold & white	50-75	25-50
turban gold & white	50-75	25-50
blue headband	20-25	15-20
white wig stand	20-25	15-20
wig blonde	15-20	10-15
wig redhead (Titian)	20-25	15-20
wig brunette	15-20	10-15
wrist tag	40-65	25-40
shoes: white open toe	20-25	15-25

Barbie
Fashion Queen
Stock # 871
Date 1963
head only w/ wigs

	NRFB	Mint/ No Box	Avg
	150-225	75-150	50-75

	Mint	Avg
blue headband	20-25	15-20
white wig stand	20-25	15-20
wig blonde	15-20	10-15
wig redhead (Titian)	20-25	15-20
wig brunette	15-20	10-15

Bubble Cut. Blonde. Never removed from box.
Author's Collection

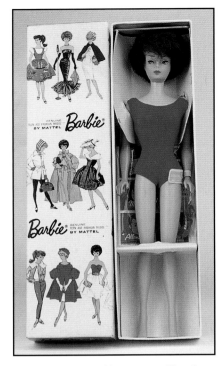

Bubble Cut. Brunette. Never removed from box.
Author's Collection

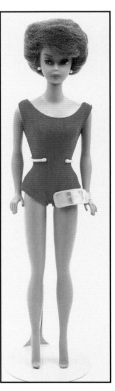

Bubble Cut. Titian. Mint
with wrist tag.
Courtesy of Anthony Alcaide

Bubble Cut. Blonde. Carnation Special Mail-Away off.
Never removed from box. *Author's Collection*

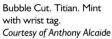

Fashion Queen. Never
removed from box.
Author's Collection

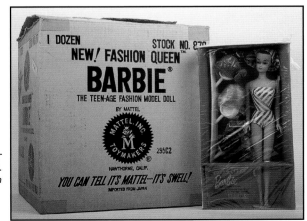

BARBIE SWIRL PONYTAIL

Barbie
Swirl Ponytail
Stock # 850
Date 1964

	NRFB	Mint/ No Box	Avg
Blonde	600-825	275-350	175-275
Brunette	650-875	285-375	175-275
Redhead	675-900	325-450	250-325
Platinum	1200-1500	450-600	225-375

	Mint	Avg
box	75-100	50-75
box liner	75-100	50-75
stand: wire	25-35	15-25
booklet in cellophane	15-20	10-15
white rimmed sunglasses	15-20	10-15
pearl earrings	15-20	10-15
swimsuit: red	20-30	15-20
yellow hair ribbon	35-45	25-35
bobby pin	35-45	25-35
wrist tag	75-100	50-75
shoes: red open toe	15-20	10-15

MISS BARBIE

Barbie
Miss Barbie
Stock # 1060
Date 1964

	NRFB	Mint/ No Box	Avg
Miss Barbie	375-600	200-275	175-275

	Mint	Avg
box	50-75	25-50
stand: wire	25-35	15-25
white wig stand	25-35	15-25

Miss Barbie.
Never removed
from box.
Author's Collection

Swirl. Blonde.
Never removed from box.
Author's Collection

wig blonde	15-20	10-15
wig redhead (Titian)	15-20	10-15
wig brunette	15-20	10-15
booklet in cellophane	25-35	15-25
orange headband	25-35	15-25
swimsuit: pink	50-75	25-50
pink swim cap	25-35	15-25
wrist tag	50-75	25-50
shoes: pink open toe	15-20	10-15

AMERICAN GIRL BARBIE

Barbie American Girl
Bendable legs
Stock # 1070
Date 1965

	NRFB	Mint/ No Box	Avg
Blonde	1550-1800	375-500	225-375
Brunette	1550-1800	375-500	225-375
Redhead	1650-1850	400-525	225-375

	Mint	Avg
box	175-250	125-175
stand: wire	25-35	15-25
booklet in cellophane	25-35	15-25
multicolored striped swimsuit	65-85	45-65
wrist tag	40-65	25-40
shoes: turquoise open toe	25-35	15-25

American Girl. Blonde.
Author's Collection

Barbie American Girl
Bendable legs
Long hair
Stock # 1070
Date 1966

	NRFB	Mint/ No Box	Avg
American Girl long hair	2000-2600	1000-1500	750-1000

	Mint	Avg
box	175-250	125-175
stand: wire	25-35	15-25
booklet in cellophane	25-35	15-25
multicolored striped swimsuit	65-85	45-65
wrist tag	40-65	25-40
shoes: turquoise open toe	25-35	15-25

Barbie American Girl
Bendable legs
High color face
Stock # 1070
Date 1966

	NRFB	Mint/ No Box	Avg
American Girl high color face	2500-3000	1100-1500	800-1100

	Mint	Avg
box	175-250	125-175
stand: wire	25-35	15-25
booklet in cellophane	25-35	15-25
multicolored striped swimsuit	65-85	45-65
wrist tag	40-65	25-40
shoes: turquoise open toe	25-35	15-25

Barbie American Girl
Bendable legs
Side part
Stock # 1070
Date 1966

	NRFB	Mint/ No Box	Avg
American Girl side part, flesh skin toned	3000-3600	1700-2400	1200-1700

	Mint	Avg
box	175-250	125-175
stand: wire	25-35	15-25
booklet in cellophane	25-35	15-25
multicolored striped swimsuit	65-85	45-65
wrist tag	40-65	25-40
shoes: turquoise open toe	25-35	15-25

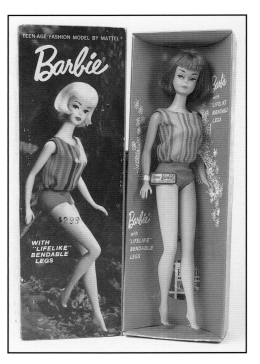

American Girl, long hair. Never removed from box.
Courtesy of Anthony Alcaide

American Girl, long hair.
Courtesy of Anthony Alcaide

American Girl, long hair, high color. Mint with wrist tag. *Author's Collection*

American Girl, side part. Rare. *Courtesy of Anthony Alcaide*

Barbie American Girl
Bendable legs
Japanese side part
Stock # 1070
Date 1966

	NRFB	Mint/ No Box	Avg
American Girl Japanese side part, pink skin toned	3000-3600	1700-2400	1200-1700

	Mint	Avg
box Japanese	200-300	175-200
stand: wire	25-35	15-25
booklet in cellophane	25-35	15-25
multicolored striped swimsuit	65-85	45-65
wrist tag	40-65	25-40
shoes: turquoise open toe	25-35	15-25

COLOR MAGIC BARBIE

Barbie Color Magic
Bendable legs
Stock # 1150
Date 1966-67

	NRFB	Mint/ No Box	Avg
Golden Blonde/Scarlet Flame cardboard box	1850-2400	475-600	375-475
plastic closet box	1500-2000	475-600	375-475
Midnight/Ruby Red cardboard box	3200-3800	775-1250	675-775
plastic closet box	2650-3100	775-1250	675-775

	NRFB	Mint/ No Box	Avg
Platinum Prototype cardboard box	3500-4000	1200-1600	775-1200

	Mint	Avg
cardboard box	175-225	125-175
plastic closet box	125-200	75-125
instruction booklet	75-100	50-75
booklet in cellophane	25-45	15-25
swimsuit: multicolored diamond print	65-85	45-65
headband multicolored diamond print	25-45	15-25
bobby pin turquoise	25-45	15-25
ribbon/pins	25-45	15-25
color changer A	25-45	15-25
color changer B	25-45	15-25
tulle tie	40-65	25-40
applicator	25-45	15-25
shoes: turquoise open toe	25-45	15-25
wrist tag	40-65	25-40

Bubble Cut, side part, bendable legs. Rare.
Courtesy of Anthony Alcaide

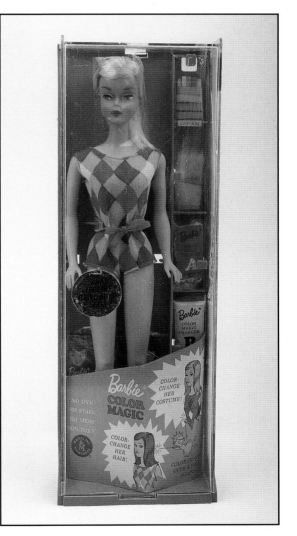

Color Magic. Golden Blonde/Scarlet Flame. Mint in box.
Author's Collection

Color Magic. Platinum. Rare.
Author's Collection

STANDARD BARBIE

Barbie
Standard Barbie
Stock # 1190
Date 1967

	NRFB	Mint/ No Box	Avg
Blonde	600-825	275-350	175-275
Brunette	650-875	275-350	175-275
Redhead	1200-1500	525-675	475-525

	Mint	Avg
box 1st issue	175-250	125-175
box 2nd issue	150-200	100-150
liner	50-75	25-50
stand: clear x	10-15	5-10
booklet in cellophane	25-45	15-25
swimsuit: 1 piece	65-85	45-65
swimsuit: 2 piece	75-100	50-75
pink hair ribbon	25-45	15-25
wrist tag	40-65	25-40

HAIR FAIR BARBIE

Barbie
Hair fair Barbie, head only
Stock # 4043
Date 1968

	NRFB	Mint/ No Box	Avg
Blonde	175-225	50-75	25-50
Brunette	200-250	75-100	50-75

Standard Barbie, 1st issue.
Courtesy of Karen Bindelglass

Standard Barbie, 2ND issue. Never removed from box.
Author's Collection

Barbie
Hair Fair Barbie head only
Stock # 4044
Date 1970

	NRFB No Box	Mint/	Avg
Blonde	75-125	35-50	25-35
Brunette	75-125	35-50	25-35

	Mint	Avg
card empty 4033	20-25	15-25
card empty 4044	20-25	15-25
wiglet brunette	20-25	15-25
ringlets brunette	20-25	15-25
hairpiece long Brunette	20-25	15-25
wig brunette	20-25	15-25
braid headband brunette	25-40	15-25
hairpiece long w/ribbon brunette	25-40	15-25
hairpiece long w/ribbon blonde	25-40	15-25
braid headband blonde	25-40	15-25
wiglet blonde	20-25	15-25
ringlets blonde	20-25	15-25
hairpiece long blonde	20-25	15-25
wig blonde	20-25	15-25
styling extras: card w/ comb, brush, 2 white flowers, 8 bobby pins	25-40	15-25
earring single	10-15	5-10

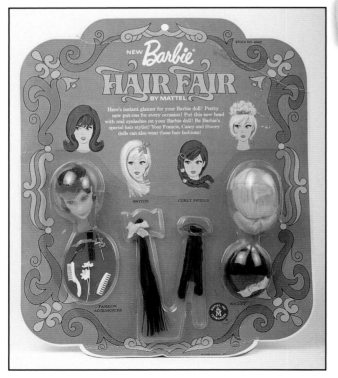

Hair Fair Barbie. Brunette. Mint on card.
Author's Collection

TWIST 'n TURN BARBIE

Barbie
Twist 'n Turn
Stock # 1160
Date 1967

	NRFB	Mint/ No Box	Avg
Blonde	600-825	275-350	175-275
Brunette	650-875	285-375	175-300
Redhead	1200-1500	450-600	225-375

	Mint	Avg
box	75-100	50-75
stand: clear x	10-15	5-10
booklet in cellophane	25-45	15-25
swimsuit: top shell	20-25	15-20
swimsuit: pink bottom	20-25	15-20
green belt	40-50	30-40
pink hair ribbon	25-45	15-25
wrist tag	40-65	30-40

Barbie
Twist 'n Turn
Trade in Box
Stock # 1160
Date 1968

	NRFB	Mint/ No Box	Avg
Blonde	475-550	275-350	175-275
Brunette	500-575	285-375	175-300
Redhead	875-975	450-600	225-375

	Mint	Avg
Trade-In Box	40-65	25-40
stand: clear x	10-15	5-10
booklet	25-45	15-25
swimsuit: top	20-25	15-20
swimsuit: bottom	25-45	15-25
fishnet cover-all	20-25	15-20
orange hair ribbon	25-45	15-25
wrist tag	40-65	25-40

Barbie
Twist 'n Turn
2nd issue
Orange bikini
Stock # 1160
Date 1968

	NRFB	Mint/ No Box	Avg
Blonde	600-825	275-350	175-275
Brunette	650-875	285-375	175-300
Redhead	1200-1500	450-600	225-375

	Mint	Avg
box	75-100	50-75
stand: clear x	10-15	5-10
booklet	25-45	15-25
swimsuit: orange top	20-25	15-20
swimsuit: orange bottom	25-45	15-25
fishnet cover-all	20-25	15-20
orange hair ribbon	25-45	15-25
wrist tag	40-65	25-40

Twist 'n Turn Barbie.
Mint with wrist tag.
Courtesy of Anthony Alcaide

Twist 'n Turn Barbie.
Redhead. Trade in box. Rare.
Courtesy of Lisa Varuolo

Twist 'n Turn Barbie.
Never removed from box.
Author's Collection

Twist 'n Turn Barbie.
Mint w/ wrist tag.
Courtesy of Karen Bindelglass

Twist 'n Turn Barbie, Blonde.
Courtesy of Karen Bindelglass

Barbie
Twist 'n Turn
Flip
Multicolor print suit
Stock # 1160
Date 1968

	NRFB	Mint/ No Box	Avg
Blonde	475-550	275-350	175-275
Brunette	500-575	285-375	175-300

	Mint	Avg
box	75-100	50-75
stand: clear x	10-15	5-10
booklet	25-45	15-25
swimsuit: multicolored knit	40-65	25-40
wrist tag	40-65	25-40

Barbie
Twist 'n Turn
Flip
Nylon pink & white suit
Stock # 1160
Date 1969

	NRFB	Mint/ No Box	Avg
Blonde	475-550	275-350	175-275
Brunette	500-575	285-375	175-300

	Mint	Avg
box	75-100	50-75
stand: clear x	10-15	5-10
booklet	25-45	15-25
swimsuit: pink & white	40-65	25-40
wrist tag	40-65	25-40

Barbie
Twist 'n Turn
Flip
Multicolor nylon suit
Stock # 1160
Date 1969

	NRFB	Mint/ No Box	Avg
Blonde	475-550	275-350	175-275
Brunette	525-600	285-375	175-300

	Mint	Avg
box	75-100	50-75
stand: clear x	10-15	5-10
booklet	25-45	15-25
swimsuit: multi- colored nylon	50-75	25-50
wrist tag	40-65	25-40

Twist 'n Turn Barbie. Brunette.
Never removed from box.
Author's Collection

Twist 'n Turn Barbie.
Blonde.
Never removed
from box.
Author's Collection

TALKING BARBIE

Barbie
Talking Barbie
Side ponytail
Clear box
Stock # 1115
Date 1967

	NRFB	Mint/ No Box	Avg
Blonde	475-550	275-350	175-275
Brunette	500-575	285-375	175-300
Redhead	875-975	450-600	225-375
Spanish	500-575	285-375	225-375

Note: prices are for repaired talking dolls. Mute deduct 10%

	Mint	Avg
box	40-65	25-40
stand: clear x	10-15	5-10
stool top	10-15	5-10
stool bottom	10-15	5-10
booklet	25-45	15-25
swimsuit: pink knit top	20-25	15-20
swimsuit: pink bottom	25-45	15-25
pink hair ribbons	25-45	15-25
wrist tag	40-65	25-40

Talking Barbie,
side ponytail.
*Courtesy of
Lisa Varuolo*

Barbie
Talking Barbie
Side ponytail
Stock # 1115
Date 1967

	NRFB	Mint/ No Box	Avg
Blonde	475-550	275-350	175-275
Brunette	500-575	285-375	175-300
Redhead	875-975	450-600	225-375
Spanish	500-575	285-375	225-375

Note: prices are for repaired talking dolls. Mute deduct 10%

	Mint	Avg
box	40-65	25-40
stand: clear x	10-15	5-10
booklet	25-45	15-25
swimsuit: pink knit top	20-25	15-20
swimsuit: pink bottom	25-45	15-25
pink hair ribbons	25-45	15-25
wrist tag	40-65	25-40

Barbie
Talking Barbie
Nape curl
Stock # 1115
Date 1968

	NRFB	Mint/ No Box	Avg
Blonde	475-550	275-350	175-275
Brunette	500-575	285-375	175-300
Redhead	875-975	450-600	225-375
Stacy face mold	500-575	285-375	175-300

	Mint	Avg
box	40-65	25-40
stand: clear x	10-15	5-10
booklet	25-45	15-25
swimsuit: top	20-25	15-20
swimsuit: bottom	25-45	15-25
cover-up	20-25	15-20
wrist tag	40-65	25-40

Talking Barbie. Redhead. Nape Curl.
Courtesy of Richard Chapman and Glenn Mandeville

Talking Barbie.
Nape Curl.
Never removed
from box.
Author's Collection

Barbie
Talking Barbie
Nape curl
Stock # 1115
Date 1969

	NRFB	Mint/ No Box	Avg
Blonde	475-550	275-350	175-275
Brunette	500-575	285-375	175-300
Redhead	875-975	450-600	225-375

	Mint	Avg
box	40-65	25-40
or baggy w/ header	25-45	15-25
stand: clear x	10-15	5-10
booklet	25-45	15-25
swimsuit: white top	25-45	15-25
swimsuit: white bottom	25-45	15-25
gold cover-up	25-45	15-25
wrist tag	40-65	25-40

DRAMATIC NEW LIVING BARBIE

Barbie
Dramatic New Living
Stock # 1116
Date 1969

	NRFB	Mint/ No Box	Avg
Blonde	175-225	50-75	25-50
Brunette	200-250	75-100	50-75
Redhead	175-225	50-75	25-50

	Mint	Avg
box	40-65	25-40
liner	25-45	15-25
stand: clear x	10-15	5-10
booklet	25-45	15-25
swimsuit	25-45	15-25
cover-up	10-15	5-10
wrist tag	40-65	25-40

LIVING BARBIE

Barbie
Living Barbie
Stock # 1116
Date 1970

	NRFB	Mint/ No Box	Avg
Blonde	475-550	275-350	175-275
Brunette	500-575	285-375	175-285
Redhead	475-550	275-350	175-275
Japanese Living	750-825	475-550	275-350

	Mint	Avg
box	40-65	25-40
stand: clear x	10-15	5-10
booklet	25-45	15-25
swimsuit	40-65	25-40
wrap skirt	25-45	15-25
wrist tag	40-65	25-40

LIVE ACTION BARBIE

Barbie
Live Action
Stock # 1155
Date 1970

	NRFB	Mint/ No Box	Avg
Blonde	275-350	100-175	75-100

	Mint	Avg
box	25-45	15-25
stand: clear Touch 'n Go	25-45	15-25
booklet	25-45	15-25
instructions	10-15	5-10
top	25-45	15-25
pants	10-15	5-10
headband	25-45	15-25

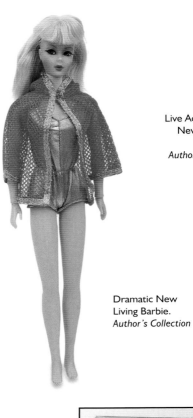

Dramatic New Living Barbie.
Author's Collection

wrist fringe pair	40-65	25-40
shoes: brown flats	15-25	15-25
wrist tag	40-65	25-40

Live Action Barbie.
Never removed from box.
Author's Collection

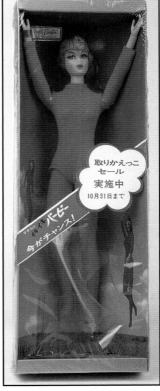

Japanese Living Barbie.
Never removed from box.
Courtesy of Karen Bindelglass

Live Action Barbie. Mint with wrist tag.
Author's Collection

Barbie
Live Action
With stage
Stock # 1152
Date 1970

	NRFB	Mint/ No Box	Avg
Blonde	300-375	150-225	75-150

	Mint	Avg
box	25-45	15-25
stand: stage	40-65	25-40
microphone	25-45	15-25
instructions	10-15	5-10
top	25-45	15-25
pants	10-15	5-10
headband	25-45	15-25
wrist fringe pair	40-65	25-40
shoes: brown flats	25-45	15-25
wrist tag	40-65	25-40

BARBIE HAIR HAPPENIN'S

Barbie
Hair Happenin's
Stock # 1174
Date 1971

	NRFB	Mint/ No Box	Avg
Redhead	2000-2500	675-950	500-675

	Mint	Avg
box	100-175	75-100
stand: clear x	10-15	5-10
booklet	25-45	15-25
dress	75-100	50-75
belt	75-100	50-75
wrist tag	40-65	25-40
mini curls	25-45	15-25
midi swirls	25-45	15-25
fashion fall	25-45	15-25
styling extras		
card w/ comb, brush,		
2 pink flowers,		
mini bobby pins,		
rubber band	25-45	15-25
shoes: t-strap black heels	40-65	25-40

BARBIE WITH GROWIN' PRETTY HAIR

Barbie
Growin' Pretty Hair
Stock # 1144
Date 1970

	NRFB	Mint/ No Box	Avg
Blonde	300-375	150-225	75-150

	Mint	Avg
box	25-45	15-25
stand: clear x	10-15	5-10

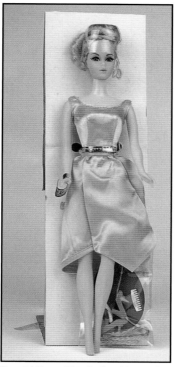

Growin' Pretty Hair Barbie. Mint with wrist tag on mailer liner. *Author's Collection*

	Mint	Avg
booklet	25-45	15-25
dress	25-45	15-25
shoes: pink pilgrim	10-15	5-10
wrist tag	40-65	25-40
braids	25-45	15-25
sausage curls	25-45	15-25
styling extras		
card w/ comb, brush,		
2 pink flowers,		
mini bobby pins	25-45	15-25

Barbie
Growin' Pretty Hair
Empire dress
Stock # 1144
Date 1972

	NRFB	Mint/ No Box	Avg
Blonde	475-550	275-350	175-275

	Mint	Avg
box	25-45	15-25
stand: clear x	10-15	5-10
booklet	25-45	15-25
dress	40-65	25-40
shoes: blue square toe	10-15	5-10

Growin' Pretty Hair Barbie, empire dress. Never removed from box. Growin' Pretty Hair Barbie, pink dress. Never removed from box. *Author's Collection*

wrist tag		40-65	25-40
braids		25-45	15-25
sausage curls		25-45	15-25
styling extras			
card w/ comb, brush,			
2 pink flowers, mini			
bobby pins		25-45	15-25

BUSY BARBIE

Barbie
Busy with Holdin' Hands
Stock # 3311
Date 1971

	NRFB	Mint/ No Box	Avg
Blonde	475-550	275-350	175-275
		Mint	Avg
box		25-45	15-25
stand: clear x		10-15	5-10
instructions		10-15	5-10
top		25-45	15-25
skirt		10-15	5-10
shoes: red pilgrim		10-15	5-10
wrist tag		40-65	25-40
barrette		10-15	5-10
record player		10-15	5-10
record		10-15	5-10
tray		10-15	5-10
cups		10-15	5-10
tv		10-15	5-10
telephone		10-15	5-10
travel case		10-15	5-10

Barbie
Talking Busy
Stock # 1195
Date 1971

	NRFB	Mint/ No Box	Avg
Blonde	300-375	150-225	75-150
		Mint	Avg
box		25-45	15-25
stand: clear x		10-15	5-10
instructions		10-15	5-10
top		25-45	15-25
overalls		40-65	25-40
belt		40-65	25-40
hat		25-45	15-25
shoes: green lace-up boots		10-15	5-10
wrist tag		40-65	25-40
record player		10-15	5-10
record		10-15	5-10
tray		10-15	5-10
cups		10-15	5-10
tv		10-15	5-10
telephone		10-15	5-10
travel case		10-15	5-10

Walk Lively Barbie. Never removed from box. *Author's Collection*

Montgomery Ward Barbie.
Author's Collection

WALK LIVELY BARBIE

Barbie
Walk Lively
Stock # 1182
Date 1971

	NRFB	Mint/ No Box	Avg
Blonde	200-275	150-225	75-150
		Mint	Avg
box		25-45	15-25
stand: walking		25-45	15-25
instructions		10-15	5-10
top		10-15	5-10
pants		25-45	15-25
purse		10-15	5-10
shoes: red pilgrim		25-45	15-25

MONTGOMERY WARD COMMEMORATIVE PONYTAIL BARBIE

Barbie
Montgomery Ward
Stock # n/a
Date 1972

	NRFB	Mint/ No Box	Avg
Brunette	475-550	275-350	175-275
		Mint	Avg
box mailer		25-45	15-25
box pink		40-65	25-40
stand: clear x		10-15	5-10
swimsuit: black & white		25-45	15-25
shoes: white open toe		25-45	15-25

MALIBU BARBIE

Barbie
Sun Set Malibu
Stock # 1067
Date 1970

	NRFB	Mint/ No Box	Avg
Blonde	175-225	50-75	25-50
		Mint	Avg
box card		25-45	15-25
swimsuit		10-15	5-10
towel		10-15	5-10
sunglasses		10-15	5-10
wrist tag *		25-45	15-25

* nrfb examples have been found without wrist tag

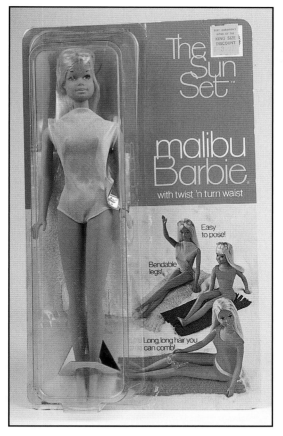

Sun Set Malibu Barbie. Never removed from box/card.
Author's Collection

Quick Curl Barbie. Never removed from box/card. Gift set UK Special By Mattel for Burbank Toys.
Courtesy of Sue Anderson

Barbie
Forget Me Not baggy
Stock # 3269
Date 1971

	NRFB	Mint/ No Box	Avg
Blonde	200-275	150-225	75-150

	Mint	Avg
header card	25-45	15-25
swimsuit	10-15	5-10
towel	10-15	5-10
sunglasses	10-15	5-10

QUICK CURL BARBIE

Barbie
Quick Curl
Stock # 4220
Date 1972

	NRFB	Mint/ No Box	Avg
Blonde	175-225	50-75	25-50
Gift set			
w/ outfit	300-375	50-75	25-50

Pink Silhouette display box, Barbie Q.
Never removed from box.
Courtesy of Anthony Alcaide

	Mint	Avg
box card	25-45	15-25
pink dress	10-15	5-10
stand: white x	10-15	5-10
hair seed beads	10-15	5-10
styling extras		
comb, brush, curler,		
barrettes, ribbons	25-45	15-25
wrist tag	25-45	15-25

STORE DISPLAY
DRESSED BOX DOLLS

Barbie
Pink Silhouette box
Display
Date 1959-60
Ponytail

Found with either #1, #2 or #3 Barbie doll Examples known are Barbie Q, Busy Gal, Commuter Set, Enchanted Evening, Evening Splendor, Friday Night Date, Gay Parisienne, Let's Dance, Nighty Negligee, Plantation Belle, Resort Set, Roman Holiday, Silken Flame, Solo in the Spotlight, Suburban Shopper, Sweater Girl, Sweet Dreams, Wedding Day Set, Winter Holiday.

Price reflects which doll, outfit, and stand. See prices for each. Add together plus box.

	Mint	Avg	Below Avg
box	775-1100	500-775	less than 500
box from Japan w/sticker	875-1175	550-875	less than 550

Barbie
Striped Display box
Display
Date 1963-65
Box date 1962
Swirl or Bubble cut

Found with either Swirl or Bubble cut Barbie doll

Examples known are After Five, American Airlines Stewardess, Black Magic, Brides Dream, Career Girl, Country Fair, Dinner at eight, Evening Splendor, Garden Party, Garden Tea Party, Ice Breaker, Knitting Pretty, Masquerade, Mood for Music, Nighty Negligee, Orange Blossom, Peachy Fleecy, Registered Nurse, Senior Prom, Sheath Sensation, Solo in the Spotlight, Swingin' Easy, Tennis Anyone?, Theatre Date, Barbie In Holland, Barbie In Mexico, Arabian Nights, Cinderella, Guinevere. Price reflects which doll, outfit, and stand. See prices for each. Add together plus box.

	Mint	Avg
box	225-300	150-225
clear id plastic lid	100-175	50-100
stand: wire	25-40	15-25
booklet in cellophane	25-45	15-25
blue panty	10-15	5-10
wrist tag*	40-65	25-40

* sometimes nrfb found with no wrist tag

Pink Silhouette display box, Plantation Belle.
Never removed from box.
Courtesy of Sherry Baloun

Left:
Striped display box, Nighty Negligee.
Never removed from box.
Courtesy of Anthony Alcaide

Above:
Striped display box, Barbie In Holland.
Never removed from box.
Author's Collection

KEN

Ken
Ken flocked hair
Stock # 750
Date 1961

	NRFB	Mint/ No Box	Avg
Blonde	200-275	150-225	75-150
Brunette	200-275	150-225	75-150
		Mint	**Avg**
box		50-75	35-50
box liner		25-40	20-35
stand: wire		25-40	15-25
booklet in cellophane		20-30	15-20
sandals		25-35	10-20
yellow towel		15-20	10-15
swimsuit: red		15-20	10-15
wrist tag		25-35	10-25

Ken
Ken painted hair
Stock # 750
Date 1962

	NRFB	Mint/ No Box	Avg
Blonde	175-225	50-75	25-50
Brunette	200-275	50-75	25-50
		Mint	**Avg**
box		50-75	35-50
box liner		25-40	20-35
stand: wire		25-40	15-25
booklet in cellophane		20-30	15-20
sandals		25-35	10-20
towel		15-20	10-15
swimsuit: trunks		15-20	10-15
wrist tag		25-35	10-25

Ken. Blonde painted hair.
Never removed from box.
Author's Collection

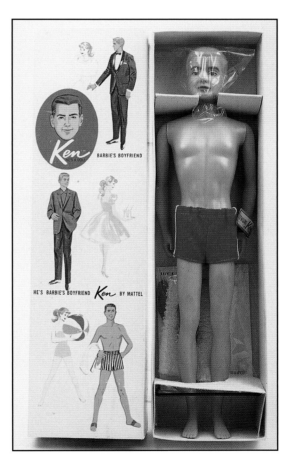

Ken. Blonde flocked hair.
Never removed from box.
Author's Collection

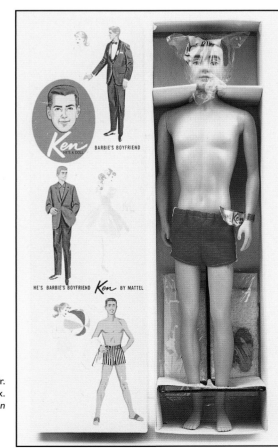

Ken. Brunette flocked hair.
Never removed from box.
Author's Collection

KEN BENDABLE LEG

Ken
Bendable Leg
Stock # 1020
Box Date 1964

	NRFB	Mint/ No Box	Avg
Blonde	475-550	275-350	175-275
Brunette	475-550	275-350	175-275

	Mint	Avg
box	50-75	35-50
stand: wire	25-40	15-25
booklet in cellophane	20-30	15-20
sandals	25-35	10-20
swimsuit: top	25-35	10-20
swimsuit: trunks	15-20	10-15
wrist tag	25-35	10-25

TALKING KEN

Ken
Talking
Stock # 1111
Date 1968

	NRFB	Mint/ No Box	Avg
Reddish brown	175-225	50-75	25-50

Note: prices are for repaired talking dolls. Mute deduct 10%

	Mint	Avg
box	25-40	20-35
stand: white x	10-15	5-10
jacket top	10-15	5-10
shorts	10-15	5-10
wrist tag	25-35	10-25

Ken
Talking Spanish
Stock # 1111
Date 1968

	NRFB	Mint/ No Box	Avg
brunette	200-275	50-75	25-50

Note: prices are for repaired talking dolls. Mute deduct 10%

	Mint	Avg
box	25-40	20-35
stand: white x	10-15	5-10
shirt	10-15	5-10
trunks	10-15	5-10
wrist tag	25-35	10-2

Ken
Talking
Stock # 1111
Date 1969

	NRFB	Mint/ No Box	Avg
Brunette	200-275	50-75	25-50

Note: prices are for repaired talking dolls. Mute deduct 10%

	Mint	Avg
box	25-40	20-35
stand: white x	10-15	5-10
shirt	10-15	5-10
trunks	10-15	5-10
wrist tag	25-35	10-25

Ken
New Good Lookin'
Stock # 1124
Date 1969

	NRFB	Mint/ No Box	Avg
Brunette	200-275	50-75	25-50

Note: prices are for repaired talking dolls. Mute deduct 10%

	Mint	Avg
box	25-40	20-35
stand: white x	10-15	5-10
shirt	10-15	5-10
trunks	10-15	5-10
wrist tag	25-35	10-25

LIVE ACTION

Ken
Live Action
Stock # 1159
Date 1970

	NRFB	Mint/ No Box	Avg
Brunette	200-275	50-75	25-50

	Mint	Avg
box	25-45	15-25
or baggy w/header no stand	25-45	15-25
stand: clear Touch 'n Go	25-45	15-25
instructions	10-15	5-10
top	10-15	5-10
pants	10-15	5-10
suede vest	25-45	15-25
shoes: brown	15-25	10-15
wrist tag	25-35	10-25

Live Action Ken.
Never removed from box.
Author's Collection

Ken
Live Action
W/ stage
Stock # 1172
Date 1970

	NRFB	Mint/ No Box	Avg
Brunette	200-275	75-100	50-75

	Mint	Avg
box	25-45	15-25
stand: stage	40-65	25-40
microphone	25-45	15-25
instructions	10-15	5-10
top	10-15	5-10
pants	10-15	5-10
suede vest	25-35	15-25
shoes: brown	15-25	10-15
wrist tag	25-35	10-25

SUN SET MALIBU KEN

Ken
Sun Set
Stock # 1088
Date 1970

	NRFB	Mint/ No Box	Avg
Blonde	75-150	25-45	15-25

	Mint	Avg
box card	25-40	20-35
towel	10-15	5-10
trunks	10-15	5-10
wrist tag	25-35	10-25

BUSY KEN

Ken
Busy w/ Holdin' Hands
Stock # 3314
Date 1971

	NRFB	Mint/ No Box	Avg
Brunette	200-275	50-75	25-50

	Mint	Avg
box	25-45	15-25
stand: clear x	10-15	5-10
instructions	10-15	5-10
top	25-45	15-25
pants	10-15	5-10
belt	10-15	5-10
shoes: white	10-15	5-10
wrist tag	25-35	10-20
record player	10-15	5-10
record	10-15	5-10
tray	10-15	5-10
cups	10-15	5-10
tv	10-15	5-10
telephone	0-15	5-10
travel case	10-15	5-10

Ken
Talking Busy w/ Holdin' Hands
Stock # 1196
Date 1971

	NRFB	Mint/ No Box	Avg
Brunette	225-300	75-100	50-75

Note: prices are for repaired talking dolls.
Mute deduct 10%

	Mint	Avg
box	25-45	15-25
stand: clear x	10-15	5-10
instructions	10-15	5-10
top	25-45	15-25
pants	25-45	15-25
belt	10-15	5-10
shoes: brown	10-15	5-10
record player	10-15	5-10
record	10-15	5-10
tray	10-15	5-10
cups	10-15	5-10
tv	10-15	5-10
telephone	10-15	5-10
travel case	10-15	5-10
wrist tag	25-35	10-25

WALK LIVELY KEN

Ken
Walk Lively
Stock # 1184
Date 1971

	NRFB	Mint/ No Box	Avg
Brunette	175-225	50-75	25-50

Note: prices are for repaired talking dolls.
Mute deduct 10%

	Mint	Avg
box	25-45	15-25
stand: walking	25-45	15-25
instructions	10-15	5-10
top	10-15	5-10
pants	10-15	5-10
shoes: brown	10-15	10-15
wrist tag	25-35	10-25

Walk Lively Ken.
Never removed from box.
Author's Collection

MOD HAIR KEN

Ken
Mod Hair
Stock # 4224
Date 1972

	NRFB	Mint/No Box	Avg
Brunette	75-125	50-75	25-50

	Mint	Avg
box card	10-15	5-10
stand: white x	10-15	5-10
jacket	10-15	5-10
pants w/ belt	10-15	5-10
dickey	10-15	5-10
shoes: brown	15-25	10-15
mustache, beard, & sideburns on sheet	10-15	5-10
wrist tag	25-35	10-25

STORE DISPLAY DRESSED BOX KEN DOLLS

Ken
Striped Display box
Display
Date 1963-65
Box date 1962
Painted Hair Ken

Found with either Blonde or Brunette painted hair Ken doll

Examples known are Campus Hero, Casuals, Dr. Ken, Fraternity Meeting, Holiday, sailor, Ski Champion, Time for Tennis, Touchdown, Ken in Holland, Mexico, Arabian Nights, King Arthur, The Prince.

Price reflects which doll, outfit, and stand. See prices for each. Add together plus box.

	Mint	Avg
box	150-225	75-150
clear id plastic lid	100-175	50-100
stand: wire	25-40	15-25
booklet in cellophane	25-45	15-25
wrist tag*	25-35	10-25

*sometimes nrfb found with no wrist tag

Mod Hair Ken with extra long hair.
Courtesy of Richard Chapman and Glenn Mandeville

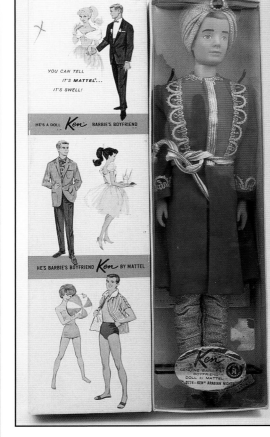

Striped display box, Ken Arabian Nights.
Never removed from box.
Author's Collection

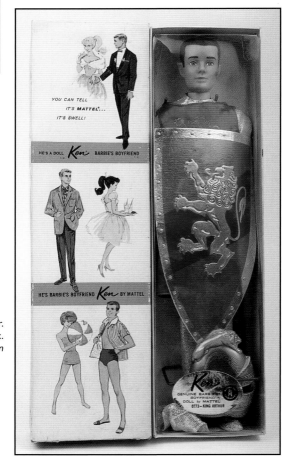

Striped display box, Ken King Arthur.
Never removed from box.
Author's Collection

MIDGE

Midge
Straight Legs
Stock # 860
Date 1963
Box date 1962

	NRFB	Mint/ No Box	Avg
Blonde	150-225	75-150	50-75
Brunette	175-250	75-150	50-75
Redhead	150-225	75-150	50-75
		Mint	Avg
box		40-65	25-40
box liner		40-65	25-40
stand: wire		25-35	15-25
booklet in cellophane		20-30	15-20
shoes: white open toe		25-35	10-20
swimsuit: 2-piece		20-25	15-20
wrist tag		40-65	25-40

Midge
Straight legs
With teeth
Stock # 860
Date 1963
Box date 1962

	NRFB	Mint/ No Box	Avg
Blonde	175-250	75-150	50-75
Brunette	225-300	75-100	50-75
Redhead	175-250	75-150	50-75
		Mint	Avg
box		40-65	25-40
box liner		40-65	25-40
stand: wire		25-35	15-25
booklet in cellophane		20-30	15-20
shoes: white open toe		25-35	10-20
swimsuit, 2-piece		20-25	15-20
wrist tag		40-65	25-40

Midge
Straight legs
With no freckles
Stock # 860
Date 1963
Box date 1962

	NRFB	Mint/ No Box	Avg
Blonde	225-300	75-100	50-75
Brunette	225-300	75-100	50-75
Redhead	225-300	75-100	50-75
		Mint	Avg
box		40-65	25-40
box liner		40-65	25-40
stand: wire		25-35	15-25
booklet in cellophane		20-30	15-20
shoes: white open toe		25-35	10-20

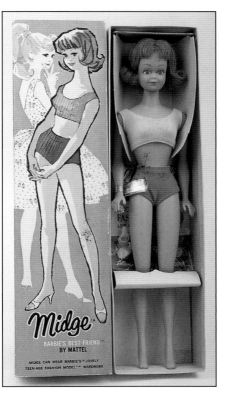

Midge Titian.
Never removed from box.
Author's Collection

Midge. Titian with teeth. Rare.
Author's Collection

swimsuit: 2 piece	20-25	15-20
wrist tag	40-65	25-40

WIG WARDROBE MIDGE

Midge
Head only w/ wigs
Stock # 1009
Date 1964

NRFB	Mint/ No Box	Avg
375-525	175-250	75-150

	Mint	Avg
box card	50-75	35-50
orange headband	25-45	15-25
wig stand	25-45	15-25
wig blonde	25-45	15-25
wig titian (redhead)	25-45	15-25
titian pigtails blue ribbons	15-20	10-15
wig brunette	25-45	15-25
brunette velvet ribbon	15-20	10-15

BENDABLE LEG MIDGE

Midge
Bendable Leg
Stock # 1080
Date 1965
Box Date 1964

	NRFB	Mint/ No Box	Avg
Blonde	550-800	225-300	75-100
Brunette	550-800	225-300	75-100
Redhead	550-800	225-300	75-100
		Mint	Avg
box		175-250	125-175
stand: wire		25-35	15-25
booklet in cellophane		20-30	15-20
blue ribbon headband		25-45	15-25
shoes: turquoise open toe		25-45	15-25
swimsuit: striped knit		65-85	45-65
wrist tag		40-65	25-40

STORE DISPLAY DRESSED BOX MIDGE DOLLS

Midge
Striped display box
Display
Date 1963-65
Box date 1962

Found with either Blonde or Brunette or Redhead doll.
Examples known are Crisp 'n Cool, Fancy Free, Orange Blossom
Price reflects which doll, outfit, and stand. See prices for each. Add together plus box.

	Mint	Avg
box	150-225	75-150
clear id plastic lid	100-175	50-100
stand: wire	25-35	15-25
booklet in cellophane	20-30	15-20
wrist tag*	40-65	25-40
blue panty	10-15	5-10

* sometimes nrfb found with no wrist tag

SKIPPER

Skipper
Straight legs
Stock # 950
Date 1964
Box date 1963

	NRFB	Mint/ No Box	Avg
Blonde	125-175	50-75	25-50
Platinum Blonde	225-300	75-100	50-75
Brunette	125-175	50-75	25-50
Titian	125-175	50-75	25-50
Titian Color Magic	225-300	75-100	50-75

	Mint	Avg
box	50-75	25-50
liner	25-45	15-25
stand: wire	25-35	15-25
booklet in cellophane	20-30	15-20
headband brass	10-15	5-10
shoes: red Japan flats	10-15	5-10
swimsuit	10-15	5-10
wrist tag	25-45	15-25

Skipper Japanese
Straight legs, pink skin tone
Black eyes
Stock # 5950
Date 1964

	NRFB	Mint/ No Box	Avg
Blonde	475-600	200-275	125-200
Brunette	475-600	200-275	125-200
Titian	475-600	200-275	125-200

	Mint	Avg
box	50-75	25-50
liner	25-45	15-25
stand: wire	25-35	15-25
booklet in cellophane	20-30	15-20
headband brass	10-15	5-10
shoes: red Japan flats	10-15	5-10
swimsuit: red & white	10-15	5-10
wrist tag	25-45	15-25

Skipper, straight legs.
Toy department in-house
sample. Rare.
NRFB price, $400.
Author's Collection

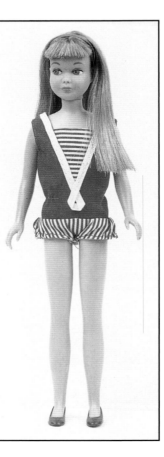

Skipper. Titian. Color Magic. Rare.
Courtesy of Lisa Varuolo

Skipper. Japanese,
Blonde, Brunette, Titian.
Author's Collection

Skipper. Japanese.
Note the black eyes.
Author's Collection

SKIPPER BENDABLE LEG

Skipper
Bendable leg
Stock # 1030
Date 1965
Box date 1964

	NRFB	Mint/ No Box	Avg
Blonde	300-375	75-125	50-75
Brunette	300-375	75-125	50-75
Titian	300-375	75-125	50-75
		Mint	**Avg**
box		75-125	50-75
stand: wire		25-35	15-25
booklet in cellophane		20-30	15-20
headband brass		10-15	5-10
shoes: red Japan flats		10-15	5-10
swimsuit: red & blue		10-15	5-10
wrist tag		25-45	15-25

SKIPPER TWIST 'n TURN

Skipper
Twist 'n Turn
Stock # 1105
Date 1968

	NRFB	Mint/ No Box	Avg
Blonde	475-600	200-275	125-200
Brunette	475-600	200-275	125-200
Titian	475-600	200-275	125-200
		Mint	**Avg**
box		25-45	15-25
stand: clear x		10-15	5-10
booklet in cellophane		25-45	15-25
headband blue		25-45	15-25
swimsuit		25-45	15-25
wrist tag		25-45	15-25

Skipper
Twist 'n Turn
Sausage curls hairstyle 1st issue
Stock # 1105
Date 1969

	NRFB	Mint/ No Box	Avg
Blonde	325-400	100-175	50-100
Brunette	325-400	100-175	50-100
		Mint	**Avg**
box		25-45	15-25
stand: clear x		10-15	5-10
booklet in cellophane		25-45	15-25
orange hair ribbons		25-45	15-25
swimsuit		25-45	15-25
wrist tag		25-45	15-25

Bendable Leg Skipper. Titian.
Never removed from box.
Author's Collection

Bendable Leg Skipper. Titian.
Never removed from box.
Courtesy of Lisa Varuolo

Skipper
Twist 'n Turn
Sausage Curls hairstyle 2nd issue
Stock # 1105
Date 1969

	NRFB	Mint/ No Box	Avg
Blonde	300-375	100-175	50-100
Brunette	300-375	100-175	50-100
		Mint	**Avg**
box		25-45	15-25
stand: clear x		10-15	5-10
booklet in cellophane		25-45	15-25
orange hair ribbons		25-45	15-25
swimsuit: bikini		25-45	15-25
wrist tag		25-45	15-25

Twist 'n Turn Skipper. Sausage Curls.
Never removed from box.
Author's Collection

DRAMATIC NEW LIVING SKIPPER

Dramatic Living & Dramatic New Living Skipper.
Author's Collection

Skipper
Dramatic New Living
Stock # 1117
Date 1970
Box date 1969

	NRFB	Mint/ No Box	Avg
Blonde	125-200	50-75	25-50

	Mint	Avg
box	25-45	15-25
stand: clear x	10-15	5-10
booklet in cellophane	25-45	15-25
pink hair ribbons	10-15	5-10
swimsuit	10-15	5-10
wrist tag	25-45	15-25

Skipper
Dramatic Living
Stock # 1117
Date 1970

	NRFB	Mint/ No Box	Avg
Blonde	250-325	75-125	25-50

	Mint	Avg
box	25-45	15-25
stand: clear x	10-15	5-10
booklet in cellophane	25-45	15-25
pink hair ribbons	10-15	5-10
swimsuit: top	10-15	5-10
swimsuit: bottoms	10-15	5-10
skateboard	10-15	5-10
wrist tag	25-45	15-25

Skipper
Special Living
Trade-in box
Stock # 1147
Date 1970

	NRFB	Mint/ No Box	Avg
Blonde	125-200	50-75	25-50

	Mint	Avg
box	25-45	15-25
stand: clear x	10-15	5-10
booklet in cellophane	25-45	15-25
pink hair ribbons	10-15	5-10
swimsuit	10-15	5-10
wrist tag	25-45	15-25

Dramatic Living Skipper.
Never removed from box.
Courtesy of Sue Anderson

SKIPPER RE-ISSUE

Skipper
Re-issue straight leg
Stock # 950
Date 1970
Box date 1963

	NRFB	Mint/ No Box	Avg
Blonde	375-475	100-175	50-75
Brunette	375-475	100-175	50-75
Titian	375-475	100-175	50-75

	Mint	Avg
box	50-75	25-50
stand: clear x	10-15	5-10
booklet in cellophane	25-45	15-25
headband brass	10-15	5-10
shoes: red Japan flats	10-15	5-10
swimsuit	25-45	15-25
wrist tag	25-45	15-25

Re-issue Skipper.
Never removed from box.
Note the Twist 'n Turn
mod graphics on the box.
Author's Collection

MALIBU SKIPPER

Skipper
Sun Set Malibu
Stock # 1069
Date 1971
Box date 1970

	NRFB	Mint/ No Box	Avg
Blonde	75-125	25-50	15-25

	Mint	Avg
box	25-45	15-25
stand: clear x	10-15	5-10
swimsuit: orange bikini	10-15	5-10
towel blue	10-15	5-10
wrist tag	25-45	15-25

SKIPPER QUICK CURL

Skipper
Quick Curl
Stock # 4223
Date 1973
Box date 1972

	NRFB	Mint/ No Box	Avg
Blonde	75-125	25-50	15-25

	Mint	Avg
box or card	25-45	15-25
dress	10-15	5-10
stand: white x	10-15	5-10
hair ribbons on card	10-15	5-10
styling extras		
comb, brush, curler,		
barrettes, ribbons	25-45	15-25
wrist tag	25-45	15-25

SKIPPER POSE 'n PLAY

Skipper
Pose 'n Play
Stock # 1972
Box Date 1973

	NRFB	Mint/ No Box	Avg
Blonde	75-125	25-50	15-25

	Mint	Avg
header card / baggy	25-45	15-25
swimsuit	10-15	5-10
blue hair ribbons	10-15	5-10
wrist tag	25-45	15-25

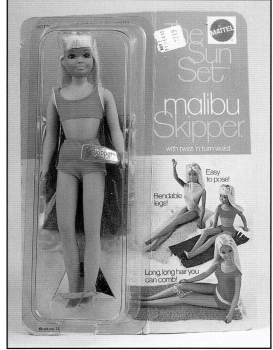

Sun Set Malibu Skipper.
Never removed
from box/card.
Author's Collection

Quick Curl Skipper.
Never removed from box/card.
Author's Collection

Pos 'n Play
Skipper. Mint
with wrist tag.
Author's Collection

Pos 'n Play Skipper.
Never removed from bag.
Courtesy of Lisa Varuolo

GROWING UP SKIPPER

Skipper
Growing Up
Stock # 7259
Date 1975
Box Date 1974

	NRFB	Mint/ No Box	Avg
Blonde	75-125	25-50	15-25

	Mint	Avg
box	25-45	15-25
red hair ribbon	10-15	5-10
body suit	5-10	3-5
blue collar	10-15	5-10
mini skirt	5-10	3-5
wrap skirt	5-10	3-5
blue scarf	10-15	5-10
red knee socks	5-10	3-5
shoes: white sandals	5-10	3-5
shoes: red flats	10-15	5-10

Growing Up Skipper. Never removed from box. *Courtesy of Lisa Varuolo*

STORE DISPLAY DRESSED BOX SKIPPER DOLLS

Skipper
Striped display box
Display
Date 1964
Box date 1964

Found with either Blonde or Brunette or Redhead doll.

Examples known are Flower Girl, Happy Birthday, Masquerade Party, Red Sensation, School Days, Silk 'n Fancy, Skating Fun.

Price reflects doll, outfit, and stand. See prices for each. Add together plus box & lid

	Avg	Below Avg
box	150-225	75-150
clear id plastic lid	100-175	50-100
stand: wire	25-35	15-25
booklet in cellophane	25-45	15-25
wrist tag*	40-65	25-40

*sometimes nrfb found with no wrist tag

ALLAN

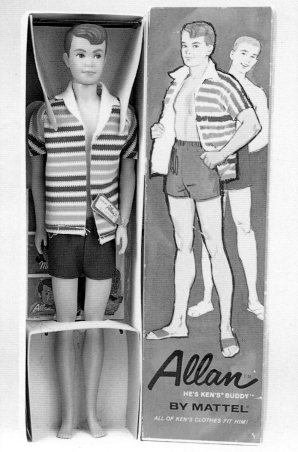

Allan. Never removed from box. *Author's Collection*

Allan
Straight legs
Stock # 1000
Date 1963
Box date 1964

	NRFB	Mint / No Box	Avg
Redhead	175-225	50-75	25-50

	Mint	Avg
box	50-75	35-50
box liner	25-40	20-35
stand: wire	25-40	15-25
booklet in cellophane	20-30	15-20

	Mint	Avg
yellow towel	15-20	10-15
multicolored stripe jacket	25-35	10-20
swimsuit: trunks	15-20	10-15
shoes: blue sandals	25-35	10-20
wrist tag	25-35	10-20

Allan
Bendable leg
Stock # 1010
Date 1965
Box date 19654

	NRFB	Mint / No Box	Avg
Redhead	475-550	275-350	175-275

	Mint	Avg
box	50-75	35-50
stand: wire	25-40	15-25
booklet in cellophane	20-30	15-20
blue jacket	25-35	10-20
swimsuit: trunks	15-20	10-15
shoes: sandals	25-35	10-25
wrist tag	25-35	10-25

STORE DISPLAY

DRESSED BOX ALLAN DOLL

Allan
Marked end panel box
Display
Stock # 1000
Date 1963
Box date 1964

Found with Allan doll Dressed in Rovin' Reporter

Box marked DRESSED BOX with clothing sticker applied to end panel

	NRFB	Mint / No Box	Avg
Redhead	475-550	275-350	175-275

	Mint	Avg
box	175-250	100-175
clear id plastic lid	100-175	50-100
stand: wire	25-40	15-25
booklet in cellophane	25-45	15-25
wrist tag*	40-65	25-40

  * sometimes nrfb found with no wrist tag

FRANCIE

Francie
Straight legs
Stock # 1160
Date 1966
Box date 1965

	NRFB	Mint/ No Box	Avg
Blonde	475-550	175-275	100-175
Brunette	475-550	175-275	100-175

	Mint	Avg
box	40-65	25-40
stand: clear x	10-15	5-10
booklet in cellophane	25-45	15-25
swimsuit: top	25-45	15-25
swimsuit: bottoms	25-45	15-25
shoes: red soft pointed heels	10-15	5-10
wrist tag	40-65	25-40

Francie
Bendable legs
Stock # 1130
Date 1966
Box date 1965

	NRFB	Mint/ No Box	Avg
Blonde	475-550	175-275	100-175
Brunette	475-550	175-275	100-175

	Mint	Avg
box	40-65	25-40
stand: clear x	10-15	5-10
booklet in cellophane	25-45	15-25
swimsuit: white	25-45	15-25
harder to find blue version	40-65	25-40
wrist tag	40-65	25-40

Francie
Japanese straight legs
Date 1966
Box date 1965

	NRFB	Mint/ No Box	Avg
Brunette	1850-2200	975-1150	850-975

	Mint	Avg
box w/ sticker	100-150	75-100
Francie stand	850-1000	650-850
Japanese booklet	100-150	75-100
blue version swimsuit	40-65	25-40
wrist tag	75-100	50-75

Japanese Francie.
Author's Collection

Francie
Bendable legs
Twist 'n Turn waist
Stock # 1170
Date 1967
Box date 1965

	NRFB	Mint/ No Box	Avg
Blonde	375-425	100-175	75-100
Brunette	375-425	100-175	75-100

	Mint	Avg
box	40-65	25-40
stand: clear x	10-15	5-10
booklet	25-45	15-25
swimsuit	25-45	15-25
wrist tag	40-65	25-40

Francie
Black
1st black version
Stock # 1100
Date 1966
Box date 1965

	NRFB	Mint/ No Box	Avg
Brunette*	2400-2850	1000-1350	875-1000

*hair usually found to have turned/oxidized to red

	Mint	Avg
box	40-65	25-40
stand: clear x	10-15	5-10
booklet	25-45	15-25
swimsuit	125-175	75-125
eyelash brush	25-45	15-25
wrist tag	40-65	25-40

Francie
Black
2nd black version
Stock # 1100
Date 1966
Box date 1965

	NRFB	Mint/ No Box	Avg
Brunette	2400-2850	1000-1350	875-1000

	Mint	Avg
box	40-65	25-40
stand: clear x	10-15	5-10
booklet	25-45	15-25
swimsuit	125-175	75-125
eyelash brush	25-45	15-25
wrist tag	40-65	25-40

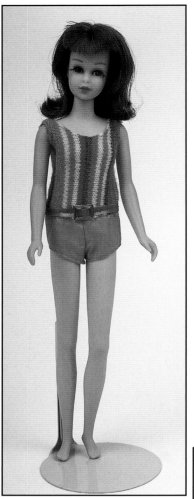

Twist 'n Turn Francie.
Author's Collection

Twist 'n Turn
Francie. Never
removed from
box.
*Author's Collec-
tion*

Twist 'n Turn Black Francie.
Never removed from box.
Author's Collection

34

FRANCIE HAIR HAPPENIN'S

Francie
Hair Happenin's
Stock # 1122
Date 1970
Box date 1969

	NRFB	Mint/ No Box	Avg
Blonde	550-800	225-300	75-100

	Mint	Avg
box	40-65	25-40
stand: clear x	10-15	5-10
booklet	25-45	15-25
turquoise dress	40-65	25-40
headband blue	40-65	25-40
mini curls hair piece	25-45	15-25
swingy swirl hair piece	25-45	15-25
fluffy whirl hair piece	25-45	15-25
twisty twirls hair piece	25-45	15-25
shoes: turquoise soft heels	25-45	15-25
wrist tag	40-65	25-40

FRANCIE NO BANGS

Francie
No Bangs
Stock # 1170
Date 191971
Box date 1969

	NRFB	Mint/ No Box	Avg
Blonde	1800-2200	850-1150	750-850
Brunette	1850-2250	875-1175	775-875

	Mint	Avg
box	40-65	25-40
stand: clear x	10-15	5-10
booklet	25-35	15-25
orange & white dress	125-175	75-125
orange panty	40-65	25-40
headband orange	65-115	40-65
shoes: white soft buckle	125-175	75-125
wrist tag	40-65	25-40

FRANCIE TWIST 'n TURN
SHORT FLIP

Francie
Short Curly Flip
Stock # 1170
Date 1969
Box date 1965

	NRFB	Mint/ No Box	Avg
Blonde	475-650	225-375	150-225
Brunette	475-650	225-375	150-225

	Mint	Avg
box	40-65	25-40
stand: clear x	10-15	5-10

Hair Happenin's Francie.
Author's Collection

booklet	25-45	15-25
swimsuit	40-65	25-40
headband yellow	40-65	25-40
or headband pink	40-65	25-40
wrist tag	40-65	25-40

Francie
Short Curly Flip
Stock # 1170
Date 1970
Box date 1965

	NRFB	Mint/ No Box	Avg
Blonde	475-650	225-375	150-225
Brunette	475-650	225-375	150-225

	Mint	Avg
box	40-65	25-40
stand: clear x	10-15	5-10
booklet	25-45	15-25
swimsuit: wrap top	40-65	25-40
pink shorts	25-45	15-25
headband yellow	40-65	25-40
or headband pink	40-65	25-40
wrist tag	40-65	25-40

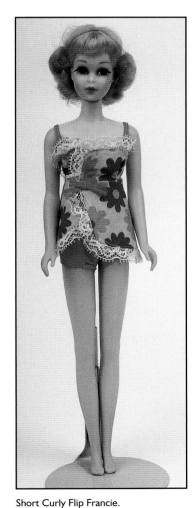

Short Curly Flip Francie.
Twist 'n Turn. Brunette.
Author's Collection

Short Curly Flip Francie.
Twist 'n Turn. Blonde.
Author's Collection

FRANCIE WITH GROWIN' PRETTY HAIR

Francie
Growin' Pretty Hair
Stock # 1129
Date 1970

	NRFB	Mint/ No Box	Avg
Blonde	225-350	125-200	75-125

	Mint	Avg
box	40-65	25-40
stand: clear x	10-15	5-10
booklet	25-45	15-25
instructions	10-15	5-10
pink lamé dress	25-45	15-25
shoes: soft pink heels	10-15	5-10
wrist tag	40-65	25-40

Growin' Pretty Hair Francie.
Never removed from box.
Author's Collection

BUSY FRANCIE

Francie
Busy with Holdin' Hands
Stock # 3313
Date 1971

	NRFB	Mint/ No Box	Avg
Blonde	475-650	225-375	150-225

	Mint	Avg
box	40-65	25-40
stand: clear x	10-15	5-10
booklet	25-45	15-25
green ribbed top	25-45	15-25
pants jeans	25-45	15-25
orange belt	25-45	15-25
hair ribbon green	25-45	15-25
shoes: square green heels	10-15	5-10
wrist tag	40-65	25-40
record player	10-15	5-10
record	10-15	5-10
tray	10-15	5-10
cups	10-15	5-10
tv	10-15	5-10
telephone	10-15	5-10
travel case	10-15	5-10

Busy with Holdin'
Hands Francie.
Author's Collection

FRANCIE SUN SET MALIBU

Francie
Malibu
Stock # 1068
Date 1971
Box Date 1970

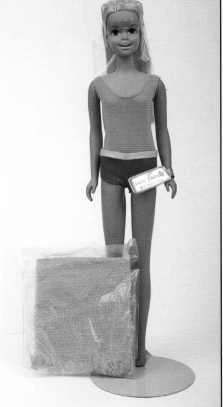

Sun Set Malibu Francie.
Mint with wrist tag.
Author's Collection

	NRFB	Mint/ No Box	Avg
Blonde	175-225	50-75	25-50

	Mint	Avg
box card	25-45	15-25
swimsuit	10-15	5-10
towel	10-15	5-10
sunglasses	10-15	5-10
wrist tag *	25-45	15-25

* nrfb examples have been found without wrist tag

Francie
Japanese Sun Sun Malibu
Date 1971
Box date 1970

	NRFB	Mint/ No Box	Avg
Brunette	3100-4000	1975-2900	1450-1975

	Mint	Avg
box card	25-45	15-25
swimsuit	10-15	5-10
towel	10-15	5-10
sunglasses	10-15	5-10
wrist tag	25-45	15-25

FRANCIE QUICK CURL

Francie
Quick Curl
Stock # 4222
Date 1972

	NRFB	Mint/ No Box	Avg
Brunette	175-225	50-75	25-50

	Mint	Avg
box card	25-45	15-25
yellow & white dress	25-45	15-25
stand: white x	10-15	5-10
styling extras comb, brush, curler, barrettes, ribbons	25-45	15-25
shoes: square white heels	10-15	5-10
wrist tag	25-45	15-25

SCOOTER

Scooter
Straight Legs
Stock # 1040
Date 1965
Box date 1964

	NRFB	Mint/ No Box	Avg
Blonde	175-225	50-75	25-50
Brunette	175-225	50-75	25-50
Redhead (Titian)	175-225	50-75	25-50

	Mint	Avg
box	50-75	35-50
box liner	25-35	15-25
stand: wire	25-35	15-25
booklet in cellophane	20-30	15-20
swimsuit: top	10-15	5-10
swimsuit: bottoms	10-15	5-10
hair ribbons: red	25-35	15-25
shoes: red Japan flats	10-15	5-10
wrist tag	25-35	15-25

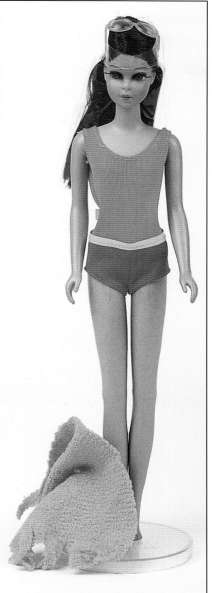

Japanese Sun Sun Malibu Francie. Rare
Courtesy of Karen Bindelglass

SCOOTER BENDABLE LEGS

Scooter
Bendable legs
Stock # 1120
Date 1966
Box date 1965

	NRFB	Mint/ No Box	Avg
Blonde	225-350	75-125	50-75
Brunette	225-350	75-125	50-75
Redhead (Titian)	225-350	75-125	50-75

	Mint	Avg
box	50-75	35-50
stand: wire	25-35	15-25
booklet in cellophane	20-30	15-20
red & white tank top	25-35	15-25
denim shorts	10-15	5-10
hair ribbons: red	25-35	15-25
shoes: red Japan flats	10-15	5-10
wrist tag	25-35	15-25

STORE DISPLAY
DRESSED BOX
SCOOTER DOLL

Scooter
Marked end panel box
Display
Stock # 1040
Date 1965
Box date 1964

Found with Scooter doll Dressed in Day At The Fair

Box marked DRESSED BOX with clothing sticker applied to end panel

	NRFB	Mint/ No Box	Avg
Blonde	475-550	275-350	175-275
Brunette	475-550	275-350	175-275
Redhead (Titian)	475-550	275-350	175-275

	Mint	Avg
box	175-250	100-175
clear id plastic lid	100-175	50-100
stand: wire	25-35	15-25
booklet in cellophane	25-45	15-25
wrist tag*	25-35	15-25
* sometimes nrfb found with no wrist tag		

FLUFF

Fluff
Living
Stock # 1143
Date 1971
Box date 1970

	NRFB	Mint/ No Box	Avg
Blonde	275-350	75-125	50-75

	Mint	Avg
box	25-45	15-25
stand: clear 2 piece	10-15	5-10
booklet in cellophane	25-45	15-25
hair ribbons: orange	10-15	5-10
swimsuit	25-45	15-25
yellow skateboard	10-15	5-10
wrist tag	25-45	15-25

TIFF

Tiff
Pose 'n Play
Stock # 1199
Date 1972
Box date 1975

	NRFB	Mint/ No Box	Avg
Redhead	375-475	200-275	150-200

	Mint	Avg
box	25-45	15-25
booklet in cellophane	25-45	15-25
white shirt w/ sticker	50-75	35-50
pants w/ stickers	50-75	35-50
red skateboard	10-15	5-10
shoes: white tennis	25-45	15-25
wrist tag	25-45	15-25

GINGER

Ginger
Growing Up
Stock # 9222
Date 1976
Box date 1975

	NRFB	Mint/ No Box	Avg
Brunette	100-175	75-125	50-75

	Mint	Avg
box	25-45	15-25
body suit	10-15	5-10
pink collar	10-15	5-10
mini skirt	10-15	5-10
skirt	10-15	5-10
pink scarf	10-15	5-10
socks	10-15	5-10
shoes: white sandals	5-10	3-5
shoes: turquoise flats	10-15	5-10

Fluff. Never removed from box.
Author's Collection

Growing Up Ginger.
Never removed from box.
Author's Collection

Fluff.
Author's Collection

Pos 'n Play Tiff. Never removed from box.
Author's Collection

RICKY

Ricky
Stock #1090
Date 1965

	NRFB	Mint/ No Box	Avg
Redhead	125-175	50-75	25-50

		Mint	Avg
box		50-75	25-50
liner		25-45	15-25
stand: wire		25-35	15-25
booklet in cellophane		25-45	15-25
shoes: red sandals		10-15	5-10
swimsuit: top		10-15	5-10
swimsuit: trunks		10-15	5-10
wrist tag		25-45	15-25

Ricky. Never removed from box.
Author's Collection

CASEY

Casey
Stock # 1180
Date 1967
Box date 1966

	NRFB	Mint/ No Box	Avg
Blonde	350-475	175-225	100-175
Brunette	350-475	175-225	100-175

		Mint	Avg
box		40-65	25-40
stand: clear x		10-15	5-10
booklet		25-45	15-25
swimsuit: gold & white		40-65	25-40
single gold triangle earring		10-15	5-10
wrist tag		40-65	25-40

Casey
Baggy
Stock # 9000
Date 1975
Box date 1974

	NRFB	Mint/ No Box	Avg
Blonde	200-275	100-175	50-100

		Mint	Avg
box / header card		25-45	15-25
swimsuit: bikini		25-45	15-25

Casey. Brunette.
Never removed from box.
Author's Collection

TWIGGY

Twiggy
Stock # 1185
Date 1967

	NRFB	Mint/ No Box	Avg
Blonde	450-525	175-225	125-175

		Mint	Avg
box		40-65	25-40
stand: clear x		10-15	5-10
booklet		25-45	15-25
yellow, green & blue dress		25-45	15-25
light blue textured panty		25-45	15-25
shoes: yellow boots		25-45	15-25
wrist tag		40-65	25-40

Twiggy. Never removed from box.
Author's Collection

P. J.

P. J.
Stock # 1113
Talking
Date 1969

	NRFB	Mint/ No Box	Avg
Blonde	275-350	*125-175	75-125

*prices are for repaired talking dolls. Mute deduct 10%

	Mint	Avg
box	40-65	25-40
stand: clear x	10-15	5-10
booklet	25-45	15-25
hair beads pair	25-45	15-25
purple round sunglasses	10-15	5-10
pink & orange dress	10-15	5-10
pink panty	25-45	15-25
shoes: hot pink pilgrims	10-15	5-10
wrist tag	25-35	10-25

P. J.
Stock # 1118
Twist 'n Turn
Date 1970
Box date 1969

	NRFB	Mint/ No Box	Avg
Blonde	275-350	125-175	75-125

	Mint	Avg
box	40-65	25-40
stand: clear x	10-15	5-10
booklet	25-45	15-25
hair beads pair	25-45	15-25
purple round sunglasses	10-15	5-10
pink w/ orange skirt swimsuit	10-15	5-10
wrist tag	25-35	10-25

LIVE ACTION P. J.

Live Action P.J.
Live Action
Stock # 1156
Date 1971
Box date 1970

	NRFB	Mint/ No Box	Avg
Blonde	275-350	75-125	50-75

	Mint	Avg
box	25-45	15-25
stand: clear Touch 'n Go	25-45	15-25
booklet	25-45	15-25
instructions	10-15	5-10
mini dress w/ hose & boots	10-15	5-10
purple suede fringe vest	25-45	15-25
hair beads pair	10-15	5-10
wrist tag	25-35	10-25

Talking P. J.
Never removed from box.
Author's Collection

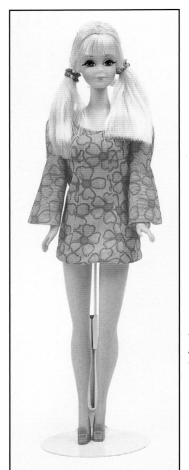

Talking P. J.
Author's Collection

Twist 'n Turn P. J.
Never removed from box.
Author's Collection

Live Action P. J.
Never removed from box.
Author's Collection

Live Action P.J.
Live Action w/ stage
Stock # 1153
Date 1971
Box date 1970

	NRFB	Mint/ No Box	Avg
Blonde	300-375	150-225	75-150

	Mint	Avg
box	25-45	15-25
stand: stage	40-65	25-40
microphone	25-45	15-25
instructions	10-15	5-10
mini dress w/ hose & boots	10-15	5-10
purple suede fringe vest	25-45	15-25
hair beads pair	10-15	5-10
wrist tag	25-35	10-25

P. J. SUN SET MALIBU

P. J.
Malibu
Stock # 1087
Date 1970

	NRFB	Mint/ No Box	Avg
Blonde	225-300	75-125	50-75

	Mint	Avg
box card	25-45	15-25
purple swimsuit	10-15	5-10
green towel	10-15	5-10
purple round sunglasses	10-15	5-10
hair beads pair	10-15	5-10
wrist tag *	25-35	10-25

* nrfb examples have been found without wrist tag

STACEY

Stacey
Twist 'n Turn
Stock # 1165
Date 1968
Box date 1967

	NRFB	Mint/ No Box	Avg
Blonde	450-525	200-275	150-200
Redhead	450-525	200-275	150-200

	Mint	Avg
box	40-65	25-40
stand: clear x	10-15	5-10
booklet	25-45	15-25
red swimsuit	25-45	15-25
red hair ribbon	25-45	15-25
wrist tag	40-65	25-40

Twist 'n Turn Stacey. Redhead. Never removed from box. Rare Great Britain box. *Author's Collection*

Twist 'n Turn Stacey. Blonde. Never removed from box.
Author's Collection

Stacey
Talking
Multicolored bikini
Stock # 1125
Date 1968

	NRFB	Mint/ No Box	Avg
Blonde	275-350	*125-175	75-125
Redhead	275-350	*125-175	75-125

*prices are for repaired talking dolls. Mute deduct 10%

	Mint	Avg
box	40-65	25-40
stand: clear x	10-15	5-10
booklet	25-45	15-25
multicolored bikini		
top & bottom	25-45	15-25
green hair ribbon	25-45	15-25
wrist tag	40-65	25-40

Stacey
Talking
Great Britain
Multicolored bikini
Stock # 1125
Date 1968

	NRFB	Mint/ No Box	Avg
Blonde	550-675	*125-175	75-125
Redhead	550-675	*125-175	75-125

*prices are for repaired talking dolls. Mute deduct 10%

	Mint	Avg
Great Britain box	75-100	50-75
stand: clear x	10-15	5-10
Great Britain booklet	75-100	50-75
multicolored bikini		
top & bottom	25-45	15-25
green hair ribbon	25-45	15-25
wrist tag	40-65	25-40

Stacey
Talking
Blue & silver swimsuit
Stock # 1125
Date 1968

	NRFB	Mint/ No Box	Avg
Blonde	375-450	*200-275	150-200
Redhead	375-450	*200-275	150-200

*prices are for repaired talking dolls. Mute deduct 10%

	Mint	Avg
box	40-65	25-40
stand: clear x	10-15	5-10
booklet	25-45	15-25
blue & silver swimsuit	40-65	25-40
green hair ribbon	25-45	15-25
wrist tag	40-65	25-40

Stacey

Twist 'n Turn
Short flip hairstyle
Aqua rose floral swimsuit
Stock # 1165
Date 1969

	NRFB	Mint/ No Box	Avg
Blonde	525-600	250-325	175-250
Redhead	525-600	250-325	175-250
		Mint	Avg
box		40-65	25-40
stand: clear x		10-15	5-10
booklet		25-45	15-25
aqua rose floral swimsuit		40-65	25-40
wrist tag		40-65	25-40

Stacey

Twist 'n Turn
Short flip hairstyle
Knit swimsuit
Stock # 1165
Date 1969
Box date 1967

	NRFB	Mint/ No Box	Avg
Blonde	450-525	200-275	150-200
Redhead	450-525	200-275	150-200
		Mint	Avg
box		40-65	25-40
stand: clear x		10-15	5-10
booklet		25-45	15-25
knit swimsuit		25-45	15-25
wrist tag		40-65	25-40

CHRISTIE

Christie

Twist 'n Turn
Date 1970
Box date 1969

	NRFB	Mint/ No Box	Avg
Brunette	300-375	150-225	75-150
		Mint	Avg
box		40-65	25-40
stand: clear x		10-15	5-10
booklet		25-45	15-25
swimsuit		25-45	15-25
wrist tag		40-65	25-40

Right: Twist 'n Turn Christie.
Never removed from box.

Far right: Twist 'n Turn Christie.
Never removed from mailer box.
Both from Author's Collection

Talking Christie. Never removed from clear box. Note: found here with Barbie pink suit top.
Author's Collection

CHRISTIE TALKING

Christie

Talking
Stock # 1126
Date 1968

	NRFB	Mint/ No Box	Avg
Brunette	375-450	*200-275	150-200

*prices are for repaired talking dolls. Mute deduct 10%

	Mint	Avg
box	40-65	25-40
stand: clear x	10-15	5-10
booklet	25-45	15-25
green knit top	25-45	15-25
pink shorts	25-45	15-25
wrist tag	40-65	25-40

Christie

Talking
Clear box
Stock # 1126
Date 1968

	NRFB	Mint/ No Box	Avg
Brunette	375-450	*200-275	150-200

*prices are for repaired talking dolls. Mute deduct 10%

	Mint	Avg
box	40-65	25-40
stand: clear x	10-15	5-10
stool top	10-15	5-10
stool bottom	10-15	5-10
booklet	25-45	15-25
green knit top	25-45	15-25
pink shorts	25-45	15-25
wrist tag	40-65	25-40

Christie
Talking
Stock # 1126
Date 1969

	NRFB	Mint/ No Box	Avg
Brunette	375-450	*200-275	150-200

*prices are for repaired talking dolls. Mute deduct 10%

	Mint	Avg
box	40-65	25-40
stand: clear x	10-15	5-10
booklet	25-45	15-25
orange swimsuit top	25-45	15-25
orange shorts	25-45	15-25
wrist tag	40-65	25-40

LIVE ACTION CHRISTIE

Christie
Live action
Stock # 1175
Date 1971
Box date 1970

	NRFB	Mint/ No Box	Avg
Brunette	375-450	200-275	150-200

	Mint	Avg
box	25-45	15-25
stand: clear Touch 'n Go	25-45	15-25
booklet	25-45	15-25
instructions	10-15	5-10
multicolored top w/ purple fringe	40-65	25-40
multicolored pants	40-65	25-40
sheer orange head scarf	40-65	25-40
shoes: purple low heels	25-45	15-25
wrist tag	25-45	15-25

CHRISTIE SUN SET MALIBU

Christie
Malibu
Stock # 7745
Date 1973

	NRFB	Mint/ No Box	Avg
Brunette	225-300	75-125	50-75

	Mint	Avg
box card	25-45	15-25
red swimsuit	10-15	5-10
towel	10-15	5-10
sunglasses	10-15	5-10
wrist tag*	25-35	10-25

*nrfb examples have been found without wrist tag

Talking Christie. Mint with wrist tag.
Author's Collection

Live Action Christie.
Never removed from box.
Author's Collection

BRAD

Brad
Talking
Stock # 1114
Date 1970
Box date 1969

	NRFB	Mint/ No Box	Avg
Brunette	100-175	50-75	50-

	Mint	Avg
box	40-65	25-40
stand: clear x	10-15	5-10
orange top	10-15	5-10
orange shorts	10-15	5-10
wrist tag	40-65	25-40

Talking Brad. Never removed from box.
Author's Collection

Brad
Talking
Stock # 1142
Date 1970
Box date 1969

	NRFB	Mint/ No Box	Avg
Brunette	100-175	50-75	50-

	Mint	Avg
box	40-65	25-40
stand: clear x	10-15	5-10
booklet	25-45	15-25
orange top	10-15	5-10
orange shorts	10-15	5-10
wrist tag	40-65	25-40

TUTTI

Tutti
Stock # 3550
Date 1965

	NRFB	Mint/ No Box	Avg
Blonde	150-200	75-150	40-75
Brunette	150-200	75-150	40-75

	Mint	Avg
box	40-65	25-40
booklet	25-45	15-25
pink & white dress	10-15	5-10
pink & white hat	10-15	5-10
pink hair ribbon	10-15	5-10
pink comb	3-5	1-3
pink brush	3-5	1-3
shoes: white bow flat	25-45	15-25
wrist tag	40-65	25-40

Tutti
Stock # 3580
Date 1965

	NRFB	Mint/ No Box	Avg
Blonde	150-200	75-150	40-75
Brunette	150-200	75-150	40-75

	Mint	Avg
box	40-65	25-40
booklet	25-45	15-25
pink & floral dress	10-15	5-10
pink hair ribbon	10-15	5-10
pink comb	3-5	1-3
pink brush	3-5	1-3
shoes: white bow flats	25-45	15-25
wrist tag	40-65	25-40

Tutti. Brunette, 1st issue.
Never removed from box.
Courtesy of Lisa Varuolo

Tutti. Blonde.
Never removed from box.
Courtesy of Lisa Varuolo

Tutti. Blonde & Brunette.
Courtesy of Lisa Varuolo

TODD

Todd
Stock # 3590
Date 1965

	NRFB	Mint/ No Box	Avg
Redhead	150-200	75-150	40-75
		Mint	**Avg**
box		40-65	25-40
booklet		25-45	15-25
blue shirt		10-15	5-10
houndstooth shorts		10-15	5-10
houndstooth hat		10-15	5-10
blue cotton socks		15-25	10-15
shoes: red tennis		25-45	15-25
wrist tag		40-65	25-40

Todd
Dressed Box
Stock # 3590
Date 1965

	NRFB	Mint/ No Box	Avg
Redhead	275-350	75-150	40-75
		Mint	**Avg**
box		40-65	25-40
booklet		25-45	15-25
red & white jacket		10-15	5-10
white shirt		10-15	5-10
blue shorts		10-15	5-10
blue cotton socks		15-25	10-15
shoes: tennis		25-45	15-25
wrist tag		40-65	25-40

Todd
Platinum prototype
Date 1965

	NRFB	Mint/ No Box	Avg
Platinum	n/a	n/a	n/a
		Mint	**Avg**
blue shirt		10-15	5-10
houndstooth shorts		10-15	5-10
houndstooth hat		10-15	5-10
blue cotton socks		15-25	10-15
shoes: red tennis		25-45	15-25
wrist tag		40-65	25-40

Todd. Never removed from box.
Author's Collection

Todd.
Courtesy of Lisa Varuolo

Todd. Platinum prototype. Rare.
Courtesy of Lisa Varuolo

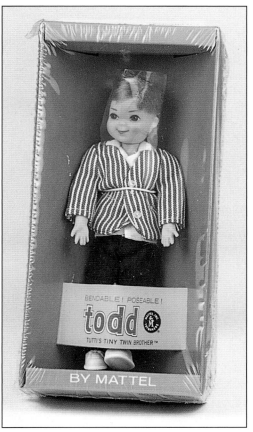

Dressed Todd.
Never removed from box rare.
Originally sold in the Mattel store.
Author's Collection

CHRIS

Chris
Stock # 3570
Date 1965

	NRFB	Mint/ No Box	Avg
Blonde	150-200	75-150	40-75
Brunette	150-200	75-150	40-75
Redhead	150-200	75-150	40-75

	Mint	Avg
box	40-65	25-40
booklet	25-45	15-25
multicolored dress	10-15	5-10
green shorts	10-15	5-10
two green hair ribbons	25-45	15-25
green hair barrette	15-25	10-15
pink comb	3-5	1-3
pink brush	3-5	1-3
shoes: orange bow flats	25-45	15-25
wrist tag	40-65	25-40

JAMIE

Jamie
Walking
Stock # 1132
Date 1970

	NRFB	Mint/ No Box	Avg
Blonde	375-450	200-275	150-200
Brunette	375-450	200-275	150-200
Redhead	375-450	200-275	150-200

	Mint	Avg
box	40-65	25-40
stand: clear x	10-15	5-10
booklet	25-45	15-25
dress w/ attached belt	25-45	15-25
yellow panty	25-45	15-25
sheer pink head scarf	45-70	25-45
shoes: orange boots	25-45	15-25
wrist tag	40-65	25-40

Chris.
Courtesy of Lisa Varuolo

Walking Jaime.
Author's Collection

Walking Jaime. Never removed from box.
Author's Collection

STEFFIE

Steffie
Walk Lively
Stock # 1183
Date 1972
Box date 1971

	NRFB	Mint/ No Box	Avg
Brunette	225-300	75-125	50-75

	Mint	Avg
box	25-45	15-25
stand: round walking	25-45	15-25
booklet	25-45	15-25
instructions	10-15	5-10
multicolored nylon jumpsuit	25-45	15-25
long red sheer scarf	40-65	25-40
shoes: red pilgrims	25-35	10-25
wrist tag	40-65	25-40

Walk Lively Steffie. Never removed from box.
Author's Collection

STEFFIE BUSY TALKING

Steffie
Busy Talking
Holdin' Hand
Stock # 1186
Date 1972
Box date 1971

	NRFB	Mint/ No Box	Avg
Blonde	375-450	200-275	150-200

*prices are for repaired talking dolls. Mute deduct 10%

	Mint	Avg
box	40-65	25-40
stand: clear x	10-15	5-10
booklet	25-45	15-25
pink & white nylon w/ blue shorts playsuit	25-45	15-25
navy blue & white belt	25-45	15-25
navy blue & white hat	25-45	15-25
pink & white nylon knee socks	25-45	15-25
shoes: white square toe	10-15	5-10
record player	10-15	5-10
record	10-15	5-10
tray	10-15	5-10
2 cups	10-15	5-10
tv	10-15	5-10
telephone	10-15	5-10
travel case	10-15	5-10
wrist tag	40-65	25-40

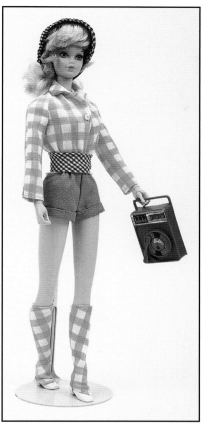

Busy Talking Steffie.
Author's Collection

STEFFIE BUSY

Steffie
Holdin' Hand
Stock # 3312
Date 1972
Box date 1971

	NRFB	Mint/ No Box	Avg
Brunette	225-300	75-125	50-75

	Mint	Avg
box	40-65	25-40
stand: white x	10-15	5-10
booklet	25-45	15-25
green floral cotton dress	25-45	15-25
shoes: green square toe	10-15	5-10
record player	10-15	5-10
record	10-15	5-10
tray	10-15	5-10
2 cups	10-15	5-10
tv	10-15	5-10
telephone	10-15	5-10
travel case	10-15	5-10
wrist tag	40-65	25-40

KELLEY

Kelley
Quick Curl
Stock # 4221
Date 1974
Box date 1972

	NRFB	Mint/ No Box	Avg
Redhead	225-300	75-125	50-75

	Mint	Avg
box card	25-45	15-25
dress	25-45	15-25
stand: white x	10-15	5-10
styling extras comb, brush, curler, barrettes, ribbons	25-45	15-25
shoes: white square toe	10-15	5-10
wrist tag	25-45	15-25

Quick Curl Kelley.
Never removed from box/card.
Author's Collection

Busy Steffie.
Never removed from box.
Author's Collection

KELLEY YELLOWSTONE

Kelley
Yellowstone
Stock # 7808
Date 1974
Box date 1973

	NRFB	Mint/ No Box	Avg
Redhead	375-450	200-275	150-200

	Mint	Avg
box card	25-45	15-25
stand: white x	10-15	5-10
shirt	25-45	15-25
shorts	25-45	15-25
pants	10-15	5-10
socks	10-15	5-10
backpack	10-15	5-10
sleeping bag	10-15	5-10
camping equipment: stove, pot, frying pan, cup, plate	25-45	15-25
shoes: sneakers	10-15	5-10
wrist tag	25-45	15-25

JULIA

Julia
Stock # 1127
Date 1969
Box date 1968

	NRFB	Mint/ No Box	Avg
Brunette	225-300	100-150	75-100

	Mint	Avg
box	40-65	25-40
stand: clear x	10-15	5-10
booklet	25-45	15-25
white dress, one piece	25-45	15-25
or two piece white suit	25-45	15-25
nurses hat	10-15	5-10
white panty	10-15	5-10
shoes: white pilgrims	10-15	5-10
wrist tag	25-45	15-25

JULIA TALKING

Julia
Talking
Stock # 1128
Date 1969-71
Box date 1968

	NRFB	Mint/ No Box	Avg
Brunette	225-300	*100-150	75-100

*prices are for repaired talking dolls. Mute deduct 10%

	Mint	Avg
box	40-65	25-40
stand: clear x	10-15	5-10
booklet	25-45	15-25
silver & gold jumpsuit	25-45	15-25
shoes: open toe clear	10-15	5-10
wrist tag	25-45	15-25

TRULY SCRUMPTIOUS

Truly Scrumptious
Talking
Stock # 1107
Date 1969

	NRFB	Mint/ No Box	Avg
Blonde	525-600	*250-325	175-250

*prices are for repaired talking dolls. Mute deduct 10%

	Mint	Avg
box	40-65	25-40
stand: clear x	10-15	5-10
booklet	25-45	15-25
pink & black lace dress	40-65	25-40
pink & black lace hat	40-65	25-40
white panty	10-15	5-10
shoes: pilgrims light pink	40-65	25-40
or pilgrims hot pink	10-15	5-10
wrist tag	40-65	25-40

Truly Scrumptious Talking.
Mint w/ wrist tag.
Author's Collection

Julia. Mint w/ wrist tag.
Author's Collection

Julia Talking.
Author's Collection

Truly Scrumptious
Stock # 1108
Date 1969

	NRFB	Mint/ No Box	Avg
Blonde	525-600	250-325	175-250

	Mint	Avg
box	40-65	25-40
stand: clear x	10-15	5-10
booklet	25-45	15-25
pink & white lace dress	40-65	25-40
pink & white lace hat	40-65	25-40
white panty	10-15	5-10
shoes: pilgrims light pink	40-65	25-40
wrist tag	40-65	25-40

MISS AMERICA

Miss America. Brunette. Kelloggs Special & Blonde Quick Curl.
Courtesy of Lisa Varuolo

Miss America
Kellogg's Special
Stock # 3194
Date 1972

	NRFB	Mint/ No Box	Avg
Brunette	225-300	100-150	75-100

	Mint	Avg
box	40-65	25-40
stand: clear x	10-15	5-10
dress w/ sash	15-25	10-15
red felt cape	15-25	10-15
red roses bouquet	15-25	10-15
scepter	15-25	10-15
shoes: white pilgrims	10-15	5-10
wrist tag band	25-45	15-25

Miss America
Walk Lively
Stock # 3200
Date 1972

	NRFB	Mint/ No Box	Avg
Brunette	275-325	100-150	75-100

	Mint	Avg
box	40-65	25-40
stand: clear x	10-15	5-10
dress w/ sash	15-25	10-15
red felt cape	15-25	10-15
red roses bouquet	15-25	10-15
scepter	15-25	10-15
shoes: white pilgrims	10-15	5-10
wrist tag band	25-45	15-25

Miss America
Walking
Stock # 3200
Date 1972

	NRFB	Mint/ No Box	Avg
Brunette	275-325	100-150	75-100

	Mint	Avg
box	40-65	25-40
stand: clear x	10-15	5-10
dress w/ sash	15-25	10-15
red felt cape	15-25	10-15
red roses bouquet	15-25	10-15
scepter	15-25	10-15
shoes: white pilgrims	10-15	5-10
wrist tag band	25-45	15-25

Miss America Walking. Brunette. Never removed from box.
Author's Collection

Miss America
Quick Curl
Stock # 8867
Date 1973

	NRFB	Mint/ No Box	Avg
Blonde	175-225	75-125	50-75

	Mint	Avg
box	40-65	25-40
stand: clear x	10-15	5-10
dress w/ sash	15-25	10-15
red felt cape	15-25	10-15
red roses bouquet	15-25	10-15
scepter	15-25	10-15
shoes: white pilgrims	10-15	5-10
wrist tag band	25-45	15-25

BUFFY & MRS. BEASLEY

Buffy & Mrs. Beasley
Stock # 3577
Date 1968

	NRFB	Mint/ No Box	Avg
Blonde	175-250	75-125	50-75

	Mint	Avg
box	25-45	15-25
red hair ribbons	10-15	5-10
Buffy red & white dress	10-15	5-10
red shorts	10-15	5-10
white tricot socks	10-15	5-10
shoes: red w/ white sole sneakers	10-15	5-10
Mrs. Beasley doll	25-45	15-25
skirt & collar	25-45	15-25
black granny glasses	25-45	15-25
wrist tag	25-45	15-25

PRETTY PAIRS

Pretty Pairs
Lori 'n Rori
Stock # 1133
Date 1970

	NRFB	Mint/ No Box	Avg
Blonde	225-300	175-225	100-150

	Mint	Avg
box card	25-45	15-25
hair ribbon	10-15	5-10
dress	25-45	15-25
socks	10-15	5-10
shoes: pink bow	10-15	5-10
Rori doll	40-65	25-40

Buffy & Mrs. Beasley.
Never removed from box.
Author's Collection

Pretty Pairs , Lori 'n Rori.

Pretty Pairs
Nan 'n Fran
Stock # 1134
Date 1970

	NRFB	Mint/ No Box	Avg
Brunette	225-300	175-225	100-150

	Mint	Avg
box card	25-45	15-25
nightcap	25-45	15-25
nightgown	10-15	5-10
shoes: hot pink scuffs	10-15	5-10
Nan doll	40-65	25-40

Pretty Pairs
Angie 'n Tangie
Stock # 1135
Date 1970

	NRFB	Mint/ No Box	Avg
Brunette	225-300	175-225	100-150

	Mint	Avg
box card	25-45	15-25
hair ribbon	10-15	5-10
dress	40-65	25-40
tights	5-45	15-25
shoes: hot pink bow	10-15	5-10
Tangie doll	40-65	25-40

Pretty Pairs, Nan 'n Fran. Never removed from box/card.
Author's Collection

Pretty Pairs, Angie 'n Tangie.
Courtesy of Lisa Varuolo

51

PART II: Outfits & Accessories

BARBIE FASHIONS
900 SERIES

Golden Girl
#911
Date 1959-62

NRFB	Mint/Complete
100-175	55-80

Add 20% for TM label versions

	Avg
gold & white brocade sheath dress	15-20
turquoise corduroy clutch bag	15-20
graduated pearl necklace	25-35
short white tricot gloves	15-20
shoes: brown open toe	25-35

Cotton Casual
#912
Date 1959-62

NRFB	Mint/Complete
100-175	40-65

Add 20% for TM label versions

	Avg
navy & white stripe dress	25-30
shoes: white open toe	10-15

Peachy Fleecy
#915
Date 1959-61

NRFB	Mint/Complete
125-200	55-80

Add 20% for TM label versions

	Avg
light beige wool coat	15-20
brown felt cloche hat w/ feather	15-20
golden clutch purse	5-7
white leatherette gloves	7-10
shoes: brown open toe	25-35

Commuter Set
#916
Date 1959-60

NRFB	Mint/Complete
875-925	350-400

Add 20% for TM label versions

	Avg
navy cotton suit jacket	20-25
navy cotton suit sheath skirt	25-30
blue & white checkered body blouse	35-40
white satin body blouse	50-75
red or rose flower silk hat	50-75
cardboard red Barbie hat box	45-50
double strand crystal bead necklace	30-35
double strand crystal bead snake bracelet	30-35
short white tricot gloves	15-20
shoes: navy open toe	25-35

Apple Print Sheath
#917
Date 1959-60

NRFB	Mint/Complete
125-200	55-80

Add 20% for TM label versions

	Avg
black w/ colorful apple print dress	25-30
shoes: black open toe	10-15

Cruise Stripes
#918
Date 1959-62

NRFB	Mint/Complete
125-200	55-80

Add 20% for TM label versions

	Avg
navy dress w/ red & white bodice	10-15
white belt	35-40
shoes: black open toe	10-15

Undergarments
#919
Date 1959-62

NRFB	Mint/Complete
50-100	20-35

Add 20% for TM label versions

	Avg
blue trunk leg panties	5-7
blue half slip	5-7
blue embroidered girdle	5-7
blue strapless bra	5-7

Floral Petticoat
#921
Date 1959-63

NRFB	Mint/Complete
75-125	30-45

Add 20% for TM label versions

	Avg
white full embroidered half slip	5-7
white embroidered panties	7-10
white strapless bra	5-7
light pink comb	3-5
light pink brush	3-5
light pink mirror	3-5

Cotton Casual. Never removed from box/card.
Courtesy of Richard Chapman and Glenn Mandeville

Barbie Doll Accessories.

Barbie Doll Accessories
Rose pink cotton swimsuit
923
Date 1961-62

	NRFB	Mint/Complete
	275-350	80-105
		Avg
rose pink cotton swimsuit		10-15
black rimmed glasses		10-15
short white tricot gloves		15-20
straw flower filled tote bag		7-10
graduated pearl necklace		25-35
pearl snake bracelet		25-35
hoop earrings		20-30
shoes: black open toe		10-15
shoes: white open toe		10-15
shoes: pink open toe		10-15

Evening Splendor
961
Date 1959-64

	NRFB	Mint/Complete
	375-425	100-125
	*Add 20% for TM label versions	
		Avg
gold & white brocade coat		15-20
gold & white brocade		
slim dress		15-20
turquoise corduroy clutch bag		15-20
woven white patterned hankie		25-30
fur & pearl hat		25-30
short white tricot gloves		15-20
graduated pearl necklace		25-35
pearl earrings		10-15
shoes: brown open toe		25-35

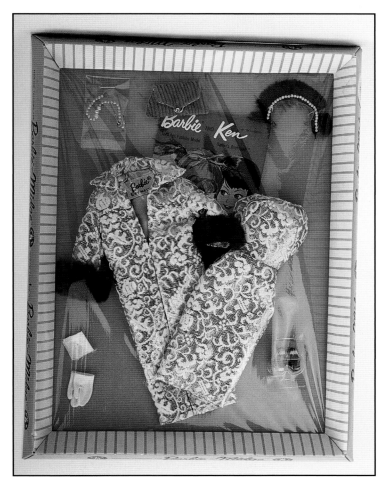

Evening Splendor. Never removed
from box/card.
Author's Collection

Barbie-Q Outfit
#962
Date 1959-62

	NRFB	Mint/Complete
	225-275	75-100

*Add 20% for TM label versions

	Avg
cotton rose dress	10-15
white apron 5-7	
white chef hat	7-10
red & white potholder	5-7
wooden rolling pin	5-7
metal spoon w/ red handle	5-7
metal spatula w/ red handle	5-7
metal knife w/ red handle	5-7
shoes: white open toe	10-15

Resort Set
#963
Date 1959-62

	NRFB	Mint/Complete
	125-175	50-75

*Add 20% for TM label versions

	Avg
red & white trim jacket	5-7
navy & white stripe shell	5-7
white cotton shorts	5-7
white sailcloth hat	5-7
charm bracelet	15-20
shoes: white cork wedges	15-20

Nighty Negligee Set
#965
Date 1959-64

	NRFB	Mint/Complete
	125-175	40-65

*Add 20% for TM label versions

	Avg
sheer pink long nightgown	7-10
sheer pink peignoir robe	5-7
stuffed pink dog	7-10
shoes: pink open toe w/ pompom	25-30

Resort Set

Nighty Negligee Set

Gay Parisienne
964
Date 1959
TM label

	NRFB	Mint/Complete
	2300-3000	975-1275
		Avg
navy blue pindot bubble dress		650-700
navy blue tulle headband hat		175-225
rabbit fur stole w/ white lining		50-75
gold velvet clutch purse		175-225
long white tricot gloves		10-15
graduated pearl necklace		25-35
pearl earrings		10-15
navy open toe #1 shoes		75-100

Plantation Belle
966
Date 1959-61

	NRFB	Mint/Complete
	525-600	150-200
	* Add 20% for TM label versions	
		Avg
sheer pink party dress		15-20
white nylon & tulle petticoat		15-20
pink & white hat		20-25
pink straw purse		15-20
pink graduated pearl necklace		25-35
pink pearl earrings		25-30
pink pearl snake bracelet		30-35
short white tricot gloves		15-20
shoes: pink open toe		15-20

Picnic Set
967
Date 1959-61

	NRFB	Mint/Complete
	575-650	175-225
	* Add 20% for TM label versions	
		Avg
red & white check body suit		7-10
clam digger jeans		5-7
straw fishing hat		20-25
fishing pole w/ fish		50-75
picnic basket		15-20
shoes: woven white cork wedges		25-30

Gay Parisienne.
Courtesy of Sherry Baloun

Plantation Belle.
Courtesy of Richard Chapman and Glenn Mandeville

Picnic Set.
Courtesy of Richard Chapman and Glenn Mandeville

Suburban Shopper
969
Date 1959-64

	NRFB	Mint/Complete
	575-650	175-225

* Add 20% for TM label versions

	Avg
blue & white striped cotton dress	15-20
straw cartwheel hat w/ blue satin ribbon	25-30
straw tote bag w/ fruit	10-15
pink telephone	10-15
pearl drop chain necklace	45-50
shoes: white open toe	10-15

Sweet Dreams
973
Date 1959-63
Yellow version

	NRFB	Mint/Complete
	125-175	40-65

* Add 20% for TM label versions

	Avg
sheer yellow baby doll pajama top	5-7
sheer yellow baby doll pajama bottom	7-10
alarm clock	5-7
"Dear Diary" book	5-7
red apple	7-10
blue hair ribbon on metal loop	10-15
shoes: blue open toe w/ pompom	25-30

Sweet Dreams
973
Date 1959-63
Pink version

	NRFB	Mint/Complete
	375-450	275-325

* Add 20% for TM label versions

	Avg
sheer pink baby doll pajama top	85-100
sheer pink baby doll pajama bottom	100-125
alarm clock	5-7
"Dear Diary" book	5-7
red apple	7-10
blue hair ribbon on metal loop	10-15
shoes: blue open toe w/ pompom	25-30

Roman Holiday
968
Date 1959
TM label

	NRFB	Mint/Complete
	4300-5000	1275-1575

	Avg
navy dress w/ red & white bodice	125-175
red & white coat	575-625
white belt	15-20
white clutch purse	5-7
red straw cord hat	125-175
black rimmed glasses	10-15
light pink comb	5-7
woven white patterned hankie	25-30
white & clear glasses case	125-175
"B" hinged compact w/ powder puff	350-400

short white tricot gloves	15-20
pearl drop chain necklace	45-50
shoes: black open toe	10-15

Easter Parade
971
Date 1959
TM label

	NRFB	Mint/Complete
	4300-5000	1275-1575

	Avg
black w/ colorful appleprint dress	125-150
black a-line coat	350-400
black clutch purse	5-7
black silk hair bow	350-400
short white tricot gloves	15-20
graduated pearl necklace	25-35
pearl earrings	10-15
shoes: black open toe	10-15

Wedding Day Set
972
Date 1959-62

	NRFB	Mint/Complete
	250-300	100-125

* Add 20% for TM label versions

	Avg
white w/ silver glitter wedding gown	15-20
white pearl crown & tulle veil	15-20
white floral bouquet	15-20
blue garter	10-15
short white tricot gloves	15-20
graduated pearl necklace	25-35
shoes: white open toe	10-15

Easter Parade.
Courtesy of Sherry Baloun

Roman Holiday.
Courtesy of Sherry Baloun

Winter Holiday
975
Date 1959-63

NRFB	Mint/Complete
175-225	60-85
* Add 20% for TM label versions	

	Avg
white leatherette coat w/ belt	15-20
blue & white striped hooded pullover w/ tie	10-15
black knit stretch pants	5-7
red plaid travel bag	5-7
red vinyl gloves	10-15
shoes: white cork wedges	15-20

Sweater Girl
976
Date 1959-62

NRFB	Mint/Complete
250-300	100-125
* Add 20% for TM label versions	

	Avg
orange wool cardigan sweater	25-30
orange wool shell sweater	25-30
gray wrap sheath skirt	5-7
"How to Knit" book	5-7
bowl of matching yarn w/ needles	10-15
silver scissors	7-10
shoes: black open toe	10-15

Silken Flame
977
Date 1960-64

NRFB	Mint/Complete
125-175	65-90

	Avg
red velvet bodice & white satin dress	25-30
wide gold belt	10-15
gold clutch purse	7-10
shoes: black open toe	10-15

Let's Dance
978
Date 1960-62

NRFB	Mint/Complete
175-225	75-100

	Avg
blue floral dress	7-10
pearl drop chain necklace	45-50
white clutch purse	5-7
shoes: black open toe	10-15

Silken Flame.
Courtesy of Richard Chapman and Glenn Mandeville

Sweater Girl

Let's Dance

Friday Night Date
979
Date 1960-64

	NRFB	Mint/Complete
	175-225	75-100
		Avg
blue corduroy jumper		10-15
white cotton underdress		5-7
black Barbie serving tray		7-10
two glasses w/ cotton fizz		20-25
two straws		15-20
shoes: black open toe		10-15

Busy Gal
981
Date 1960-61

	NRFB	Mint/Complete
	375-450	225-300
		Avg
red linen suit jacket		10-15
red linen suit skirt		10-15
red & white body blouse		15-20
navy belt		15-20
navy blue open crown hat		15-20
black fashion designer portfolio		10-15
two paper illustrations sheets		25-30
black rimmed glasses		15-20
shoes: navy open toe		25-30

Solo In The Spotlight
982
Date 1960-61

	NRFB	Mint/Complete
	375-450	150-200
		Avg
black snug glitter gown		10-15
pink chiffon scarf		10-15
long black tricot gloves		15-20
silver microphone w/ stand		50-75
four strand clear bead necklace		40-45
shoes: black open toe		10-15

Enchanted Evening
983
Date 1960-63

	NRFB	Mint/Complete
	200-275	100-150
		Avg
pink satin gown w/ rose trim		15-20
or pink satin gown w/ sequin trim		15-20
fur stole w/ pink lining		7-10
long white tricot gloves		10-15
three strand pearl choker		40-45
pearl earrings w/ drops		20-25
shoes: clear w/ gold glitter open toe		20-25

Friday Night Date.
Courtesy of Anthony Alcaide

Solo In The Spotlight.
Courtesy of Richard Chapman and Glenn Mandeville

Enchanted Evening.
Courtesy of Richard Chapman and Glenn Mandeville

American Airlines Stewardess
984
Date 1961-64

NRFB	Mint/Complete
275-350	80-105
	Avg

navy cotton suit jacket w/ wings	10-15
navy cotton suit skirt	7-10
white nylon body blouse	15-20
navy cotton hat w/AA insignia	15-20
navy AA flight bag	7-10
black shoulder purse	10-15
shoes: black open toe	10-15

Open Road
985
Date 1961-62

NRFB	Mint/Complete
375-450	150-200
	Avg

khaki car coat w/ three toggles	25-30
beige wool sweater	25-30
red, black & grey stripe pants	7-10
straw hat w/ red chiffon scarf	25-30
red sunglasses	25-30
Mattel Road Map	5-7
shoes: red cork wedges	20-25

Sheath Sensation
986
Date 1961-64

NRFB	Mint/Complete
175-225	50-75
	Avg

red cotton sheath dress	10-15
straw hat w/ red ribbon trim	15-20
short white tricot gloves	15-20
shoes: white open toe	10-15

Orange Blossom
987
Date 1961-64

NRFB	Mint/Complete
200-275	50-75
	Avg

yellow cotton sheath dress	5-7
white lace overdress	5-7
yellow tulle hat	10-15
bouquet w/ white & yellow streamers	10-15
short white tricot gloves	15-20
shoes: white open toe	10-15

Singing In The Shower
988
Date 1961-62

NRFB	Mint/Complete
175-225	40-65
	Avg

yellow terry robe	5-7
yellow terry robe belt	5-7
blue terry "Hers" towel	7-10
blue terry washcloth	7-10
blue shower cap	5-7
pink soap	5-7
gold talc box	5-7
blue powder puff	3-5
pink wash stick w/orange sponge	7-10
shoes: yellow terry scuffs	7-10

Ballerina
989
Date 1961-65

NRFB	Mint/Complete
175-225	50-75
	Avg

silver & white tulle tutu	5-7
black leotard	7-10
black tights	7-10
silver crown	10-15
ballet "Nutcracker" poster	10-15
pink satin ballet shoe bag	5-7
shoes: white ballet slippers	5-7

Registered Nurse
991
Date 1961-64

NRFB	Mint/Complete
275-350	80-105
	Avg

white dress uniform w/ pin	10-15
navy blue cape	7-10
white nurse's cap	10-15
black rimmed glasses	15-20
Barbie "Nursing Diploma"	10-15
red hot water bottle	7-10
medicine bottle	7-10
medal spoon	10-15
shoes: white open toe	10-15

Open Road.
Courtesy of Lisa Varuolo

Registered Nurse.
Author's Collection

Garden Party
931
Date 1962-63

NRFB	Mint/Complete
125-200	35-60
	Avg
cotton dress w/ eyelet inset panel	10-15
short white tricot gloves	15-20
shoes: white open toe	10-15

Movie Date
933
Date 1962-63

NRFB	Mint/Complete
75-125	20-45
	Avg
cotton dress w/ sheer overskirt	15-20

After Five
934
Date 1962-64

NRFB	Mint/Complete
125-200	35-60
	Avg
black dress w/ white organdy collar	10-15
white organdy hat w/ black velvet ribbon	10-15
shoes: black open toe	10-15

Sorority Meeting
937
Date 1962-63

NRFB	Mint/Complete
125-200	50-75
	Avg
brown cotton sleeveless dress	7-10
brown sweater vest	10-15
brown pillbox hat	7-10
graduated pearl necklace	25-35
pearl earrings	10-15
short white tricot gloves	15-20
shoes: brown open toe	25-35

Red Flare
939
Date 1962-65

NRFB	Mint/Complete
125-200	35-60
	Avg
red a-line velvet coat	5-7
red velvet clutch purse w/ diamond closure	5-7
red velvet pillbox hat	5-7
long white tricot gloves	10-15
shoes: red open toe	10-15

Mood For Music
940
Date 1962-63

NRFB	Mint/Complete
125-200	50-75
	Avg
blue & white cardigan	10-15
white knit halter	7-10
blue velvet pants	7-10
three strand pearl choker	40-45
shoes: gold cork wedges	10-15

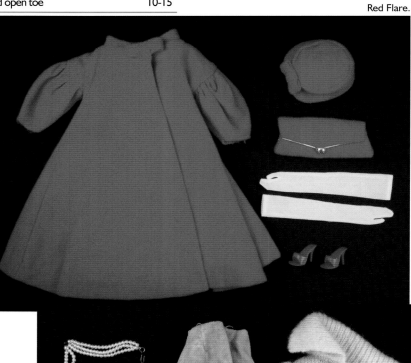

Red Flare.

Sorority Meeting.

Mood for Music.

Tennis Anyone?
941
Date 1962-64

	NRFB	Mint/Complete
	125-200	35-60
		Avg
white tennis dress		5-7
white cotton tennis sweater		7-10
"Tennis Rules" book		5-7
blue goggles sunglasses		10-15
tennis racquet		5-7
two tennis balls		5-7
white cotton socks		5-7
shoes: white tennis sneakers		5-7

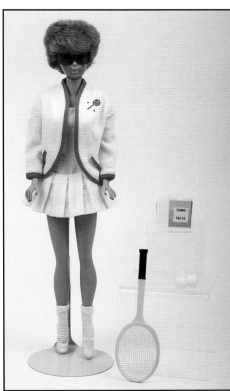

Tennis Anyone?
Author's Collection

Icebreaker
942
Date 1962-64

	NRFB	Mint/Complete
	125-200	35-60
		Avg
red cotton turtleneck body blouse		5-7
white fur jacket		7-10
red velvet skirt		5-7
nude panty hose		7-10
shoes: white skates		10-15

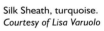

Icebreaker. Never removed from box/card.
Author's Collection

Accessory Pak
Date 1962-63

	NRFB	Mint/Complete
	175-225	90-115
		Avg
short white tricot gloves		15-20
white sunglasses w/ red/gold glitter		25-30
three strand pearl choker		40-45
pearl earrings w/ drops		20-25
pearl snake bracelet		25-35
shoes: clear w/ gold glitter open toe		20-25
shoes: red open toe		10-15
shoes: white open toe		10-15
shoes: orange open toe		10-15

Purse Pak
Date 1962-63

	NRFB	Mint/Complete
	75-125	20-45
		Avg
straw flower filled tote bag		7-10
red velvet clutch purse w/ pearl closure		5-7
black clutch purse		5-7

Silk Sheath
Pak
Date 1962-63

	NRFB	Mint/Complete
	125-225	20-150
		Avg
red silk sheath dress		75-125
shoes: red open toe		10-15
black silk sheath dress		75-125
shoes: black open toe		10-15
white silk sheath dress		50-75
shoes: white open toe		10-15
pale yellow silk sheath dress		20-45
shoes: pale yellow open toe		10-15
golden yellow silk sheath dress		65-100
shoes: golden yellow open toe		10-15
turquoise silk sheath dress		20-45
shoes: turquoise open toe		10-15
green silk sheath dress		20-45
shoes: green open toe		10-15

Slip, Panties, Bra
Pak
Date 1962-63

	NRFB	Mint/Complete
	50-75	15-30
		Avg
white full embroidered half slip		5-7
white embroidered panty		7-10
white strapless bra		5-7

Silk Sheath, turquoise.
Courtesy of Lisa Varuolo

Tee Shirt And Shorts
Pak
Date 1962-63

	NRFB	Mint/Complete
	50-75	15-30
		Avg
red & white stripe tee		5-7
navy cotton shorts		5-7
navy & white stripe tee		5-7
white cotton shorts		5-7
black & white stripe tee		5-7
red cotton shorts		5-7

Helenca Swimsuit
Pak
Date 1962-63

	NRFB	Mint/Complete
	65-90	20-45
		Avg
red swimsuit		15-20
white rimmed sunglasses		10-15
shoes: gold cork wedges		10-15
navy swimsuit		20-25
white rimmed sunglasses		10-15
shoes: gold cork wedges		10-15
black swimsuit		20-25
white rimmed sunglasses		10-15
shoes: gold cork wedges		10-15

Sheath With Gold Buttons
Pak
Date 1962-63

	NRFB	Mint/Complete
	65-90	20-45
		Avg
rust & white polka dot sheath dress		15-20
green & white polka dot sheath dress		15-20
blue & white polka dot sheath dress		15-20

Two Piece Pajamas
Pak
Date 1962-63

	NRFB	Mint/Complete
	40-65	10-25
		Avg
pink pj top		5-7
pink pj pants		5-7
yellow pj top		5-7
yellow pj pants		5-7
light blue pj top		5-7
light blue pj pants		5-7

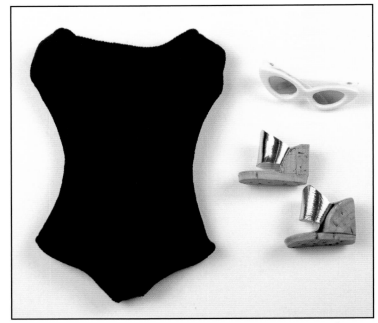

Helenca Swimsuit.

Sheath with Gold Buttons.

Two Piece Pajamas, pink. Never removed from box/card.
Author's Collection

Scoop Neck Playsuit
Pak
Date 1962-63

NRFB	Mint/Complete
65-90	20-45
	Avg
black cotton playsuit	5-7
wide blue belt	7-10
charm bracelet	15-20
red cotton playsuit	5-7
wide yellow belt	7-10
charm bracelet	15-20
white cotton playsuit	5-7
wide orange belt	7-10
charm bracelet	15-20
black & white floral cotton playsuit	5-7
wide red belt	7-10
charm bracelet	15-20
pink cotton playsuit	5-7
wide black belt	7-10
charm bracelet	15-20

Sheath Skirt And Telephone
Pak
Date 1962-63

NRFB	Mint/Complete
65-90	15-30
	Avg
black cotton sheath skirt	5-7
white telephone	7-10
white cotton sheath skirt	5-7
black telephone	7-10
black & white floral cotton sheath skirt	5-7
white telephone	7-10
pink cotton sheath skirt	5-7
black telephone	7-10
orange cotton sheath skirt	5-7
black telephone	7-10

Plain Blouse
Pak
Date 1962-63

NRFB	Mint/Complete
50-75	15-30
	Avg
red cotton blouse	5-7
yellow clutch purse	7-10

white cotton blouse	5-7
red clutch purse	7-10
pink cotton blouse	5-7
white clutch purse	7-10
black & white floral cotton blouse	5-7
blue clutch purse	7-10
orange cotton blouse	5-7
pink clutch purse	7-10

Slacks
Pak
Date 1962-63

NRFB	Mint/Complete
50-75	15-30
	Avg
red cotton pants	5-7
yellow belt	7-10
white cotton pants	5-7
orange belt	7-10
black cotton pants	5-7
blue belt	7-10
black & white floral cotton pants	5-7
red belt	7-10
orange cotton pants	5-7
pink belt	7-10

Gathered Skirt
Pak
Date 1962-63

NRFB	Mint/Complete
50-75	15-30
	Avg
red cotton full skirt	5-7
shoes: red open toe	10-15
black & white floral cotton full skirt	5-7
shoes: black open toe	10-15
orange cotton full skirt	5-7
shoes: orange open toe	10-15
black cotton full skirt	5-7
shoes: black open toe	10-15
pink cotton full skirt	5-7
shoes: pink open toe	10-15

Cardigan
Pak
Date 1962-63

NRFB	Mint/Complete
40-65	10-25
	Avg
blue & white cardigan sweater	15-20
black & white cardigan sweater	15-20
white & white cardigan sweater	15-20
pink & white cardigan sweater	15-20

Black & white cardigan & white square neck sweater.
Never removed from box/card.
Author's Collection

Lingerie Set
Pak
Date 1962-63

	NRFB	Mint/Complete
	60-85	20-45
		Avg
blue trunk leg panties		5-7
blue half slip		5-7
blue strapless bra		5-7
light pink mirror		3-5
shoes: blue open toe w/ pompom		20-25
white trunk leg panties		5-7
white half slip		5-7
white strapless bra		5-7
light pink mirror		3-5
shoes: white open toe w/ pompom		20-25
pink trunk leg panties		5-7
pink half slip		5-7
pink strapless bra		5-7
light pink mirror		3-5
shoes: pink open toe w/ pompom		20-25
black trunk leg panties		5-7
black half slip		5-7
black strapless bra		5-7
light pink mirror		3-5
shoes: black open toe w/ pompom		20-25

Apron and Utensils
Pak
Date 1962-63

	NRFB	Mint/Complete
	60-85	20-45
		Avg
white apron		5-7
red & white potholder		5-7
wooden rolling pin		5-7
metal spoon w/ red handle		5-7
metal spatula w/ red handle		5-7
metal knife w/ red handle		5-7
red apron		5-7
red & white potholder		5-7
wooden rolling pin		5-7
metal spoon w/ red handle		5-7
metal spatula w/ red handle		5-7
metal knife w/ red handle		5-7
blue apron		5-7
red & white potholder		5-7
wooden rolling pin		5-7
metal spoon w/ red handle		5-7
metal spatula w/ red handle		5-7
metal knife w/ red handle		5-7

Belle Dress
Pak
Date 1962-63

	NRFB	Mint/Complete
	70-95	25-40
		Avg
orange polished cotton dress		20-25
pink polished cotton dress		20-25
blue polished cotton dress		20-25

Belle Dress, pink.
Courtesy of Anthony Alcaide

Square Neck Sweater
Pak
Date 1962-63

	NRFB	Mint/Complete
	40-65	10-25
		Avg
white square neck sweater		10-15
pink square neck sweater		10-15
black square neck sweater		10-15

Fur Stole With Bag
Pak
Date 1962-63

	NRFB	Mint/Complete
	40-65	10-25
		Avg
fur stole w/ pink lining		7-10
gold clutch purse		7-10

Rain Coat
949
Date 1963

	NRFB	Mint/Complete
	125-225	40-65
		Avg
yellow cotton raincoat		5-7
yellow cotton raincoat belt		7-10
yellow cotton rain hat		7-10
yellow umbrella w/ tassel		7-10
shoes: white boots		7-10

Rain Coat. Never removed from box/card.
Author's Collection

Fancy Free
943
Date 1963-64

	NRFB	Mint/Complete
	100-175	35-40
		Avg
cotton red & blue dress		35-40

Fancy Free.

Orange Blossom
#987
Date 1963-64
Different gloves than 1959-62 version

	NRFB	Mint/Complete
	175-225	40-65
		Avg
yellow cotton sheath dress		5-7
white lace overdress		5-7
yellow tulle hat		10-15
bouquet w/ white & yellow streamers		10-15
long white tricot gloves		10-15
shoes: white open toe		10-15

Masquerade
#944
Date 1963-64

	NRFB	Mint/Complete
	150-200	50-75
		Avg
black & yellow halter costume		5-7
black & yellow clown hat		5-7
black mask		7-10
black pantyhose		15-20
"Come To My Party" invitation		7-10
shoes: black open toe w/ yellow pompom		25-30

Graduation
945
Date 1963-64

	NRFB	Mint/Complete
	75-125	20-45
		Avg
black graduation gown		5-7
black graduation hat		5-7
white felt collar		7-10
paper diploma w/ ribbon		7-10

Dinner At Eight
946
Date 1963-64

	NRFB	Mint/Complete
	175-225	75-100
		Avg
orange & gold hostess coat		15-20
orange jumpsuit		35-40
shoes: gold cork wedges		10-15

Masquerade.

Dinner At Eight.

Orange Blossom.
Courtesy of Richard Chapman and Glenn Mandeville

Bride's Dream
947
Date 1963-65

	NRFB	Mint/Complete
	225-300	125-150
		Avg
wedding gown w/ satin bodice		15-20
white pearl crown & tulle veil		15-20
white floral bouquet		15-20
blue garter		10-15
long white tricot gloves		10-15
graduated pearl necklace		25-35
shoes: white open toe		10-15

Ski Queen
948
Date 1963-64

	NRFB	Mint/Complete
	225-300	75-100
		Avg
blue parka w/ hood		10-15
turquoise ski pants		5-7
two skis w/ rubber bands		10-15
two ski poles		10-15
blue goggles glasses		15-20
red cotton ski gloves		7-10
shoes: black ski boots		7-10

Senior Prom
951
Date 1963-64

	NRFB	Mint/Complete
	225-300	60-85
		Avg
blue and green gown		15-20
shoes: green open toe w/ pearl		40-45

Barbie Baby-Sits
953
Date 1963-64

	NRFB	Mint/Complete
	225-300	75-100
		Avg
babysitter pink & white apron		7-10
Blonde baby		15-20
white diaper		7-10
baby robe		7-10
"Telephone Numbers" paper		10-15
blue & white baby blanket		7-10
pink pillow		7-10
coke bottle		5-7
baby bottle		5-7
pretzels box		7-10
white telephone		7-10
pink bassinet		5-7
bassinet liner sheet		5-7
alarm clock		5-7
black rimmed glasses		15-20
black book strap		5-7
"How To Loose Weight" book		5-7
"How To Get A Raise" book		5-7
"How To Travel" book		5-7

Bride's Dream.
Never removed from box/card.
Author's Collection

Ski Queen.

Senior Prom.
*Courtesy of Richard Chapman
and Glenn Mandeville*

Barbie Baby-Sits.
Never removed
from box/card.
Courtesy of Anthony Alcaide

Career Girl
954
Date 1963-64

NRFB	Mint/Complete
225-300	75-100
	Avg
black & white tweed jacket	10-15
black & white tweed skirt	7-10
black & white tweed hat w/ velvet	10-15
red cotton body blouse	10-15
long tricot black gloves	15-20
shoes: black open toe	10-15

Swingin' Easy
955
Date 1963

NRFB	Mint/Complete
250-325	100-125
	Avg
green floral dress	25-30
pearl drop chain necklace	45-50
white clutch purse	5-7
shoes: black open toe	10-15

Busy Morning
956
Date 1963

NRFB	Mint/Complete
250-300	150-175
	Avg
deep rose & white stripedcotton dress	15-20
straw cartwheel hat w/ deep rose satin ribbon	25-30
straw tote bag w/ fruit	10-15
white telephone	7-10
pearl drop chain necklace	45-50
shoes: white open toe	10-15

Knitting Pretty
957
Date 1963

NRFB	Mint/Complete
250-325	150-175
	Avg
blue wool cardigan sweater	25-30
blue wool shell sweater	25-30
blue wrap sheath skirt	7-10
"How to Knit" book	5-7
bowl of matching yarn w/ needles	10-15
silver scissors	7-10
shoes: blue open toe	10-15

Party Date
958
Date 1963

NRFB	Mint/Complete
150-200	75-100
	Avg
white dress w/ gold glitter skirt	25-30
wide gold belt	10-15
gold clutch purse	7-10
shoes: clear w/ gold glitter open toe	25-30

Theatre Date
959
Date 1963

NRFB	Mint/Complete
150-200	75-100
	Avg
green satin bolero jacket	15-20
green satin skirt	10-15
white satin sleeveless top	15-20
green satin pillbox hat	15-20
shoes: green open toe	10-15

Golden Elegance
922
Date 1963

NRFB	Mint/Complete
300-350	175-225
	Avg
gold & red brocade coat	20-25
gold & red brocade slim dress	20-25
red velvet clutch bag	15-20
woven white patterned hankie	25-30
fur & pearl hat	25-30
short white tricot gloves	15-20
graduated pearl necklace	25-35
pearl earrings	10-15
shoes: brown open toe	25-35

Career Girl.

Knitting Pretty, blue.
Courtesy of Anthony Alcaide

Busy Morning.

Golden Elegance.
Courtesy of Anthony Alcaide

Sophisticated Lady
993
Date 1963-64

NRFB	Mint/Complete
350-400	125-150
	Avg
pink silk gown	20-25
dark pink velvet coat	25-30
clear w/ solver tiara	35-40
long white tricot gloves	10-15
pink graduated pearl necklace	25-35
shoes: pink open toe	10-15

Satin Blouse
Pak
Date 1963

NRFB	Mint/Complete
75-125	35-50
	Avg
black satin blouse	20-25
diamond stud earrings	20-25
white satin blouse	15-20
diamond stud earrings	20-25
pink w/ glitter satin blouse	15-20
diamond stud earrings	20-25
rose satin blouse	15-20
diamond stud earrings	20-25

Satin Slacks
Pak
Date 1963

NRFB	Mint/Complete
75-125	35-50
	Avg.
black satin slacks	25-30
shoes: white open toe w/ silver glitter	20-25
white satin slacks	20-25
shoes: white open toe w/ silver glitter	20-25
pink w/ silver glitter satin slacks	20-25
shoes: pink open toe w/ silver glitter	20-25
rose satin slacks	20-25
shoes: pink open toe w/ silver glitter	20-25

Satin Skirt
Pak
Date 1963

NRFB	Mint/Complete
75-125	40-55
	Avg
black satin long skirt	35-40
white satin long skirt	25-30
pink w/ silver glitter satin long skirt	20-25
rose satin long skirt	20-25

Satin Wrap Skirt
Pak
Date 1963

NRFB	Mint/Complete
75-125	40-55
	Avg
black satin wrap skirt	35-40
white satin wrap skirt	25-30
pink w/ silver glitter satin wrap skirt	15-20
rose satin wrap skirt	20-25

Satin Bolero
Pak
Date 1963

NRFB	Mint/Complete
75-125	45-60
	Avg
black satin bolero jacket	25-30
black satin bolero hat	25-30
white satin bolero jacket	25-30
white satin bolero hat	20-25
pink w/ silver glitter satin bolero jacket	20-25
pink w/ silver glitter satin bolero hat	20-25
rose satin bolero jacket	25-30
rose satin bolero hat	20-25

Satin Coat
Pak
Date 1963

NRFB	Mint/Complete
100-150	50-75
	Avg
black satin coat	60-75
white satin coat	40-55
pink w/ silver glitter satin coat	30-35
rose satin coat	40-55

Knit Top
Pak
Date 1963

NRFB	Mint/Complete
40-65	25-40
	Avg
blue cotton knit blouse	10-15
charm bracelet	15-20
white sunglasses	10-15
gold cotton knit blouse	10-15
charm bracelet	15-20
white sunglasses	10-15
multicolored stripe cotton knit blouse	10-15
charm bracelet	15-20
white sunglasses	10-15

Satin Wrap Skirt.

Satin Bolero.

Knit Skirt w/ Glitter
Pak
Date 1963

	NRFB	Mint/Complete
	75-100	15-45
		Avg
blue cotton knit skirt w/ gold glitter		35-40
gold cotton knit skirt w/ gold glitter		15-20
multicolored stripe skirt w/ gold glitter		35-40

Knit Slacks
Pak
Date 1963

	NRFB	Mint/Complete
	40-65	25-40
		Avg
blue cotton knit slacks		10-15
shoes: blue & brown wedges		10-15
gold cotton knit slacks		10-15
shoes: gold & brown wedges		10-15
multicolored stripe cotton knit slacks		10-15
shoes: red & brown wedges		10-15

Knit Dress
Pak
Date 1963

	NRFB	Mint/Complete
	75-100	40-65
		Avg
blue cotton knit dress w/ cord belt		35-40
gold clutch purse		7-10
gold cotton knit dress w/ cord belt		35-40
gold clutch purse		7-10
multicolored stripe cotton knit dress w/ cord belt		35-40
gold clutch purse		7-10

Knit Top And Shorts
Pak
Date 1963

	NRFB	Mint/Complete
	40-65	25-40
		Avg
blue cotton knit crop top		10-15
gold cotton knit shorts		10-15
gold cotton knit crop top		10-15
multicolored stripe cotton knit shorts		10-15
multicolored stripe cotton knit crop top		10-15
blue cotton knit shorts		10-15

Knit Skirt with Glitter. Never removed from box/card.
Author's Collection

Knit Dress. Never removed from box/card.
Author's Collection

Pak assorted items make a cute outfit.
Courtesy of Richard Chapman and Glenn Mandeville

Knit Skirt
Pak
Date 1963

NRFB	Mint/Complete
60-85	15-45
	Avg
blue cotton knit sheath skirt	7-10
blue cotton knit sash belt	10-15
white w/ glitter sunglasses	10-15
gold cotton knit sheath skirt	7-10
gold cotton knit sash belt	10-15
white w/ glitter sunglasses	10-15
multicolored stripe cotton knit sheath skirt	7-10
multicolored stripe cotton knit sash belt	10-15
white w/ glitter sunglasses	10-15

Knit Accessories
Pak
Date 1963

NRFB	Mint/Complete
100-175	50-75
	Avg
straw hat w/ multicolored stripe cotton knit scarf	35-40
multicolored stripe cotton knit clutch purse	25-30
shoes: green open toe	10-15

Square Neck Sweater
Pak
Date 1963

NRFB	Mint/Complete
60-85	15-45
	Avg
black square neck sweater	7-10
pink chiffon scarf	10-15
white square neck sweater	7-10
pink chiffon scarf	10-15
pink square neck sweater	7-10
pink chiffon scarf	10-15

Peachy Fleecy Coat
Pak
Date 1963

NRFB	Mint/Complete
60-85	15-45
	Avg
light beige wool coat	15-20

Lamé Sheath
Pak
Date 1963

NRFB	Mint/Complete
100-175	50-75
	Avg
navy & gold lamé sheath dress	40-45
gold clutch purse	7-10
shoes: navy open toe	25-30

Lamé Sheath shown with Genuine Mink Stole. Rare. Shown missing gold purse.
Courtesy of Richard Chapman and Glenn Mandeville

Bathrobe
Pak
Date 1963

NRFB	Mint/Complete
60-85	15-45
	Avg
yellow terry robe	5-7
yellow terry robe belt	5-7
blue shower cap	5-7
shoes: yellow terry scuffs	7-10

Shoe Pak
Pak
Date 1963

NRFB	Mint/Complete
175-225	75-100
	Avg
shoes: red open toe	10-15
shoes: green open toe	10-15
shoes: white open toe	10-15
shoes: mustard open toe	10-15
shoes: black open toe	10-15
shoes: orange open toe	10-15
shoes: turquoise open toe	10-15
shoes: pink open toe	10-15
shoes: brown open toe	10-15
shoes: clear w/ glitter open toe	20-25
shoes: blue & brown wedges	10-15

In The Swim
Pak
Date 1964-65

NRFB	Mint/Complete
125-175	75-100
	Avg
orange swimsuit	20-25
straw hat w/ orange scarf	35-40
white sunglasses	10-15
shoes: gold & tan wedges	10-15
pink swimsuit	20-25
straw hat w/ pink scarf	35-40
white sunglasses	10-15
shoes: gold & tan wedges	10-15
blue swimsuit	20-25
straw hat w/ blue scarf	35-40
white sunglasses	10-15
shoes: gold & tan wedges	10-15

Shoe Wardrobe
Pak
Date 1964-65

NRFB	Mint/Complete
175-225	75-100
	Avg
shoes: red open toe	10-15
shoes: green open toe	10-15
shoes: white open toe	10-15
shoes: mustard open toe	10-15
shoes: two pair black open toe	10-15 ea
shoes: orange open toe	10-15
shoes: deep blue open toe	10-15
shoes: pink open toe	10-15
shoes: brown open toe	10-15
shoes: clear w/ glitter open toe	20-25
shoes: blue & tan wedges	10-15
shoes: gold & tan wedges	10-15

For Barbie Dressmakers
1831
Date 1964-67

NRFB	Mint/Complete
15-40	10-35
	Avg
white zippers	5-7
12 white buttons	5-7
12 red buttons	5-7
12 gold beads	5-7
12 yellow buttons	5-7
12 blue buttons	5-7
12 black buttons	5-7
12 red shanks	5-7
12 brown buttons	5-7

For Rink And Court
Pak
Date 1964-65

NRFB	Mint/Complete
40-65	25-40
	Avg
blue goggles sunglasses	10-15
tennis racquet	5-7
two tennis balls	5-7
shoes: red ice skates	10-15
shoes: white roller skates	10-15

Going To The Ball
Pak
Date 1964-65

NRFB	Mint/Complete
40-65	25-40
	Avg
white fur jacket w/ corsage	20-25
short white tricot gloves	15-20
shoes: white open toe	10-15

Costume Completers
Pak
Date 1964-65

NRFB	Mint/Complete
75-100	40-65
	Avg
long black tricot gloves	15-20
long white tricot gloves	10-15
short white tricot gloves	15-20
black clutch purse	7-10
white clutch purse	7-10
shoes: white open toe	10-15
shoes: black open toe	10-15

Dress Up Hats
Pak
Date 1964-65

NRFB	Mint/Complete
75-100	40-65
	Avg
fur & pearl hat	25-30
white organdy hat w/ black velvet ribbon	10-15
green satin pillbox hat	15-20

Fashion Accents
1830
Date 1964-65

NRFB	Mint/Complete
100-125	50-75
	Avg
gold clutch purse	7-10
white sunglasses w/ gold glitter	25-30
two graduated pearl necklace	25-35 ea
two pair pearl earrings	10-15 ea
gold & blue bead necklace	15-20
gold drop earrings	15-20
two blue bracelets	15-20
gold bracelet	10-15

Sweet Dreams
Pak
Date 1964-65

NRFB	Mint/Complete
60-85	15-40
	Avg
sheer yellow baby doll pajama top	5-7
sheer yellow baby doll pajama bottom	7-10
alarm clock	5-7
blue hair ribbon on metal loop	10-15
shoes: blue open toe w/ pompom	25-30

Boudoir
Pak
Date 1964-65

NRFB	Mint/Complete
100-125	50-75
	Avg
blue terry "Hers" towel	7-10
blue terry washcloth	7-10
blue shower cap	5-7
gold talc box	5-7
blue powder puff	3-5
pink wash stick w/ orange sponge	7-10
white princess telephone	7-10
hot water bottle	7-10
grey razor	7-10
or pink razor	25-30
light pink comb	3-5
light pink brush	3-5
light pink mirror	3-5

Color Coordinates
1832
Date 1964-65

NRFB	Mint/Complete
100-125	50-75
	Avg
blue clutch purse	7-10
pink clutch purse	7-10
orange clutch purse	7-10
red clutch purse	7-10
yellow clutch purse	7-10
shoes: blue open toe	10-15
shoes: pink open toe	10-15
shoes: orange open toe	10-15
shoes: red open toe	10-15
shoes: yellow open toe	10-15

On The Go
Pak
Date 1964-65

NRFB	Mint/Complete
65-90	20-45
	Avg
rust & white polka dot sheath dress	15-20
green & white polka dot sheath dress	15-20
blue & white polka dot sheath dress	15-20

On The Go
Pak
Floral version
Date 1964-65

NRFB	Mint/Complete
75-125	40-65
	Avg
floral multicolor sheath dress	35-50

Jumpin Jeans
Pak
Date 1964-65

	NRFB	Mint/Complete
	40-65	15-30
		Avg
white tee w/ red stripe		5-7
clam digger jeans		5-7

Spectator Sport
Pak
Date 1964-65

	NRFB	Mint/Complete
	75-100	40-65
		Avg
blue cotton knit dress w/ cord belt		35-40
gold clutch purse		7-10
gold cotton knit dress w/ cord belt		35-40
gold clutch purse		7-10
multicolored stripe cotton knit dress w/ cord belt		35-40
gold clutch purse		7-10

Fashion Feet
Pak
Date 1964-65

	NRFB	Mint/Complete
	40-65	15-30
		Avg
shoes: red ballet slippers		7-10
shoes: white tennis sneakers		5-7
shoes: yellow boots		7-10
shoes: black majorette boots		7-10
shoes: gold & tan wedges		7-10

Fashion Feet. Never removed from box/card.
Author's Collection

Leisure Hours
Pak
Date 1964-65

	NRFB	Mint/Complete
	75-100	40-65
		Avg
tan princess telephone		7-10
bowl of yarn w/ needles		10-15
"Cinderella" broom		20-25
tan television set		7-10
black Barbie tray		7-10
two glasses w/ cotton fizz		20-25
two straws		15-20

Campus Belle
Pak
Date 1964-65

	NRFB	Mint/Complete
	100-150	60-85
		Avg
rose silk belle dress		35-40
graduated pearl necklace		25-35
white short tricot gloves		15-20
shoes: white open toe		10-15
deep blue silk belle dress		35-40
graduated pearl necklace		25-35
white short tricot gloves		15-20
shoes: white open toe		10-15

Campus Belle, rose.
*Courtesy of Richard Chapman
and Glenn Mandeville*

Lovely Lingerie
Pak
Date 1964-67

	NRFB	Mint/Complete
	60-85	20-45
		Avg
blue trunk leg panties		5-7
blue half slip		5-7
blue strapless bra		5-7
light pink mirror		3-5
light pink comb		3-5
light pink brush		3-5
shoes: blue open toe w/ pompom		20-25
white trunk leg panties		5-7
white half slip		5-7
white strapless bra		5-7
light pink mirror		3-5
light pink comb		3-5
light pink brush		3-5
shoes: white open toe w/ pompom		20-25
pink trunk leg panties		5-7
pink half slip		5-7
pink strapless bra		5-7
light pink mirror		3-5
light pink comb		3-5
light pink brush		3-5
shoes: pink open toe w/ pompom		20-25
black trunk leg panties		5-7
black half slip		5-7
black strapless bra		5-7
light pink mirror		3-5
light pink comb		3-5
light pink brush		3-5
shoes: black open toe w/ pompom		20-25

Ruffles 'n Lace
Pak
Date 1964-65

	NRFB	Mint/Complete
	50-75	20-35
		Avg
white sheer w/ lace wide slip		5-7
white sheer panty		5-7
white half slip		5-7
white strapless bra		5-7
light pink mirror		3-5
light pink comb		3-5
light pink brush		3-5

What's Cookin?

Date 1964-65

	NRFB	Mint/Complete
	75-100	30-55
		Avg
white apron		5-7
white chef's hat		7-10
red & white potholder		5-7
wooden rolling pin		5-7
metal spoon w/ red handle		5-7
metal spatula w/ red handle		5-7
metal knife w/ red handle		5-7
red apron		5-7
white chef's hat		7-10
red & white potholder		5-7
wooden rolling pin		5-7
metal spoon w/ red handle		5-7
metal spatula w/ red handle		5-7
metal knife w/ red handle		5-7
blue apron		5-7
white chef's hat		7-10
red & white potholder		5-7
wooden rolling pin		5-7
metal spoon w/ red handle		5-7
metal spatula w/ red handle		5-7
metal knife w/ red handle		5-7

It's Cold Outside

#0819
Red version
Date 1964-66

	NRFB	Mint/Complete
	75-125	40-65
		Avg
red felt coat w/ belt & fur trim		10-15
red felt hat w/ fur trim		15-20

It's Cold Outside, red.
Author's Collection

It's Cold Outside

#0819
Tan version
Date 1964-66

	NRFB	Mint/Complete
	75-125	40-65
		Avg
tan felt coat w/ belt & fur trim		15-20
tan felt hat w/ fur trim		15-20

Drum Majorette

#0875
Date 1964-65

	NRFB	Mint/Complete
	75-125	40-65
		Avg
red velvet jacket		7-10
white pleated skirt		10-15

red fur tall hat	7-10
sheer tan pantyhose	15-20
baton w/ gold glitter	7-10
short white tricot gloves	15-20
shoes: white majorette boots	7-10

Cheerleader

#0876
Date 1964-65

	NRFB	Mint/Complete
	75-125	40-65
		Avg
"M" letter sweater		7-10
red corduroy skirt		7-10
two red & white pompons		25-30
megaphone w/ handle		7-10
white knit socks		5-7
shoes: red tennis sneakers		7-10

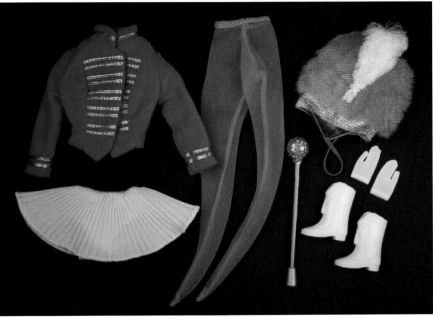

Drum Majorette.

Cheerleader.

Candy Striper Volunteer
0889
Date 1964

	NRFB	Mint/Complete
	275-325	125-150
		Avg
white cotton blouse		15-20
red & white striped pinafore		10-15
white cotton nurse's cap		15-20
pink "B" soap		7-10
hot water bottle		7-10
Kleenex box		7-10
white terry washcloth		20-25
white serving tray		10-15
blue plate		7-10
watermelon slice		10-15
glass w/ cotton fizz		10-15
straw		10-15
metal knife		7-10
metal spoon		7-10
metal fork		7-10

Lunch Date
1600
Date 1964

	NRFB	Mint/Complete
	125-175	40-65
		Avg
red & yellow print dress		35-50

Pajama Party. Never removed from box/card.
Author's Collection

Lunch Date.
Courtesy of Richard Chapman and Glenn Mandeville

Pajama Party
1601
Date 1964-65

	NRFB	Mint/Complete
	75-125	35-60
		Avg
turquoise pajama top		7-10
turquoise pajama bottom		7-10
alarm clock		5-7

Knit Separates
1602
Date 1964

	NRFB	Mint/Complete
	125-175	40-65
		Avg
multicolored stripe cotton knit blouse		10-15
gold cotton knit sheath pants		7-10
blue cotton knit sash belt		10-15
blue cotton knit sheath skirt		7-10
shoes: blue open toe		10-15

Knitting Pretty
0957
Date 1964

	NRFB	Mint/Complete
	275-325	125-150
		Avg
pink wool cardigan sweater		35-40
pink wool shell sweater		35-40
pink wrap sheath skirt		25-30
"How to Knit" book		5-7
bowl of matching yarn w/ needles		15-20
silver scissors		7-10
shoes: pink open toe		10-15

Stormy Weather
0949
Date 1964-65

	NRFB	Mint/Complete
	125-200	40-65
		Avg
yellow cotton raincoat		5-7
yellow cotton raincoat belt		7-10
yellow cotton rain hat		7-10
yellow umbrella w/ tassel		7-10
shoes: white boots		7-10

Evening Splendour
0961
Date 1964

	NRFB	Mint/Complete
	250-300	100-125
		Avg
gold & white brocade coat		15-20
gold & white brocade slim dress		15-20
turquoise corduroy clutch bag		15-20
woven white patterned hankie		25-30
fur & pearl hat		25-30
short white tricot gloves		15-20
graduated pearl necklace		25-35
pearl earrings		10-15
shoes: brown open toe		25-35

Country Fair
1603
Date 1964

	NRFB	Mint/Complete
	125-200	40-65
		Avg
yellow cotton blouse		10-15
orange multicolored floral skirt		10-15
orange clutch purse		7-10

Crisp 'n Cool
1604
Date 1964-65

	NRFB	Mint/Complete
	125-200	40-65
		Avg
white blouse w/ attached ascot		10-15
red cotton sheath skirt		7-10
red & white purse		10-15
short white tricot gloves		15-20
shoes: white open toe		10-15

Garden Tea Party
1606
Date 1964

	NRFB	Mint/Complete
	150-225	50-75
		Avg
red & white dress w/ eyelet panel		20-25
short white tricot gloves		15-20
shoes: white open toe		10-15

White Magic
1607
Date 1964

	NRFB	Mint/Complete
	150-225	40-65
		Avg
white satin coat		15-20
white satin pillbox hat		20-25
silver dimple clutch purse		7-10
shoes: white open toe		10-15

Black Magic Ensemble
1609
Date 1964-65

	NRFB	Mint/Complete
	250-300	100-125
		Avg
black silk sheath dress		15-20
black tulle coat		20-25
gold clutch purse		7-10
short black tricot gloves		40-45
shoes: black open toe		10-15

Crisp 'n Cool.
*Courtesy of Richard Chapman and
Glenn Mandeville*

Garden Tea Party.
Courtesy of Anthony Alcaide

Black Magic Ensemble.
*Courtesy of Richard Chapman and
Glenn Mandeville*

Satin 'n Rose
#1611
Date 1964v

NRFB	Mint/Complete
250-300	125-150
	Avg
rose satin bolero jacket	25-30
rose satin bolero hat	20-25
rose satin wrap skirt	20-25
rose satin slacks	20-25
rose satin blouse	15-20
diamond stud earrings	20-25
shoes: pink open toe w/ silver glitter	20-25

Barbie Skin Diver
#1608
Date 1964-65

NRFB	Mint/Complete
150-225	40-65
	Avg
yellow bikini top	10-15
orange bikini bottom	10-15
orange hooded sweatshirt	7-10
green snorkel mask	5-7
green snorkel	5-7
shoes: green fins	7-10

Golden Evening
#1610
Date 1964

NRFB	Mint/Complete
125-225	40-65
	Avg
gold skirt w/ gold glitter	35-40
gold cotton knit blouse	10-15
charm bracelet	15-20
wide gold belt	10-15
shoes: mustard open toe	10-15

Theatre Date
#1612
Date 1964

NRFB	Mint/Complete
125-175	50-75
	Avg
green satin bolero jacket	15-20
green satin skirt	10-15
white satin sleeveless top	15-20
shoes: green open toe	10-15

Dog 'n Duds
#1613
Date 1964-65

NRFB	Mint/Complete
275-325	75-100
	Avg
gray poodle dog	25-30
red leash	10-15
red collar w/ gold chain	10-15
bone	10-15
dog food in bowl	10-15
dog food box	10-15
ear muffs	15-20
yellow & black hat	10-15
black mask	7-10
pink tulle tutu	15-20
white collar	10-15
plaid coat	10-15
red velvet coat	10-15

Barbie In Japan
#0821
Date 1964

NRFB	Mint/Complete
350-400	150-175
	Avg
red kimono	15-20
gold & white obi	20-25
stick hair ornament	25-30
flower w/ silver dangles hair ornament	25-30
flower buds hair ornament	25-30
gold fan	15-20
samisen instrument	15-20
Japan travel pamphlet	25-30
shoes: thong w/ attached socks	35-40

Barbie In Mexico
#0820
Date 1964

NRFB	Mint/Complete
275-350	75-125
	Avg
white dress w/ lace trim	10-15
red & green satin skirt	10-15
black lace mantilla	10-15
Mexico travel pamphlet	25-30
crystal long double strand necklace	20-25
pearl earrings w/ crystal hoop	20-25
shoes: red open toe	10-15

Barbie In Switzerland
#0822
Date 1964

NRFB	Mint/Complete
175-250	50-100
	Avg
white dress w/ pink skirt	7-10
white eyelet bonnet	10-15
green felt corset	10-15
flower bouquet	15-20
Switzerland travel pamphlet	25-30
shoes: white open toe	10-15

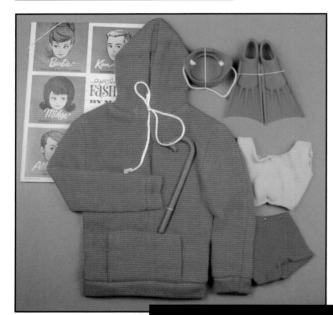

Barbie Skin Diver

Barbie In Switzerland.

Barbie In Holland
0823
Date 1964

NRFB	Mint/Complete
175-250	50-100
	Avg
blue blouse	7-10
multicolored full skirt	7-10
white apron	7-10
Dutch girl white hat	10-15
long white cotton socks	15-20
Holland travel pamphlet	25-30
shoes: wooden clogs	15-20

Barbie In Hawaii
1605
Date 1964

NRFB	Mint/Complete
200-275	75-125
	Avg
red & white bikini top	10-15
red & white bikini bottom	10-15
grass skirt	15-20
flower lei	10-15
flower lei bracelet	25-30
pineapple	10-15
Hawaii travel pamphlet	25-30

Little Red Riding Hood and The Wolf
0880
Date 1964

NRFB	Mint/Complete
275-350	75-125
	Avg
blue dress w/ white polka dots	7-10
red cape	10-15
black felt corset	10-15
straw hand basket	15-20
checked napkin	10-15
six molded rolls	10-15
wolf hood for Ken	15-20
hunter's red cap	10-15
Grandma's cap	10-15
white socks	10-15
Red Riding Hood & The Wolf theatre program	25-30
shoes: black slippers	15-20

Cinderella
0872
Date 1964-65

NRFB	Mint/Complete
275-350	100-175
	Avg
Cinderella poor dress	10-15
Cinderella rich yellow satin gown	15-20
broom	15-20
long white tricot gloves	10-15
Cinderella theatre program	25-30
shoes: clear open toe w/ glitter	20-25

Guinevere
0873
Date 1964-65

NRFB	Mint/Complete
275-350	125-175
	Avg
navy/purple velvet gown w/ chain belt	15-20
royal crown hat	15-20
red knit armlets	15-20
Guinevere theatre program	25-30
shoes: red brocade slippers	20-25

Barbie In Hawaii.

Guinevere.

Barbie Arabian Nights
0874
Date 1964-65

	NRFB	Mint/Complete
	275-350	125-175
		Avg
pink satin blouse		15-20
pink chiffon long skirt		10-15
pink chiffon sari		15-20
golden lamp		10-15
gold & blue bead necklace		15-20
gold drop earrings		15-20
two blue bracelets		15-20
gold bracelet		10-15
Arabian Nights theatre program		25-30
shoes: gold slippers		15-20

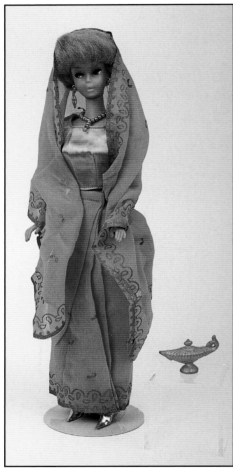

Barbie Arabian Nights.
Author's Collection

The Genuine Mink Stole
Sears Exclusive
Date 1964-65

	NRFB	Mint/Complete
	3275-3350	1500-2000
		Avg
mink fur stole		1500-2000
(see picture on page 72)		

Shoe Wardrobe
1833
Date 1964-65

	NRFB	Mint/Complete
	175-225	75-100
		Avg
shoes: red open toe		10-15
shoes: green open toe		10-15
shoes: white open toe		10-15
shoes: mustard open toe		10-15
shoes: two pair black open toe		10-15 ea
shoes: orange open toe		10-15
shoes: deep blue open toe		10-15
shoes: pink open toe		10-15
shoes: brown open toe		10-15
shoes: clear w/ glitter open toe		20-25
shoes: blue & tan wedges		10-15
shoes: gold & tan wedges		10-15

Barbie Hostess Set
1034
Date 1965

	NRFB	Mint/Complete
	3275-3350	1500-2000
		Avg
"Barbie" print dress		35-40
red vinyl belt		35-40
red taffeta hostess pajama		50-75
red lamé tabard		35-40
gold belt		50-75
silver "B" teapot w/ lid		20-25
metal teapot		10-15
two pink teacups		20-25
two pink saucers		20-25
two pink plates		50-75
two knifes		50-75
two forks		50-75
two spoons		50-75
two cake slices		40-45
two place mats		40-45
white Barbie print potholder		25-30
"Easy as Pie" cookbook		15-20
white toaster		10-15
silver serving tray		50-75
medium silver pot w/ lid		10-15
small silver pot w/ lid		10-15
metal bowl		7-10
two toast slices		15-20
blue record player		10-15
record blue Barbie label		10-15
record red Barbie label		10-15
two candelabras		75-100
blue bowl with flowers		35-40
small casserole w/ lid		20-25
medium casserole w/ lid		20-25
large casserole w/ lid		20-25
casserole handle		30-35
coffeepot w/ lid		20-25
six candles		15-20
paper doily		30-35
plastic cake, brown icing		12-15
shoes: red open toe		10-15
shoes: clear open toe with/ glitter		20-25

Fun 'n Games
1619
Date 1964-66

	NRFB	Mint/Complete
	275-325	100-150
		Avg
rainbow striped dress		10-15
two metal wickets		20-25
wooden mallet		10-15
wooden ball		10-15
wooden stake		15-20

Fun 'n Games.
Author's Collection

Junior Prom
1614
Date 1964-66

	NRFB	Mint/Complete
	475-525	175-225
		Avg
red chiffon gown		60-75
white fur stole w/ white lining		35-40
pearl drop chain necklace		45-50
long white tricot gloves		10-15
shoes: red open toe		10-15

Saturday Matinee
1615
Date 1965

	NRFB	Mint/Complete
	475-525	225-275
		Avg
brown & gold tweed fur trimmed jacket		40-45
brown & gold tweed skirt		35-40
brown & gold tweed hat		40-45
gold and fur trimmed purse		40-45
short brown tricot gloves		60-75
shoes: brown open toe		10-15

Campus Sweetheart
1616
Date 1965

	NRFB	Mint/Complete
	1550-1850	450-525
		Avg
white satin gown w/ pink & red tulle		100-150
"B" silver loving cup trophy		75-100
red roses bouquet		75-100
pink graduated pearl necklace		25-35
long white tricot gloves		10-15
shoes: red open toe		15-20

Midnight Blue
1617
Date 1965

	NRFB	Mint/Complete
	1550-1625	375-450
		Avg
blue satin gown w/ silver bodice		75-100
blue satin coat w/ fur collar		75-100
silver dimple clutch purse		7-10
long white tricot gloves		10-15
graduated pearl necklace		25-35
shoes: blue open toe		10-15

Junior Prom.
Courtesy of Richard Chapman and Glenn Mandeville

Midnight Blue.
Courtesy of Karen Bindelglass

Junior Designer
1620
Date 1965

NRFB	Mint/Complete
275-350	150-200
	Avg

turquoise sheath	15-20
green belt	35-40
floral satin appliques	35-40
silver metal iron	20-25
"How To Design Your Own Fashions" book	25-30
shoes: closed toe green	25-30

Knit Hit
1621
Date 1965

NRFB	Mint/Complete
275-350	125-150
	Avg

knit argyle top w/ blue sleeves	15-20
knit blue sheath skirt	15-20
Mattel Daily Newspaper	15-20
shoes: red soft pointed flats	20-25

Knit Hit.

Student Teacher
1622
Date 1965-66

NRFB	Mint/Complete
275-350	125-150
	Avg

red dress w/ white inset collar	25-30
"Geography" book	7-10
globe on white pedestal	10-15
black pointer	20-25
black rimmed glasses	15-20
shoes: red closed toe	15-20

Vacation Time
1623
Date 1965

NRFB	Mint/Complete
225-300	100-125
	Avg

pink knit sweater	15-20
pink & white checkered shorts	20-25
black camera	15-20
shoes: pink squishy flats	20-25

Fun At The Fair
1624
Date 1965

NRFB	Mint/Complete
275-350	125-150
	Avg

Barbie print shirt	20-25

red wrap skirt w/ Barbie print lining	15-20
Barbie print head scarf	20-25
pink cotton candy	35-40
shoes: red sneakers	10-15

Modern Art
1625
Date 1965

NRFB	Mint/Complete
400-450	275-325
	Avg

green dress w/ sheer organza	100-125
framed painting by Barbie	75-100
Painting's by Barbie show program	50-75
shoes: closed toe green	25-30

Modern Art.
Courtesy of Richard Chapman and Glenn Mandeville

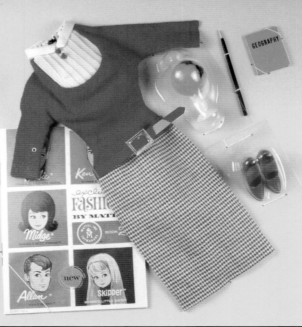

Student Teacher.

Dancing Doll
1626
Date 1965

	NRFB	Mint/Complete
	300-350	200-275
		Avg
pink checked dress w/ white collar		35-40
pink belt		25-30
blue record player		10-15
record blue Barbie label		10-15
record red Barbie label		10-15
shoes: white closed toe		15-20

Country Club Dance
1627
Date 1965

	NRFB	Mint/Complete
	300-350	200-275
		Avg
gold & white dress		35-40
gold clutch purse		7-10
long white tricot gloves		10-15
graduated pearl necklace		25-35
shoes: white closed toe		15-20

Brunch Time
1628
Date 1965

	NRFB	Mint/Complete
	300-350	175-225
		Avg
white w/ butterfly pattern dress		15-20
small casserole w/ lid		20-25
medium casserole w/ lid		20-25
large casserole w/ lid		20-25
casserole handle		30-35
coffeepot w/ lid		20-25
shoes: orange closed toe		15-20

Skater's Waltz
1629
Date 1965-66

	NRFB	Mint/Complete
	300-350	200-275
		Avg
pink knit skating costume		35-40
pink fuzzy collar		25-30
pink fuzzy mittens		25-30
tan pantyhose		15-20
shoes: white skates		10-15

Aboard Ship
1631
Date 1965

	NRFB	Mint/Complete
	300-350	175-225
		Avg
red, white & blue pleated dress		15-20
blue vest w/ red lining		10-15
red belt		15-20
"How To Travel" book		7-10
Hawaii travel brochure		15-20
Mexico travel brochure		20-25
Niagra Falls travel brochure		20-25
black camera		15-20
"Travel" poster		25-30
shoes: red closed toe		15-20

Invitation To Tea
1632
Date 1965

	NRFB	Mint/Complete
	300-350	200-275
		Avg
pink taffeta hostess pajama		35-40
pink lamé tabard		15-20
silver belt		35-40
silver "B" teapot w/ lid		20-25
two pink teacups		20-25
two pink saucers		20-25
shoes: clear open toe w/ glitter		20-25

Disc Date
1633
Date 1965

	NRFB	Mint/Complete
	150-200	75-100
		Avg
sheer white organdy body blouse		20-25
fuchsia velvet long skirt		15-20
blue record player		10-15
record blue Barbie label		10-15
record red Barbie label		10-15
rose closed toe shoes		15-20

Barbie Learns to Cook!
1634
Date 1965

	NRFB	Mint/Complete
	300-350	200-275
		Avg
white Barbie print dress		35-40
hot pink belt		15-20
white Barbie print potholder		25-30
"Easy as Pie" cookbook		15-20
white toaster		10-15
large silver pot w/ lid		10-15
medium silver pot w/ lid		10-15
small silver pot w/ lid		10-15
metal bowl		7-10
two toast slices		15-20
shoes: light blue open toe		15-20

Country Club Dance.
Courtesy of Anthony Alcaide

Fashion Editor
1635
Date 1965

	NRFB	Mint/Complete
	300-350	175-225
		Avg
turquoise silk suit dress		35-40
turquoise silk suit jacket		35-40
turquoise silk pillbox hat		35-40
black camera		15-20
shoes: turquoise closed toe		15-20

Sleeping Pretty
1636
Date 1965

	NRFB	Mint/Complete
	275-325	150-200
		Avg
light blue nylon robe		35-40
light blue nylon nightgown		35-40
blue satin pillow		25-30
white brush		3-5
shoes: blue open toe w/ pompom		20-25

Outdoor Life
1637
Date 1965

	NRFB	Mint/Complete
	275-325	150-200
		Avg
blue & white checked jacket		30-35
blue knit top		30-35
blue & white pants		30-35
white cotton duck hat		20-25
shoes: white tennis		10-15

Outdoor Life

Fashion Editor.
*Courtesy of Richard Chapman and
Glenn Mandeville*

Fraternity Dance
1638
Date 1965

	NRFB	Mint/Complete
	275-325	150-200
		Avg
pink silk taffeta gown w/ white bodice		50-75
pearl drop chain necklace		45-50
long white tricot gloves		10-15
shoes: pink open toe		10-15

Fraternity Dance.
*Courtesy of Richard Chapman and
Glenn Mandeville*

Holiday Dance
1639
Date 1964-65

	NRFB	Mint/Complete
	450-500	275-325
		Avg
gold & white gown w/ orange silk sash		150-175
gold dimple clutch purse		10-15
long white tricot gloves		10-15
shoes: white closed toe		15-20

Matinee Fashion.

Holiday Dance.
Courtesy of Richard Chapman and Glenn Mandeville

Poodle Parade.
Courtesy of Anthony Alcaide

Matinee Fashion
1640
Date 1965

	NRFB	Mint/Complete
	450-500	275-325
		Avg
red short jacket w/ fur trim		40-45
red sheath dress		40-45
red pillbox hat w/ attached scarf		50-75
shoes: red closed toe		15-20

Slumber Party
1642
Date 1965

	NRFB	Mint/Complete
	275-325	150-200
		Avg
pink long robe		15-20
pink satin pajama top		15-20
pink satin pajama bottom		15-20
"How To Loose Weight" book		5-7
six pink rollers		10-15
pink scale		7-10
blue comb		5-7
blue brush		5-7
shoes: pink open toe w/ blue pompom		35-40

Poodle Parade
1643
Date 1965

	NRFB	Mint/Complete
	550-600	275-325
		Avg
olive green & white knit coat		15-20
olive green jumper dress		20-25
pink knit dickie		20-25
pink head scarf		25-30
"First Prize" certificate		20-25
poodle purse		25-30
brown rimmed sunglasses		35-40
metal trophy		75-100
shoes: olive closed toe		50-75

On The Avenue
1644
Date 1965

	NRFB	Mint/Complete
	275-325	150-200
		Avg
white & gold knit jacket		25-30
white & gold knit dress		25-30
graduated pearl necklace		25-35
gold clutch purse		10-15
long white tricot gloves		10-15
shoes: white closed toe		15-20

Golden Glory
1645
Date 1965-66

	NRFB	Mint/Complete
	450-525	275-325
		Avg
gold lamé dress w/ green chiffon scarf		45-50
gold lamé coat w/ fur trim		45-50
green & gold clutch purse		35-40
short white tricot gloves		15-20
shoes: clear open toe w/glitter		15-20

On The Avenue.

Magnificience
1646
Date 1965

	NRFB	Mint/Complete
	650-725	275-325
		Avg
pink taffeta gown w/ red satin bodice		65-90
red satin coat w/ white fur trim		45-50
pink tulle slip		65-90
shoes: pink open toe		10-15
or clear open toe w/ glitter		20-25

Gold 'n Glamour
1647
Date 1965

	NRFB	Mint/Complete
	550-625	350-400
		Avg
tan dress w/ blue taffeta bodice		50-75
tan coat w/ attached scarf & fur trim		40-65
tan hat w/ fur trim		50-75
long brown tricot gloves		100-150
shoes: brown closed toe		40-65

Golden Glory.
Courtesy of Karen Bindelglass

Gold 'n Glamour.
*Courtesy of
Anthony Alcaide*

Photo Fashion
1648
Date 1965

NRFB	Mint/Complete
200-275	75-125
	Avg
turquoise sweater	20-25
turquoise dickie	40-45
turquoise capri pants	15-20
shoes: turquoise squishy flats	15-20

Barbie Baby Sits
0953
Date 1965

NRFB	Mint/Complete
300-375	175-225
	Avg
blonde baby	15-20
white diaper	7-10
baby robe	7-10
white bonnet	15-20
white christening gown	15-20
pink bunting	15-20
"Barbie baby Sitter's Manual" book	20-25
"Formula" paper	10-15
blue & white baby blanket	7-10
pink pillow	7-10
baby bottle	5-7
pink bassinet	5-7
bassinet liner sheet	5-7

Miss Astronaut
1641
Date 1965

NRFB	Mint/Complete
300-350	175-225
	Avg
metallic spacesuit jumper	25-30
white helmet	65-80
brown space gloves	65-80
American flag	75-100
shoes: brown boots	50-65

Pink Formal
Sears Exclusive
Date 1966

NRFB	Mint/Complete
800-875	550-600
	Avg
pink satin top w/ silver glitter detail	150-175
pink satin skirt w/ pink tulle	150-175
pink marabou boa	150-175
shoes: clear open toe w/ silver glitter	20-25

Lunch Date
Pak
Date 1966-67

NRFB	Mint/Complete
175-250	75-125
	Avg
Poodle Parade fabric dress	75-100
shoes: white open toe	10-15
Knit Hit fabric dress	75-100
shoes: red open toe	10-15

Above left:
Photo Fashion.
Courtesy of Richard Chapman and Glenn Mandeville

Above right:
Pink Formal. Rare.
Courtesy of Karen Bindelglass

Far left:
Lunch Date Knit Hit fabric.
Courtesy of Richard Chapman and Glenn Mandeville

Left:
Lunch Date Poodle Parade fabric.
Courtesy of Richard Chapman and Glenn Mandeville

Red Delight
Pak
Date 1966-67

NRFB	Mint/Complete
175-250	75-125
	Avg
red dress	65-80
shoes: red closed toe	15-20

Match Mates
Pak
Date 1966-67

NRFB	Mint/Complete
200-275	100-125
	Avg
orange purse	15-20
white purse	15-20
red purse	15-20
blue purse	15-20
shoes: orange closed toe	15-20
shoes: white closed toe	15-20
shoes: red closed toe	15-20
shoes: blue closed toe	15-20

Tailored Tops
Pak
Date 1966-67

NRFB	Mint/Complete
200-275	100-125
	Avg
Barbie print body blouse	25-30
white tank top w/ red stitching	35-40
white silk body blouse	35-40
red tank top w/ white stitching	40-65

Pert Skirts
Pak
Date 1966-67

NRFB	Mint/Complete
200-275	100-125
	Avg
dark blue pleated skirt	25-30
pink velvet sheath skirt	40-65
red plaid wrap skirt	25-30
blue linen sheath skirt	40-65

Set 'n Serve
Pak
Date 1966-67

NRFB	Mint/Complete
200-275	100-125
	Avg
silver "B" teapot w/ lid	20-25
two turquoise teacups	10-15
two turquoise saucers	10-15
two spoons	20-25
two place mats	20-25
two turquoise plates	35-40
small casserole w/ lid	20-25
medium casserole w/ lid	20-25
large casserole w/ lid	20-25
casserole handle	30-35
coffeepot w/ lid	20-25

Have Fun
Pak
Date 1966-67

NRFB	Mint/Complete
150-200	75-100
	Avg
two spoons	20-25
glass w/ pink drink	15-20
glass w/ brown drink	15-20
two straws	15-20
blue record player	10-15
record blue Barbie label	10-15
record red Barbie label	10-15
brown serving tray	15-20
tan television	10-15
two plain napkins	25-30

Kitchen Magic
Pak
Date 1966-67

NRFB	Mint/Complete
125-175	60-85
	Avg
white toaster	10-15
large silver pot w/ lid	10-15
medium silver pot w/ lid	10-15
small silver pot w/ lid	10-15
two toast slices	15-20

Glamour Hats
Pak
Date 1966-67

NRFB	Mint/Complete
175-225	100-150
	Avg
red wide brim satin hat	40-65
pink satin hat w/ white edging	35-50
white felt molded hat w/ gold band	40-65

Tailored Tops & Pert Skirts.
Courtesy of Anthony Alcaide

Tailored Tops & Pert Skirts.
Courtesy of Anthony Alcaide

Flats 'n Heels
1837
Date 1966-67

	NRFB	Mint/Complete
	175-225	100-150
		Avg
shoes: green open toe		10-15
shoes: white open toe		10-15
shoes: turquoise open toe		10-15
shoes: hot pink open toe		10-15
shoes: orange closed toe		15-20
shoes: off white closed toe		15-20
shoes: red closed toe		15-20
shoes: turquoise closed toe		15-20
shoes: black closed toe		15-20
shoes: pale pink closed toe		15-20
shoes: gold & tan wedges		10-15
shoes: light pink squishy flats		15-20

Lunch On The Terrace
1649
Date 1966-67

	NRFB	Mint/Complete
	300-350	175-225
		Avg
green & white checked dress w/ polka dot bodice		40-65
green & white checked hat w/ polka dot brim		65-90
shoes: white closed toe		15-20

Outdoor Art Show
1650
Date 1966-67

	NRFB	Mint/Complete
	375-425	175-225
		Avg
multicolored nylon sheath dress		40-65
turquoise felt molded hat w/ red band		85-105

Outdoor Art Show.

Beau Time
1651
Date 1966-67

	NRFB	Mint/Complete
	300-350	175-225
		Avg
red & blue taffeta dress w/ red bow		175-225

Pretty As A picture
1652
Date 1966-67

	NRFB	Mint/Complete
	300-350	125-175
		Avg
black & white checked taffeta dress w/ black bodice		50-75
black & white checked taffeta large brim hat		50-75
shoes: black closed toe		15-20

International Fair
1653
Date 1966-67

	NRFB	Mint/Complete
	300-350	125-175
		Avg
white crepe blouse w/ gold buttons		35-60
red & white stripe pleated skirt		40-45
black camera		10-15
shoes: white closed toe		15-20

Reception Line
1654
Date 1966-67

	NRFB	Mint/Complete
	325-400	125-175
		Avg
light blue taffeta dress		35-60
light blue taffeta hat w/ white edging		35-60
shoes: blue closed toe		15-20

Under Fashions
1655
Date 1966-67

	NRFB	Mint/Complete
	300-350	125-175
		Avg
pink corselet w/ sheer ruffle		35-40
pink sheer bra		20-25
pink tricot panty		20-25
pink nylon half slip w/ sheer ruffle		20-25
tan textured hose		20-25

Lunch On The Terrace.
Courtesy of Anthony Alcaide

Lunch On The Terrace.

Fashion Luncheon
1656
Date 1966-67

	NRFB	Mint/Complete
	550-625	350-400
		Avg
pink satin & cotton weave dress		40-60
pink satin & cotton weave jacket		40-60
pink satin hat w/ flowers		90-115
long white tricot gloves		10-15
shoes: pink closed toe		15-20

Garden Wedding
1658
Date 1966-67

	NRFB	Mint/Complete
	350-425	125-175
		Avg
rose satin sheath dress		40-60
white lace overdress		30-55
shoes: rose closed toe		15-20

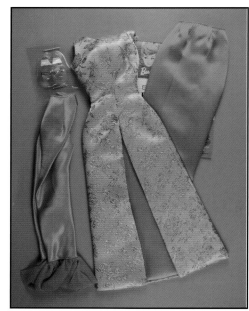
Evening Gala.

Evening Gala
1660
Date 1966-67

	NRFB	Mint/Complete
	550-625	225-275
		Avg
silver & gold brocade over-dress w/ turquoise lining		50-75
turquoise satin long skirt		40-65
turquoise satin pants w/ chiffon cuffs		50-75
shoes: clear open toe w/ silver glitter		20-25

London Tour
1661
Date 1966-67

	NRFB	Mint/Complete
	550-625	225-275
		Avg
bone leatherette coat		25-50
bone leatherette hat		25-50
bone leatherette purse		25-50
sheer organza turquoise scarf		85-115
shoes: off white closed toe		15-20

Fashion Luncheon.
Courtesy of Richard Chapman and Glenn Mandeville

Garden Wedding.
Courtesy of Richard Chapman and Glenn Mandeville

London Tour.

Music Center Matinee
1663
Date 1966-67

	NRFB	Mint/Complete
	550-625	350-400
		Avg
red chiffon over taffeta tunic w/ pin		75-100
red chiffon over taffeta skirt		50-75
rose satin large brim hat		75-100
long white tricot gloves		10-15
shoes: red closed toe		15-20

Benefit Performance.
Courtesy of Karen Bindelglass

Music Center Matinee.
Courtesy of Anthony Alcaide

Debutante Ball
1666
Date 1966-67

	NRFB	Mint/Complete
	1450-1525	550-600
		Avg
light blue satin w/ blue organza gown		75-100
white fur w/ blue organza tie		50-75
gold dimple clutch purse		10-15
pearl drop chain necklace		45-50
long white tricot gloves		10-15
shoes: clear open toe w/ silver glitter		20-25

Benefit Performance
1667
Date 1966-67

	NRFB	Mint/Complete
	1450-1525	550-600
		Avg
red velvet tunic w/ diamond buttons		75-100
white tulle underskirt w/ red bows		100-125
long white tricot gloves		10-15
shoes: red open toe		10-15

Shimmering Magic
1664
Date 1966-67

	NRFB	Mint/Complete
	1625-1850	675-725
		Avg
white & silver lamé sheath dress		75-100
red satin coat		75-100
white & silver large brim hat w/ roses		225-275
shoes: red closed toe		15-20
or closed toe clear w/ silver glitter (rare)		175-225

Shimmering Magic. Never removed from box/card.
Author's Collection

Riding In The Park.

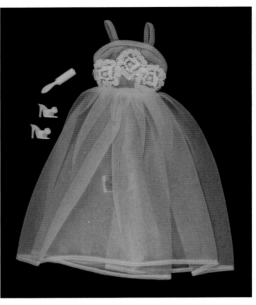

Dreamland.

Riding In The Park
1668
Date 1966-67

NRFB	Mint/Complete
550-625	275-325

	Avg
brown & tan checked jacket	20-25
white cotton body blouse w/ ascot	40-65
yellow riding pants	35-40
brown riding crop	75-100
brown riding hat	35-40
shoes: brown tall boots	35-40

Dreamland
1669
Date 1966-67

NRFB	Mint/Complete
175-250	75-125

	Avg
peach sheer nightgown	35-40
white comb	3-5
white brush	3-5
shoes: white scuff w/ peach pompoms	25-30

Coffee's On
1670
Date 1966-67

NRFB	Mint/Complete
175-250	75-125

	Avg
white w/ butterfly pattern dress	15-20
medium casserole w/ lid	20-25
coffeepot w/ lid	20-25

Sporting Casuals
1671
Date 1966-67

NRFB	Mint/Complete
175-250	50-100

	Avg
turquoise sweater	20-25
turquoise capri pants	15-20
shoes: turquoise squishy flats	15-20

Club Meeting
1672
Date 1966-67

NRFB	Mint/Complete
175-250	75-125

	Avg
turquoise silk suit dress	35-40
turquoise silk suit jacket	35-40
black camera	15-20
shoes: turquoise closed toe	15-20

Lunchtime
1673
Date 1966-67

NRFB	Mint/Complete
175-250	75-125

	Avg
white Barbie print dress	35-40
hot pink belt	15-20
white toaster	10-15
medium silver pot w/ lid	10-15
metal teapot	10-15
two toast slices	15-20

Sleepytime Gal
1674
Date 1966-67

NRFB	Mint/Complete
175-250	100-150

	Avg
pink long robe	15-20
pink satin pajama top	15-20
pink satin pajama bottom	15-20
"How To Loose Weight" book	5-7

	Avg
six pink rollers	10-15
blue comb	5-7
blue brush	5-7
shoes: pink open toe w/ blue pompon	35-40

Sunday Visit
1675
Date 1966-67

NRFB	Mint/Complete
200-275	75-125

	Avg
white & gold knit jacket	25-30
white & gold knit dress	25-30
gold dimple clutch purse	10-15
shoes: white closed toe	15-20

Fabulous Fashion
1676
Date 1966-67

NRFB	Mint/Complete
625-700	200-275

	Avg
pink taffeta gown w/ red satin bodice	65-90
red satin coat w/ white fur trim	45-50
shoes: clear w/ silver glitter open toe	20-25

Pan American Airways Stewardess
1678
Date 1966

NRFB	Mint/Complete
4200-4700	800-875

	Avg
blue/gray twill suit jacket w/ wings	125-175
blue/gray twill suit skirt	125-175
white cotton blouse	125-175
blue/gray twill hat w/ Pan Am insignia	125-175
black shoulder purse	10-15
short white tricot gloves	15-20
shoes: black closed toe	15-20

Here Comes The Bride
1665
Date 1966-67

NRFB	Mint/Complete
1250-1325	400-450
	Avg
white satin slim gown	100-125
white tulle train veil	100-125
pale pink orchids bouquet	100-125
blue garter	10-15
long white tricot gloves	10-15
shoes: white closed toe	15-20

Here Comes The Bride.
Courtesy of Karen Bindelglass

Pink Sparkle
1440
Date 1967

NRFB	Mint/Complete
250-300	75-125
	Avg
pink brocade dress w/ pink metallic detail	45-50
sheer pink chiffon cover-up	45-50
shoes: magenta open toe	10-15

Tropicana
1460
Date 1967-68

NRFB	Mint/Complete
200-275	50-75
	Avg
orange, yellow & white linen dress w/ flower	45-50
shoes: orange closed toe	15-20

Intrigue
1470
Date 1967-68

NRFB	Mint/Complete
550-625	200-250
	Avg
metallic gold & white knit mini dress	45-50
metallic gold trench coat	45-50
metallic gold trench coat belt	45-50
shoes: white closed toe	15-20

Intrigue.
Courtesy of Karen Bindelglass

Sunflower
1983
Date 1967-68

NRFB	Mint/Complete
250-325	75-125
	Avg
large flower print halter dress	30-45
two pink bracelets	25-30
pink drop w/ navy round earrings	25-30
shoes: hot pink closed toe	15-20

Underprints
1685
Date 1967-68

NRFB	Mint/Complete
175-250	50-75
	Avg
pink floral print slip	15-20
pink floral print bra	15-20
pink floral print girdle	15-20
turquoise princess phone	10-15
turquoise mirror	7-10
turquoise comb	5-7
turquoise brush	5-7

Print Aplenty
1686
Date 1967-68

NRFB	Mint/Complete
250-325	75-125
	Avg
block print dress	30-45
hot pink rectangular drop earrings	30-45
shoes: hot pink closed toe	15-20

Caribbean Cruise
1687
Date 1967-68

NRFB	Mint/Complete
225-300	50-100
	Avg
yellow silk jumpsuit	30-45
shoes: yellow squishy flats	35-40

Caribbean Cruise.

Travel Togethers
#1688
Date 1967

NRFB	Mint/Complete
250-325	75-125
	Avg
yellow & red floral suit jacket	30-45
yellow & red floral suit skirt	25-30
yellow & red floral hat	25-30
shoes: red closed toe	15-20

Studio Tour
#1690
Date 1967

NRFB	Mint/Complete
250-325	75-125
	Avg
yellow, green & red w/ pin dots dress	30-45
yellow, green & red w/ pin dots hat	30-45
shoes: red closed toe	15-20

Fashion Shiner
#1691
Date 1967-68

NRFB	Mint/Complete
250-325	75-125
	Avg
stripe knit halter dress	40-55
red vinyl raincoat	35-45
red purse	15-20
short white tricot gloves	15-20
shoes: red closed toe	15-20

Patio Party
#1692
Date 1967-68

NRFB	Mint/Complete
375-450	150-200
	Avg
nylon multicolored jumpsuit	40-55
green & blue satin hostess dress	35-40
blue round disc w/ gold detail drop earrings	40-55
shoes: blue closed toe	15-20

Pink Moonbeams
Light pink
#1694
Date 1967-68

NRFB	Mint/Complete
375-450	75-125
	Avg
light pink tricot robe w/ feather trim	35-40
light pink tricot night gown	35-40
shoes: light pink open toe	10-15

Pink Moonbeams
Hot pink
#1694
Date 1967-68

NRFB	Mint/Complete
375-450	100-150
	Avg
hot pink tricot robe w/ feather trim	45-50
hot pink tricot night gown	45-50
shoes: light pink open toe	10-15

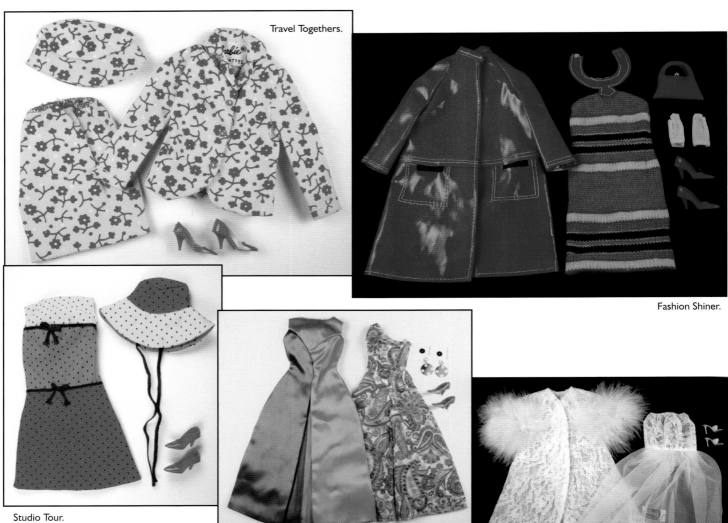

Travel Togethers.

Fashion Shiner.

Studio Tour.

Patio Party.

Pink Moonbeams.

Evening Enchantment
1695
Date 1967

	NRFB	Mint/Complete
	950-1250	350-425
		Avg
red chiffon gown w/ white fur trim		75-100
red chiffon cape w/ white fur trim		75-100
shoes: red closed toe		15-20

Floating Gardens
1696
Date 1967

	NRFB	Mint/Complete
	675-750	375-425
		Avg
floral nylon long dress		75-100
red chiffon hooded wrap		100-125
red cuff bracelet		15-20
pink cuff bracelet		15-20
red & pink interlocking earrings		35-40
shoes: red closed toe		15-20

Formal Occasion
1697
Date 1967

	NRFB	Mint/Complete
	375-450	150-200
		Avg
white crepe gown w/ gold embroidery		50-75
gold cape w/ pink chiffon lining		40-55
shoes: white closed toe		15-20

Beautiful Bride
1698
Date 1967

	NRFB	Mint/Complete
	1750-1825	675-750
		Avg
white satin gown w/ petal bodice		100-125
white satin & tulle underskirt		100-125
white satin bow veil w/ tulle train		100-125
white flowers w/ pearls bouquet		100-125
blue garter		10-15
short white tricot gloves		15-20
shoes: white closed toe		15-20

Stripes Away
Color Magic
1775
Date 1967

	NRFB	Mint/Complete
	375-450	175-225
		Avg
long olive cotton dress		50-75
olive cotton head scarf		50-75
two pink snake bracelets		25-30
red applicator stick w/ sponge		20-25
color changer package A		15-20
color changer package B		15-20

Evening Enchantment.
Courtesy of Karen Bindelglass

Floating Gardens.

Beautiful Bride. Never removed from box/card.
Courtesy of Karen Bindelglass

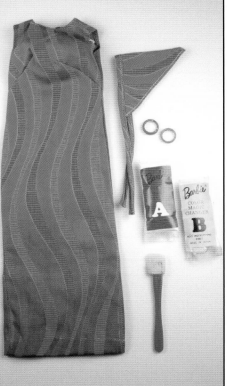

Stripes Away.

Smart Switch
Color Magic
1776
Date 1967

	NRFB	Mint/Complete
	375-450	200-250
		Avg
yellow top w/ pink multicolored belt		75-100
pink multicolored skirt		50-75
pink multicolored head scarf		75-100
red applicator stick w/ sponge		20-25
color changer package A		15-20
color changer package B		15-20

Pretty Wild!
Color Magic
1777
Date 1967

	NRFB	Mint/Complete
	400-475	225-275
		Avg
block print dress w/ flower design		75-100
block print hat w/ yellow brim		75-100
flower design purse handbag		75-100
red applicator stick w/ sponge		20-25
color changer package A		15-20
color changer package B		15-20

Bloom Bursts
Color Magic
1778
Date 1967

	NRFB	Mint/Complete
	375-450	200-250
		Avg
floral sun dress		75-100
sheer pink chiffon bonnet		75-100
yellow applicator stick w/ sponge		20-25
color changer package A		15-20
color changer package B		15-20

Mix 'n Matchers
Color Magic
1779
Date 1967

	NRFB	Mint/Complete
	375-450	200-250
		Avg
yellow stripe & floral pattern shirt		30-45
yellow stripe & floral pattern skirt		30-45
pink pants w/ yellow stripe & floral pattern		30-45
straw hat w/ attached yellow scarf		40-45
yellow mixing bowl		25-30
metal spoon w/ red handle		5-7
yellow applicator stick w/ sponge		20-25
red applicator stick w/ sponge		20-25
color changer package A		15-20
color changer package B		15-20
shoes: pink squishy flats		20-25

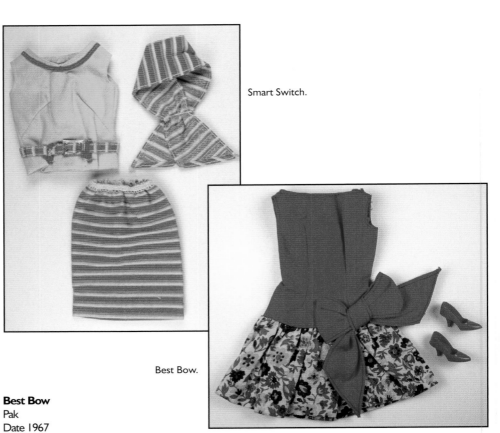

Smart Switch.

Best Bow.

Best Bow
Pak
Date 1967

	NRFB	Mint/Complete
	175-550	75-375
		Avg
red dress w/ "On the Go" fabric		225-275
red dress w/ "Sledding Fun" fabric		350-400
red dress w/ "Time To Turn In" fabric		350-400
red dress w/blue & white fabric		225-275
red dress w/ "Gay Parisienne" fabric		375-425
red dress w/ Allan's original outfit fabric		225-275

Skirt Styles
Pak
Date 1967

	NRFB	Mint/Complete
	175-250	75-125
		Avg
red & white stripe pleated skirt		40-45
yellow cotton sheath skirt		40-45

Top Twosome
Pak
Date 1967

	NRFB	Mint/Complete
	175-250	75-125
		Avg
yellow cotton tank shirt		40-45
white crepe body blouse		40-45

Fancy Trimmings
Pak
Date 1967

	NRFB	Mint/Complete
	175-250	75-125
		Avg
Blonde hair braid w/ red ribbon		20-25
red umbrella		10-15
red purse		10-15
blue textured purse		10-15
white lace stockings		20-25
short white tricot gloves		15-20
shoes: red open toe		10-15
shoes: blue closed toe		15-20

Cook Ups
Pak
Date 1967

	NRFB	Mint/Complete
	175-250	75-125
		Avg
white toaster		10-15
two toast slices		15-20
silver "B" teapot w/ lid		20-25
two turquoise teacups		10-15
two turquoise saucers		10-15
two turquoise plates		35-40
small casserole w/ lid		20-25
medium casserole w/ lid		20-25
large casserole w/ lid		20-25
casserole handle		30-35
coffeepot w/ lid		20-25

Bouncy-Flouncy
1805
Date 1967-68

	NRFB	Mint/Complete
	375-450	200-250
		Avg
multicolored floral summer dress		60-75
multicolored floral tote bag		35-50
shoes: orange closed toe		15-20

Disco Dater
1807
Date 1967-68

	NRFB	Mint/Complete
	275-350	100-150
		Avg
orange satin dress w/ pleated skirt		20-25
orange lace over-blouse		25-30
shoes: orange closed toe		15-20

Mini Prints
1809
Date 1967-68

	NRFB	Mint/Complete
	275-350	75-125
		Avg
multicolored jersey dress		40-45
multicolored jersey hose		20-25
shoes: royal blue bow		20-25

Bouncy-Flouncy.

Disco Dater.

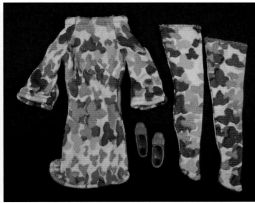

Mini Prints.

Pajama Pow!
1806
Date 1967-68

	NRFB	Mint/Complete
	375-450	200-250
		Avg
multicolored floral jumpsuit		20-25
gold, pink & red round dangle earrings		50-75
hoes: yellow soft flats		30-35S

Drizzle Dash!
1808
Date 1967-68

	NRFB	Mint/Complete
	75-125	35-60
		Avg
orange & pink raincoat		15-20
orange & pink head scarf		25-30
shoes: orange rain boots		15-20

Bermuda Holidays
1810
Date 1967-68

	NRFB	Mint/Complete
	300-375	100-150
		Avg
multicolored floral tunic		30-35
green shorts		40-45
multicolored floral hat		40-45
shoes: hot pink flats		20-25

Pajama Pow!

Drizzle Dash!

Bermuda Holidays.

Weekenders

Sears Exclusive
1815
Date 1967

	NRFB	Mint/Complete
	400-475	225-275
		Avg
pink, wine & green striped jacket		40-45
pink, wine & green print top w/ belt		40-45
pink, wine & green print pants		40-45
pink, wine & green hat w/ green visor		50-75
shoes: hot pink flats		20-25
or fluorescent hot pink flats		20-25

The Yellow Go

Sears Exclusive
1816
Date 1967

	NRFB	Mint/Complete
	775-850	475-525
		Avg
yellow cotton raincoat		60-85
yellow cotton hood w/ attached scarf		75-100
pale yellow lace hose		100-125
blue purse w/ chain strap		60-85
shoes: aqua soft bow		75-100

Red Fantastic

Sears Exclusive
1817
Date 1967

	NRFB	Mint/Complete
	850-1250	475-525
		Avg
coral pink satin gown w/ crepe insert		175-225
coral pink satin shawl w/ fur trim		150-200
shoes: coral pink closed toe		15-20
or hot pink		15-20

Velvet-Teens

Sears Exclusive
1818
Date 1967

	NRFB	Mint/Complete
	775-850	275-350
		Avg
red velvet jumpsuit w/ crepe blouse insert		175-225
red velvet jacket		175-225
shoes: fluorescent hot pink flats		20-25

Beautiful Blues

Gift Set
Sears Exclusive
3303
Date 1967

	NRFB	Mint/Complete
	2800-3500	850-1250
		Avg
blue lamé one shoulder dress		175-225
blue satin coat w/ fur trim		250-300
blue vinyl clutch purse		250-300
shoes: blue closed toe		15-20

Beautiful Blues.
Courtesy of Karen Bindelglass

Travel In Style

Gift Set
Sears Exclusive
3303
Date 1968

	NRFB	Mint/Complete
	2800-3500	675-750
		Avg
blue & green floral coat		100-125
blue & green floral skirt		100-125
blue knit top		150-175
green & blue travel hatbox		50-75
royal blue hose		150-175
shoes: royal blue bow		15-20

Red Fantastic. Rare. Never removed from box/card.
Author's Collection

Velvet-Teens.
Courtesy of Karen Bindelglass

Stripes Are Happening
Gift Set
Sears Exclusive
1545
Date 1968

	NRFB	Mint/Complete
	2000-2600	675-750
		Avg
pink jacket w/ multicolored sleeves		100-125
multicolored shell		100-175
multicolored mini skirt		75-150
multicolored socks		100-175
shoes: low soft pink boots		15-20

Glimmer Glamour
Gift Set
Sears Exclusive
1547
Date 1968

	NRFB	Mint/Complete
	4000-4500	900-1500
		Avg
blue taffeta dress w/ gold glitter		600-725
gold coat w/ yellow lining		100-125
gold sheer nylon hose		500-650
wide gold belt		10-15
gold dimple clutch purse		10-15
shoes: clear open toe w/ gold glitter		20-25

Dinner Dazzle
Gift Set
Sears Exclusive
1551
Date 1968

	NRFB	Mint/Complete
	1850-2200	400-500
		Avg
blue & pink lamé jacket w/ fur trim		150-200
blue & pink lamé skirt		75-100
pink satin blouse w/ ruffles		75-100
sheer pink hose		30-35
shoes: pink closed toe		15-20

Silver 'n Satin
Gift Set
Sears Exclusive
1552
Date 1968

	NRFB	Mint/Complete
	1850-2200	400-500
		Avg
silver lamé dress w/ pink satin waist		200-225
pink satin coat		150-200
pink nylon petticoat		15-20
long silver belt		75-125
hot pink hose		30-35
shoes: hot pink closed toe		15-20

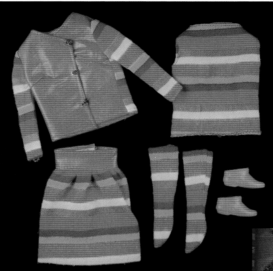

Stripes Are Happening

Glimmer Glamour.

Dinner Dazzle

Knit Hit
1804
Date 1968-69

	NRFB	Mint/Complete
	100-175	35-50
		Avg
blue & pink knit mini dress		15-20
shoes: light blue closed toe		15-20

Knit Hit
Japanese Exclusive
Date 1968-69

	NRFB	Mint/Complete
	650-800	250-350
		Avg
white, red & green knit mini dress		250-350

Knit Hit. Japanese exclusive.
Courtesy of Karen Bindelglass

Snugg Fuzz
1813
Date 1968-69

	NRFB	Mint/Complete
	275-350	85-115
		Avg
pink fuzzy jacket		15-20
white belt		20-25
pink fuzzy mini skirt		15-20
silver mesh top		40-45
silver mesh hose		15-20
shoes: gray soft low boots		15-20

Sparkle Squares
1814
Date 1968-69

	NRFB	Mint/Complete
	200-275	100-125
		Avg
checkerboard pattern dress w/ ruffle skirt		25-30
checkerboard pattern coat w/ ruffle trim		45-50
silver dimple clutch purse		15-20
sheer white hose		30-35
shoes: soft bow		25-30

Snugg Fuzz.
Courtesy of Karen Bindel-glass

Underliners
1821
Date 1968-69

	NRFB	Mint/Complete
	200-275	50-75
		Avg
multicolored negligee w/ lace trim		10-15
multicolored garter belt		20-25
sheer beige hose		20-25
shoes: pink open toe		10-15

Swirly-Cue
1822
Date 1968-69

	NRFB	Mint/Complete
	200-275	75-100
		Avg
multicolored silk mini dress		25-30
green & pink triangle dangle earrings		35-40
shoes: hot pink closed toe		15-20

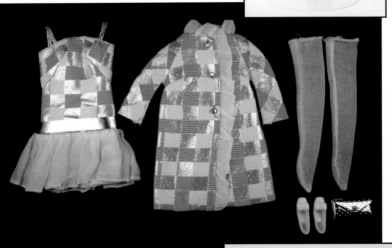

Sparkle Squares

Swirly-Cue

Zokko!
1820
Date 1968-69

	NRFB	Mint/Complete
	200-275	75-100
		Avg
silver & blue lamé dress		25-30
orange rectangular dangle earrings		35-40
shoes: silver & orange boots		15-20

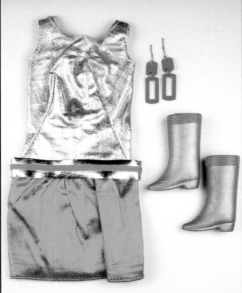

Zokko!

Jump Into Lace
1823
Date 1968

	NRFB	Mint/Complete
	200-275	40-65
		Avg
hot pink jumpsuit cover in white lace		15-20
shoes: hot pink open toe		10-15

Snap Dash
1824
Date 1968

NRFB	Mint/Complete
125-175	50-75
	Avg
green dress w/ yellow trim	10-15
green felt hat w/ yellow band	25-30
yellow cotton knee socks	20-25
shoes: yellow ankle boots	20-25
or soft yellow bow	15-20

Night Clouds
1841
Date 1968

NRFB	Mint/Complete
75-125	30-55
	Avg
yellow, pink & orange ruffled nighty	15-20
sheer yellow robe	10-15
shoes: yellow open toe	10-15

Togetherness
1842
Date 1968

NRFB	Mint/Complete
125-175	50-75
	Avg
aqua blue knit dress	15-20
aqua blue knit bonnet	15-20
aqua blue knit hose	25-30
shoes: soft pink bow	15-20

Dancing Stripes
1843
Date 1968

NRFB	Mint/Complete
175-225	75-100
	Avg
pink, purple & white striped dress	25-30
pink, purple & white striped coat	20-25
shoes: hot pink closed toe	15-20

Extravaganza
1844
Date 1968

NRFB	Mint/Complete
450-575	100-125
	Avg
pink gown w/ glitter net overlay	50-75
silver dimple clutch purse	15-20
long hot pink tricot gloves	35-40
shoes: hot pink open toe	10-15

All That Jazz.

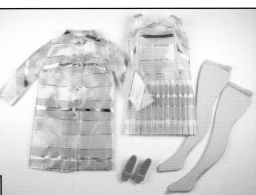

Snap Dash. Never removed from box/card.
Courtesy of Karen Bindelglass

Trailblazers

Scene-Stealers
1845
Date 1968

NRFB	Mint/Complete
275-325	150-175
	Avg
green lamé shell w/ pink satin trim	15-20
pink sheer silk coat w/ pink satin trim	65-90
pink silk & satin ruffled skirt	35-40
shoes: hot pink closed toe	15-20

Trailblazers
1846
Date 1968

NRFB	Mint/Complete
275-325	125-150
	Avg
yellow knit top w/ flwer design	15-20
multicolored striped corduroy jacket	15-20
multicolored striped corduroy pants	15-20
green sunglasses w/ pink stripes	60-85
shoes: acid green low boots	15-20

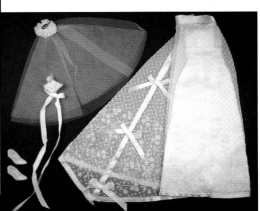

Wedding Wonder.
Courtesy of Karen Bindelglass

All That Jazz
1847
Date 1968-69

NRFB	Mint/Complete
275-325	150-175
	Avg
pink, orange, yellow & gold striped dress	25-30
pink, orange, yellow & gold striped coat	20-25
thin gold belt	35-40
sheer beige hose	20-25
shoes: soft orange bow	15-20

Wedding Wonder
1849
Date 1968-69

NRFB	Mint/Complete
350-400	175-225
	Avg
long white satin gown w/ sheer dotted overlay	45-50
white two tiered veil w/ gold barrette	35-40
white floral bouquet w/ satin streamers	25-30
shoes: white closed toe	15-20

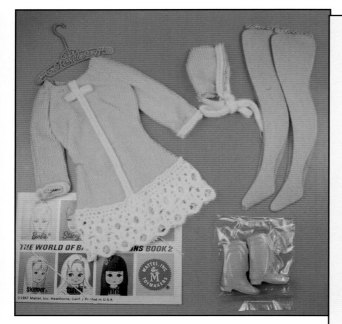

Now Wow!

Now Wow!
1853
Date 1968-69

NRFB	Mint/Complete
125-150	50-75
	Avg
light blue corduroy mini dress	10-15
light blue corduroy bonnet	15-20
light blue sheer hose	25-30
shoes: light blue majorette boots w/ chartreuse trim	15-20

Twinkle Togs
1854
Date 1968-69

NRFB	Mint/Complete
125-150	50-75
	Avg
blue lamé top with multicolored skirt	25-30
lime green sheer hose	25-30
shoes: blue closed toe	15-20

Team-Ups
1855
Date 1968-69

NRFB	Mint/Complete
125-150	60-85
	Avg
pink knit dress w/ multicolored top	15-20
pink knit jacket	10-15
thin gold belt w/ gold buckle	30-35
shoes: hot pink closed toe	15-20

Wild 'n Wonderful
1856
Date 1968-69

NRFB	Mint/Complete
175-225	75-100
	Avg
multicolored cotton top	15-20
multicolored cotton skirt	15-20
orange panty	25-30
shoes: tall orange sandals	35-40

Wild 'n Wonderful
Courtesy of Karen Bindelglass

Dreamy Pink
1857
Hot pink
Date 1968-69

NRFB	Mint/Complete
125-150	50-75
	Avg
hot pink nylon nightgown	10-15
hot pink nylon robe	10-15
shoes: hot pink slippers	10-15

Dreamy Pink
1857
Light pink
Date 1968-69

NRFB	Mint/Complete
125-150	50-75
	Avg
light pink nylon nightgown	10-15
light pink nylon robe	10-15
shoes: hot pink slippers	10-15

Fancy Dancy
1858
Date 1968-69

NRFB	Mint/Complete
175-225	75-100
	Avg
hot pink & green knit dress	15-20
hot pink & green knit jacket	15-20
sheer w/ flowers pink hose	25-30
shoes: soft hot pink bow	10-15

Tunic 'n Tights
1859
Date 1968-69

NRFB	Mint/Complete
175-225	75-100
	Avg
hot pink & yellow knit top	15-20
yellow tunic top	15-20
yellow shorts	20-25
hot pink & yellow knit tights	15-20
shoes: yellow squishy low boots	15-20

Fancy Dancy.

Smasheroo
#1860
Date 1968-69

	NRFB	Mint/Complete
	175-225	85-115
		Avg
red striped shirt dress		15-20
gold chain belt		20-25
yellow fur jacket		10-15
yellow fur hat		15-20
yellow textured hose		15-20
shoes: tall red riding boots		20-25

Dressed-Up!
Pak
Date 1968

	NRFB	Mint/Complete
	175-225	75-150
		Avg
dress & bodice in many assorted colors		75-150

Smasheroo.

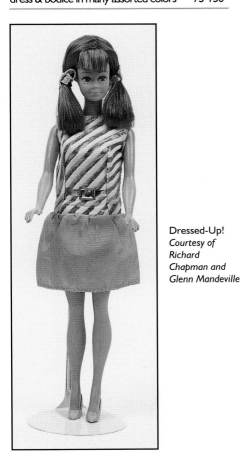

Dressed-Up!
*Courtesy of
Richard
Chapman and
Glenn Mandeville*

Extra Casuals
Pak
Date 1968

	NRFB	Mint/Complete
	60-110	50-75
		Avg
yellow cotton hat		30-35
pink tote w/ large flower		10-15
two pink snake bracelets		25-30
hot pink rectangular drop earrings		30-45
shoes: hard pointed yellow w/ cut outs		15-20
shoes: hard pointed hot pink w/ cut outs		15-20

Pedal Pushers
Pak
Date 1968

	NRFB	Mint/Complete
	50-100	40-65
		Avg
blue cotton denim shell		10-15
blue cotton denim shorts		10-15
shoes: soft yellow flats		15-20

Change-Abouts
Pak
Date 1968

	NRFB	Mint/Complete
	175-250	75-125
		Avg
blonde hair braid w/ red ribbon		20-25
red umbrella		10-15
red purse		10-15
blue textured purse		10-15
white lace stockings		20-25
short white tricot gloves		15-20
shoes: red open toe		10-15
shoes: blue closed toe		15-20

Add-Ons
Pak
Date 1968

	NRFB	Mint/Complete
	175-250	75-125
		Avg
black granny glasses		25-35
black eyelash brush		20-25
brown pencil		10-15
pink shoulder purse		10-15
green & white double strand necklace		25-30
hot pink small case		15-20
red cuff bracelet		15-20
pink cuff bracelet		15-20
red & pink interlocking earrings		35-40
pair gold triangle earrings		15-20

Flats 'n Heels
Pak
Date 1968

	NRFB	Mint/Complete
	175-225	100-150
		Avg
shoes: green open toe		10-15
shoes: white open toe		10-15
shoes: aqua open toe		15-20
shoes: hot pink open toe		10-15
shoes: orange closed toe		15-20
shoes: off white closed toe		15-20
shoes: red closed toe		15-20
shoes: blue closed toe		15-20
shoes: black closed toe		15-20
shoes: soft blue bows		15-20
shoes: gold & tan wedges		10-15
shoes: light pink squishy flats		15-20

Dream Wrap
#1476
Date 1969-70

	NRFB	Mint/Complete
	65-90	30-55
		Avg
pink & white shorty robe w/ lace trim		10-15
pink & white panty w/ lace trim		5-10
shoes: pink felt scuffs w/ white flower		10-15

Hurray For Leather
#1477
Date 1969-70

	NRFB	Mint/Complete
	75-100	30-55
		Avg
orange knit cotton sweater		10-15
yellow skirt w/ orange trim		10-15
shoes: yellow pilgrim		5-10

Shift Into Knit
1478
Date 1969-70

	NRFB	Mint/Complete
	75-100	30-55
		Avg
orange & navy knit dress		10-15
gold belt w/ round accent		10-15
orange knit scarf		10-15
shoes: red pilgrim		5-10
or soft red bows		10-15

Leisure Leopard
1479
Date 1969-70

	NRFB	Mint/Complete
	75-100	30-55
		Avg
leopard print dress		10-15
shoes: yellow pilgrim		5-10
or yellow open toe		10-15

Firelights
1481
Date 1969-70

	NRFB	Mint/Complete
	75-100	30-55
		Avg
silver & turquoise brocade jumpsuit		15-20
shoes: turquoise open toe		10-15

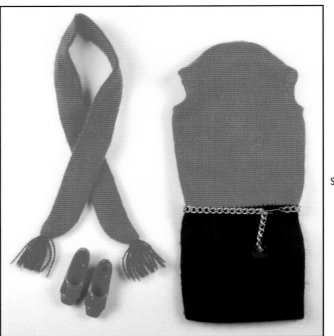

Shift Into Knit.

Important In-Vestment
1481
Date 1969-70

	NRFB	Mint/Complete
	75-100	40-65
		Avg
green knit dress		10-15
gold chain belt w/ flower clasp		15-20
white fluffy vest		10-15
shoes: green pilgrim		5-10

Important In-Vestment
Yellow variation
1481
Date 1969-70

	NRFB	Mint/Complete
	125-175	80-115
		Avg
yellow knit dress		55-60
gold chain belt w/ flower clasp		15-20
white fluffy vest		10-15
shoes: yellow pilgrim		5-10

Important In-Vestment.

Important In-Vestment.

Firelights.
Author's Collection

Little Bow-Pink
#1483
Date 1969-70

	NRFB	Mint/Complete
	75-100	40-65
		Avg
pink satin dress		30-35
hot pink mesh hose		15-20
shoes: pink pilgrims		5-10
or soft pink bow		10-15

Yellow Mellow
#1484
Date 1969-70

	NRFB	Mint/Complete
	75-100	40-65
		Avg
yellow velour dress		15-20
yellow lacy hose		15-20
shoes: yellow pilgrim		5-10

Shirt Dressy
#1487
Date 1969-70

	NRFB	Mint/Complete
	100-175	75-100
		Avg
sheer yellow dress w/ white lace detail		15-20
yellow satin underdress		15-20
sheer yellow hose		25-30
shoes: yellow pilgrim		5-10

Velvet Venture
#1488
Date 1969-70

	NRFB	Mint/Complete
	100-175	75-100
		Avg
gold & pink brocade dress		30-35
acid green velour coat		40-45
shoes: acid green pilgrim		5-10

Cloud 9
#1489
Date 1969-70

	NRFB	Mint/Complete
	75-100	40-65
		Avg
light blue & coral satin robe		5-10
light blue & coral satin nighty		5-10
light blue panty		15-20
shoes: light blue & coral satin slippers		10-15

Red , White 'n Warm
1491
Date 1969-70

	NRFB	Mint/Complete
	150-200	100-125
		Avg
orange & pink block dress		20-25
white vinyl coat w/ fur trim		15-20
white vinyl belt		15-20
white vinyl hat w/ fur hat		15-20
shoes: white vinyl boots w/ fur		20-25

Silver Polish
#1492
Date 1969-70

	NRFB	Mint/Complete
	75-100	40-65
		Avg
silver lamé jumpsuit		15-20
yellow hostess coat		15-20
shoes: yellow pilgrim		5-10

Yellow Mellow.

Winter Wow
#1486
Date 1969-70

	NRFB	Mint/Complete
	100-175	75-100
		Avg
orange cotton jacket w/ brown fur trim		10-15
gold belt w/ large gold buckle		15-20
orange cotton pleated skirt		10-15
brown fur bonnet		15-20
brown fur muff		15-20
shoes: gold lamé tall boots		25-30

Winter Wow.
Courtesy of Karen Bindelglass

Silver Polish. Never removed from box/card.
Courtesy of Karen Bindelglass

Fab Fur
1493
Date 1969-70

	NRFB	Mint/Complete
	150-200	100-125
		Avg
coral satin shell		30-35
tan & beige fur coat		20-25
tan & beige fur skirt		15-20
shoes: gold lamé pantyhose boots		20-25

Fab Fur
1493
Date 1969-70
Variation leopard print

	NRFB	Mint/Complete
	200-250	150-175
		Avg
coral satin shell		30-35
tan & beige black leopard fur coat		50-55
tan & beige black leopard fur skirt		50-55
shoes: gold lamé pantyhose boots		20-25

Goldswinger
1494
Date 1969-70

	NRFB	Mint/Complete
	200-250	150-175
		Avg
orange & gold lamé gown		50-55
orange & gold lamé coat		50-55
shoes: orange closed toe		15-20

Nite Lightning.

Nite Lightning
Gift Set
Sears Exclusive
1591
Date 1969

	NRFB	Mint/Complete
	2500-3000	850-950
		Avg
pink satin & multicolored dress		150-175
royal blue satin swing coat w/ rhinestone		100-175
royal blue hose		150-175
shoes: royal blue closed toe		15-20
or blue open toe		10-15

Twinkle Town
Gift Set
Sears Exclusive
1592
Date 1969

	NRFB	Mint/Complete
	1500-1850	40-65
		Avg
silver & pink top		5-10
pink satin skirt		10-15
pink hose		15-20
shoes: soft pink bow		15-20

Golden Groove
Gift Set
Sears Exclusive
1593
Date 1969

	NRFB	Mint/Complete
	2000-2500	400-450
		Avg
pink & gold brocade jacket w/ fur trim		150-175
pink & gold brocade skirt		100-175
shoes: gold lamé tall boots		25-30

Simply Wow
Gift Set for Julia
Sears Exclusive
1594
Date 1969

	NRFB	Mint/Complete
	1500-2000	400-450
		Avg
white satin & aqua knit skirt dress		150-175
aqua knit jacket		150-175
shoes: aqua pilgrim		5-10

Goldswinger.
Courtesy of Karen Bindelglass

Golden Groove.
Courtesy of Richard Chapman and Glenn Mandeville

Fabulous Formal
Gift Set for Barbie & Ken
Sears Exclusive
1595
Date 1969

NRFB	Mint/Complete
2000-2500	550-575

Barbie

	Avg
yellow ruffled gown w/ silver top	100-125
silver purse w/ yellow lining	75-100
yellow flower earrings	75-100
shoes: yellow pilgrim	5-10

Ken

	Avg
gold nylon jacket	75-100
red & gold brocade vest	5-10
white shirt w/ gold & white ascot	10-15
white pants	10-15
white cotton socks	7-10
shoes: white loafer	5-10

Pink Premier
Gift Set
JC Penney Exclusive
1596
Date 1969

NRFB	Mint/Complete
1500-2000	400-450

	Avg
pink & gold satin jacket	100-125
pink satin w/ white ruffles dress	100-125
pink & gold satin purse	10-15
pink sheer pantyhose w/ fishnet panty	15-20
gold lamé gloves	10-15
shoes: pink pilgrim	5-10

Leather Weather
Julia outfit
1751
Date 1969-70

NRFB	Mint/Complete
150-200	75-100

	Avg
red vinyl coat w/ fur trim	20-25
pink knit shell	15-20
plaid yarn mini skirt	15-20
red vinyl purse	20-25
shoes: red pilgrim	5-10

Brrr-Furrr
Julia outfit
1752
Date 1969-70

NRFB	Mint/Complete
150-200	75-100

	Avg
lime green & aqua dress	20-25
aqua coat w/ lime green fur trim	20-25
lime green fur hat	20-25
shoes: aqua pilgrim	5-10

Fabulous Formal, Barbie & Ken.
Courtesy of Richard Chapman and Glenn Mandeville

Brrr-Furrr
Julia outfit
1752
Date 1969-70
Variation green metallic bodice

NRFB	Mint/Complete
175-225	125-150

	Avg
green metallic bodice & aqua dress	40-45
aqua coat w/ green fur trim	40-45
green fur hat	40-45
shoes: aqua pilgrim	5-10

Leather Weather.

Brrr-Furrr
Julia outfit
1752
Date 1969-70
Variation red & white

NRFB	Mint/Complete
250-300	175-200

	Avg
red & white dress	60-65
red & white coat w/ white fur trim	60-65
white fur hat	60-65
shoes: red pilgrim	5-10

Candlelight Capers
Julia outfit
1753
Date 1969-70

NRFB	Mint/Complete
150-200	75-100

	Avg
orange bodice & yellow velour dress	20-25
yellow velour cape	15-20
yellow velour hat w/ fur trim	20-25
shoes: yellow pilgrim	5-10

Candlelight Capers.

Candlelight Capers
Julia outfit
1753
Date 1969-70
Variation gold lamé bodice

	NRFB	Mint/Complete
	150-200	75-100
		Avg
gold lamé bodice & yellow velour dress		20-25
yellow velour cape		15-20
yellow velour hat w/ fur trim		20-25
shoes: yellow pilgrim		5-10

Pink Fantasy
Julia outfit
1754
Date 1969-70

	NRFB	Mint/Complete
	100-150	50-75
		Avg
hot pink nylon long nightgown		15-20
hot pink nylon robe		15-20
shoes: gold lamé slippers		10-15
or pink pilgrim		5-10

Make Mine Midi
#1861
Date 1969

	NRFB	Mint/Complete
	75-100	40-65
		Avg
white cotton blouse		20-25
pink skirt w/ pink poufs		15-20
pink nylon slip		15-20
shoes: soft pink bow		10-1

Country Caper
#1862
Date 1969

	NRFB	Mint/Complete
	75-100	40-65
		Avg
white, orange, & yellow sweater		10-15
yellow cotton shorts		10-15
shoes: soft yellow flats		10-15

Pretty Power
#1863
Date 1969

	NRFB	Mint/Complete
	75-100	40-65
		Avg
white dress w/ pink & white print skirt		20-25
shoes: black closed toe		15-20
or black pilgrim		10-15

Close-Ups
#1864
Date 1969

	NRFB	Mint/Complete
	50-75	15-40
		Avg
sheer yellow & hot pink slip		5-10
pink lace bra		5-10
pink sheer pantyhose w/ lace panty		15-20

Pink Fantasy.

Pink Fantasy.
Author's Collection

Make Mine Midi.
Author's Collection

Country Caper on a rare pink skin toned bend leg Midge.
Courtesy of Richard Chapman and Glenn Mandeville

Close-Ups

Glo-Go
#1865
Date 1969

	NRFB	Mint/Complete
	150-200	75-100

		Avg
red lamé dress w/ pink & white print skirt		50-65
shoes: red closed toe		15-20

Movie Groovie
#1866
Date 1969

	NRFB	Mint/Complete
	50-100	40-65
		Avg
silver & pink top		5-10
pink satin skirt		10-15
pink hose		15-20
shoes: soft pink bow		15-20

Dream-Inns
#1867
Date 1969

	NRFB	Mint/Complete
	50-100	30-45
		Avg
peach & pink short nighty		10-15
pink fuzzy robe		10-15

Happy Go Pink
#1868
Date 1969

	NRFB	Mint/Complete
	50-100	40-65
		Avg
pink long sleeve dress w/ white skirt		15-20
sheer hot pink hose		15-20
or sheer light pink hose		15-20
shoes: pink closed toe		15-20

Midi-Magic
#1869
Date 1969

	NRFB	Mint/Complete
	100-150	50-75
		Avg
black taffeta skirt w/ white bodice dress		15-20
sheer black hose		30-35
shoes: black closed toe		15-20
or black pilgrim		10-15

Midi-Marvelous
#1870
Date 1969

	NRFB	Mint/Complete
	100-150	50-75
		Avg
white dress w/ pink satin trim		20-25
white hat w/ pink satin trim		15-20
sheer white hose		30-35
shoes: white closed toe		15-20
or white pilgrim		10-15
or soft white bow		15-20

Romantic Ruffles
#1871
Date 1969

	NRFB	Mint/Complete
	175-225	75-125
		Avg
pink ruffled gown w/ silver top		20-25
silver purse w/ pink lining		10-15
pink flower earrings		20-25
shoes: pink closed toe		15-20
or pink pilgrim		10-15
or soft pink bow		15-20

See-Worthy
#1872
Date 1969

	NRFB	Mint/Complete
	150-200	100-125
		Avg
aqua blue sailor dress w/ yellow fabric stars		50-75
aqua blue hat w/ yellow pompom		20-25
aqua blue cotton socks		20-25
yellow satin neck tie		35-40
black camera		15-20
shoes: aqua sneakers		10-15

Romantic Ruffles.

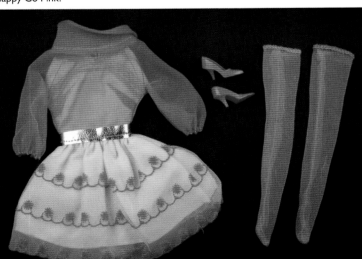

Midi-Magic.
Courtesy of Lisa Varuolo

Happy Go Pink.

See-Worthy

Plush Pony
#1873
Date 1969

	NRFB	Mint/Complete
	150-200	75-100
		Avg
orange dress w/ black & white plush skirt		35-40
black & white plush coat		20-25
gold chain belt		30-35
shoes: orange boots		10-15

Fab City
#1874
Date 1969

	NRFB	Mint/Complete
	250-300	150-175
		Avg
pink, white and silver gown		40-45
silver stole pink lining		20-25
short pink tricot gloves		20-25
shoes: pink closed toe		15-20
or pink pilgrim		10-15

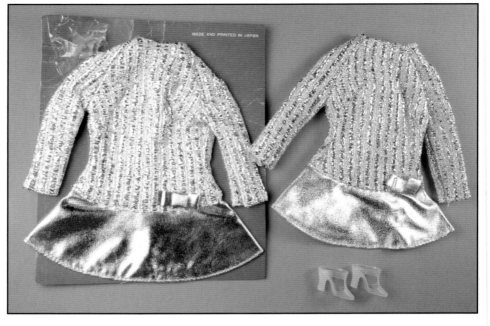

Silver Sparkle.

Fab City.
Courtesy of Karen Bindelglass

Let's Have A Ball
#1879
Date 1969

	NRFB	Mint/Complete
	275-325	200-225
		Avg
aqua velvet w/ white chiffon gown		100-125
aqua velvet w/ white fur trim		50-75
shoes: aqua closed toe		15-20
or aqua pilgrim		10-15

Winter Wedding
#1880
Date 1969-70

	NRFB	Mint/Complete
	100-150	50-75
		Avg
off white brocade gown w/ fur trim		20-25
off white veil brocade cap w/ fur trim		10-15
pink velvet floral bouquet		10-15
shoes: white closed toe		15-20
or white pilgrim		10-15

Made For Each Other
#1881
Date 1969

	NRFB	Mint/Complete
	250-300	150-175
		Avg
yellow cotton ribbed shell		15-20
yellow, orange & white woven coat		15-20
yellow, orange & white woven skirt		20-25
orange belt w/ gold buckle		25-30
orange plush hat		20-25
yellow & orange double strand necklace		20-25
shoes: orange riding boots		20-25

Silver Sparkle
#1885
Date 1969

	NRFB	Mint/Complete
	100-150	25-50
		Avg
silver dress w/ silver lamé skirt		15-20
shoes: clear open toe		15-20
or clear t-strap		30-35

Terrific Twosome
Pak
Date 1969

	NRFB	Mint/Complete
	175-250	75-150
		Avg
white shell		30-45
yellow linen skirt w/ black velvet waistband		30-45
white & green double strand necklace		20-25
shoes: white closed toe		15-20
white shell		30-45
aqua linen skirt w/ black velvet waistband		30-45
white & green double strand necklace		20-25
shoes: white closed toe		15-20
white shell		30-45
red, white & green floral print skirt		
w/ black velvet waistband		50-75
white & green double strand necklace		20-25
shoes: white closed toe		15-20
white shell		30-45
blue, white & green floral print skirt		
w/ black velvet waistband		75-100
white & green double strand necklace		20-25
shoes: white closed toe		15-20

Sun-Shiner. Green with black dots.

Sun-Shiner. Yellow
with black dots.
Author's Collection

Sun-Shiner
Pak
Date 1969

	NRFB	Mint/Complete
	175-350	75-225
		Avg
red w/ black dots cotton dress		50-75
shoes: red closed toe		15-20
yellow w/ black dots cotton dress		50-75
shoes: red closed toe		15-20
green w/ black dots cotton dress		50-75
shoes: red closed toe		15-20
blue w/ white dots cotton dress		200-225
shoes: red closed toe		15-20
yellow w/ red flowers cotton dress		50-75
shoes: red closed toe		15-20
yellow w/ red & white flowers cotton dress		175-200
shoes: red closed toe		15-20

Petti-Pinks
Pak
Date 1969

	NRFB	Mint/Complete
	100-150	50-75
		Avg
pink nylon petticoat		15-20
pink fuzzy scale		7-10
gold talc box		5-7
hot pink powder puff		7-10
hot pink comb		3-5
hot pink brush		3-5
hand mirror		7-10
shoes: pink felt slippers		10-15

Finishing Touches
Pak
Date 1969

	NRFB	Mint/Complete
	100-150	50-75
		Avg
silver belt		15-20
brown eyeliner pencil		10-15
black eyelash brush		10-15
silver dimple purse		10-15
flower corsage w/ satin bow		25-30
silver mesh hose		20-25
long white tricot gloves		10-15
graduated pearl necklace		25-35

Tour-Ins
Pak
Date 1969

	NRFB	Mint/Complete
	100-150	50-75
		Avg
orange umbrella w/ tassel		15-20
green, blue & white hat box		15-20
black camera		15-20
yellow & orange double strand necklace		20-25
orange purse		10-15
pink round sunglasses		7-10
shoes: soft lime green bow		10-15

Flats 'n Heels
Pak
Date 1969

	NRFB	Mint/Complete
	100-150	50-75
		Avg
shoes: soft light blue bow		10-15
shoes: soft royal blue bow		10-15
shoes: soft orange bow		10-15
shoes: soft hot pink bow		10-15
shoes: white pilgrim		10-15
shoes: hot pink pilgrim		10-15
shoes: aqua pilgrim		10-15
shoes: aqua sneakers		10-15
shoes: orange ankle boots		10-15
shoes: yellow ankle boots		20-25

Tangerine Scene
#1451
Date 1970

	NRFB	Mint/Complete
	75-125	25-50
		Avg
orange long sleeve body suit		10-15
orange & white plaid skirt		10-15
shoes: soft orange flats		15-20
or orange pilgrim		10-15

Tangerine Scene.

Now Knit.

Loop Scoop.

Dreamy Blues.
*Courtesy of
Lisa Varuolo*

Now Knit
#1452
Date 1970

	NRFB	Mint/Complete
	75-125	50-75
		Avg
green, blue & silver knit dress w/ attached belt		20-25
green plush hat w/ blue band		10-15
blue neckerchief w/ silver thread ring		20-25
shoes: royal blue t-strap		10-15
or royal blue pilgrim		10-15

Flower Wower
#1453
Date 1970

	NRFB	Mint/Complete
	75-125	50-75
		Avg
multicolored floral dress w/ flower accent		10-15
shoes: lime green t-strap		10-15
or lime green pilgrim		10-15

Loop Scoop
#1454
Date 1970

	NRFB	Mint/Complete
	75-125	50-75
		Avg
yellow dress w/ multicolored knit skirt		10-15
shoes: yellow t-strap		10-15
or yellow pilgrim		10-15

Dreamy Blues
#1456
Date 1970

	NRFB	Mint/Complete
	75-125	50-75
		Avg
blue satin dress w/ chiffon skirt		15-20
shoes: blue t-strap		10-15
or blue pilgrim		10-15

City Sparkler
#1457
Date 1970

	NRFB	Mint/Complete
	75-125	50-75
		Avg
green metallic dress w/ chiffon skirt		15-20
shoes: lime green t-strap		10-15
or lime green pilgrim		10-15

Gypsy Spirit.

Lovely Sleep-Ins
#1463
Date 1970

NRFB	Mint/Complete
40-90	25-40
	Avg
pink nighty	15-20
pink lace robe w/ plush cuffs	10-15
shoes: pink plush slippers	10-15

Anti-Freezers
#1464
Date 1970

NRFB	Mint/Complete
75-125	50-75
	Avg
yellow cotton shell	20-25
orange, yellow & white knit plaid skirt	10-15
orange knit jacket w/ attached belt	15-20
orange, yellow & white knit plaid scarf	10-15
shoes: yellow boots	15-20

Lemon Kick
#1465
Date 1970

NRFB	Mint/Complete
75-125	50-75
	Avg
yellow pleated top	10-15
yellow pleated pants	10-15
yellow undershorts	25-20
shoes: yellow t-strap	10-15
or yellow pilgrim	10-15
or soft yellow bow	10-15

Gypsy Spirit
#1458
Date 1970

NRFB	Mint/Complete
75-125	50-75
	Avg
pink nylon long sleeve body suit	10-15
aqua suede skirt	10-15
aqua suede vest w/ gold ties	10-15
shoes: blue t-strap	10-15
or blue pilgrim	10-15
or pink t-strap	10-15
or pink pilgrim	10-15

Great Coat
#1459
Date 1970

NRFB	Mint/Complete
75-125	50-75
	Avg
yellow vinyl coat w/ leopard trim	10-15
yellow vinyl hat w/ leopard trim	15-20
shoes: yellow t-strap	10-15
or yellow pilgrim	10-15
or soft yellow bow	10-15

Rare Pair
#1462
Date 1970

NRFB	Mint/Complete
75-125	50-75
	Avg
yellow & pink knit dress	10-15
yellow & pink knit jacket	15-20
sheer yellow hose	20-25
shoes: yellow t-strap	10-15
or soft yellow bow	10-15

Great Coat.
Author's Collection

Rare Pair.
*Courtesy of
Lisa Varuolo*

Lemon Kick.
*Courtesy of Richard
Chapman & Glenn Mandeville*

Lamb 'n Leather. *Author's Collection*

Lamb 'n Leather
#1467
Date 1970

	NRFB	Mint/Complete
	150-200	75-100
		Avg
white fuzzy plush coat w/ pink lining		15-20
white fuzzy plush hat		20-25
black & pink vinyl belt		15-20
black & pink vinyl purse		15-20
short black tricot gloves		25-30
shoes: black & pink vinyl boots		25-30

Special Sparkle
#1468
Date 1970

	NRFB	Mint/Complete
	175-225	75-100
		Avg
gold & pink brocade coat w/ medallion		25-30
pink chiffon shell		20-25
gold lamé skirt		15-20
shoes: pink t-strap		10-15
or pink pilgrim		10-15

Blue Royalty
#1469
Date 1970

	NRFB	Mint/Complete
	175-225	50-75
		Avg
blue gown w/ gold braid trim		25-30
white plush coat		10-15
shoes: blue t-strap		10-15
or blue pilgrim		10-15

Shoe Bag
#1498
JC Penny Exclusive
Date 1970-71

	NRFB	Mint/Complete
	325-375	250-300
		Avg
orange umbrella w/ tassel		15-20
pink sheer pantyhose w/ fishnet panty		15-20
green, blue & white hat box		15-20
red visor hat w/ scarf		15-20
14 Barbie hangers		10-15
shoes: soft royal blue bow		10-15
shoes: soft hot pink ballerina slippers		10-15
shoes: white sneakers		10-15
shoes: hot pink open toe		10-15
shoes: hot pink open toe		10-15
shoes: aqua boots		10-15
shoes: royal blue ankle boots		10-15
shoes: orange ankle boots		10-15
shoes: gray ankle boots		10-15
shoes: green ankle boots		10-15
shoes: hot pink closed toe		15-20
shoes: black closed toe		15-20
shoes: royal blue closed toe		15-20
shoes: blue closed toe		15-20
shoes: aqua closed toe		15-20
shoes: orange closed toe		15-20
shoes: yellow closed toe		150-200
shoes: acid green closed toe		150-200
shoes: lime green closed toe		150-200
or grape closed toe		75-125
orange boots		10-15
or white boots		20-25
pink snow boots		20-25
pink round sunglasses		7-10
shoes: soft lime green bow		10-15

Glamour Group
#1510
Date 1970-73

	NRFB	Mint/Complete
	175-225	50-75
		Avg
cotton shift dress		15-20
party dress		20-25
knit dress w/ tie belt		15-20
coat w/ tie belt		15-20
fluorescent swimsuit bikini		40-45
or short pajama top & bottom		15-20
blue clutch purse		10-15
4 pink curlers		7-10
pink comb		3-5
pink brush		3-5
shoes: pink t-strap		10-15
or white t-strap		10-15
pink pilgrim		10-15
or white pilgrim		10-15

Fashion Bouquet
#1511
Sears Exclusive
Date 1970

	NRFB	Mint/Complete
	175-225	50-75
		Avg
coat w/ three buttons		15-20
wrap dress w/ tie belt		15-20
nylon shell		20-25
cotton pants		10-15
shoes: white pilgrim		10-15

Fashion Bouquet.

Fashion Bouquet

#1511
Sears Exclusive
Date 1970

NRFB	Mint/Complete
175-225	50-75
	Avg
sun dress	15-20
short pajama top & bottom	15-20
cotton jacket	15-20
nylon shell	20-25
cotton pants	10-15
cotton skirt	15-20
4 pink curlers	7-10
pink comb	3-5
pink brush	3-5
shoes: green pilgrim	10-15

Goodies Galore

#1518
Sears Exclusive
Date 1970-73

NRFB	Mint/Complete
175-225	50-75
	Avg
red visor hat w/ scarf	15-20
tennis racket	5-7
tennis ball	5-7
chocolate sundae	10-15
red princess phone	10-15
hand mirror	10-15
eyelash brush	10-15
brown pencil	10-15
10 Barbie hangers	7-10
blue clutch purse	10-15
white clutch purse	10-15
pink round sunglasses	7-10
red round sunglasses	25-30
blue round sunglasses	45-50
shoes: soft hot pink ballerina slippers	10-15
shoes: white sneakers	10-15
aqua boots	10-15
aqua riding cap	10-15
white ice skates	10-15
red ice skates	10-15
shoes: lime green pilgrim	10-15
shoes: hot pink pilgrim	10-15
shoes: orange pilgrim	10-15
shoes: red pilgrim	10-15
shoes: yellow pilgrim	10-15
shoes: blue pilgrim	10-15
shoes: white pilgrim	10-15
or t-strap shoes avail in 1971	10-15

Fashion Accents

#1521
Sears Exclusive
Date 1970-73

NRFB	Mint/Complete
175-225	50-75
	Avg
shoes: red pilgrim	10-15
shoes: blue pilgrim	10-15
shoes: white pilgrim	10-15
shoes: soft red bow	10-15
shoes: soft light blue bow	10-15
shoes: soft orange bow	10-15
shoes: soft royal blue bow	10-15
shoes: royal blue ankle boots	10-15
shoes: orange ankle boots	10-15
shoes: yellow ankle boots	10-15
shoes: aqua sneakers	10-15
short white tricot gloves	15-20
silver dimple purse	10-15
silver mesh hose	15-20
silver belt	15-20

Furry Friends

Gift Set
For Jamie
Sears Exclusive
1584
Date 1970-71

NRFB	Mint/Complete
1800-2200	275-350
	Avg
orange, yellow & pink knit dress	20-25
pink sheer head scarf	40-45
yellow nylon panty	20-25
orange plush coat w/ pink belt	10-15
orange plush hat	15-20
grey poodle	15-20
hot pink dog collar	15-20
dog bone	15-20
dog food box	10-15
yellow bowl w/ dog food	30-35
shoes: orange boots	10-15
shoes: orange pilgrims	10-15

Action Accents

Gift Set
Sears Exclusive
1585
Date 1970-72

NRFB	Mint/Complete
700-850	175-225
	Avg
orange & aqua nylon bathing suit	20-25
hot pink knit leotard	40-45
hot pink knit tights	30-35
hot pink jacket	10-15
hot pink & orange tulle skirt	20-25
aqua skirt w/ pink trim	20-25
hot pink plush bonnet	20-25
hot pink skis	20-25
ski poles w/ pink hand grips	20-25
black elastic exercise cord	10-15
aqua snorkel	10-15
aqua diving mask	10-15
shoes: aqua swim fins	10-15
shoes: pink ski boots	15-20
shoes: pink ballerina slippers	10-15
shoes: aqua ice skates	10-15

Mad About Plaid

Gift Set
Sears Exclusive
1587
Date 1970

NRFB	Mint/Complete
1500-1850	200-250
	Avg
red, green & blue plaid dress w/ belt	40-45
red, green & blue plaid coat	20-25
red plush hat	35-40
red, green & blue plaid purse	40-45
shoes: red pilgrim	10-15

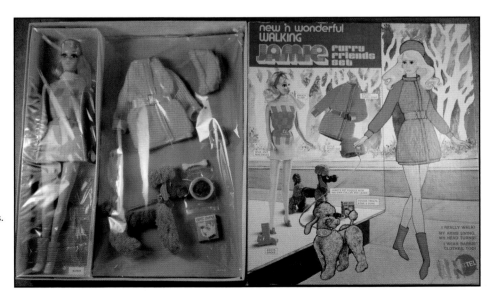

Furry Friends.

Swingin' In Silver
Gift Set
For P.J.
Sears Exclusive
1588
Date 1970

NRFB	Mint/Complete
1500-1750	275-350
	Avg
pink satin dress w/ silver lamé skirt	75-90
silver lamé coat w/white fur trim	25-30
shoes: silver lamé boots w/ white fur trim	45-50

Tennis Team
#1781
Date 1970-71

NRFB	Mint/Complete
35-85	15-25
	Avg
white tennis dress w/ orange bows	5-10
tennis racket	5-7
tennis ball	5-7
shoes: white sneakers	10-15

Shape Ups
#1782
Date 1970-71

NRFB	Mint/Complete
50-100	25-50
	Avg
red long sleeve leotard	10-15
red sheer pantyhose	15-20
black elastic exercise cord	10-15
"Living Barbie" book	7-10
exercise twist board	7-10
shoes: red soft buckle flats	10-15

Ruffles 'n Swirls
#1783
Date 1970-71

NRFB	Mint/Complete
35-85	15-25
	Avg
pink & blue wrap dress	10-15
pink vinyl belt	25-30
shoes: blue pilgrim	10-15
or blue t-strap	10-15

Ruffles 'n Swirls
#1783
Date 1970-71
Variation pink w/ flowers

NRFB	Mint/Complete
100-150	50-75
	Avg
pink w/ flowers wrap dress	45-50
pink vinyl belt	25-30
shoes: pink pilgrim	10-15
or pink t-strap	10-15

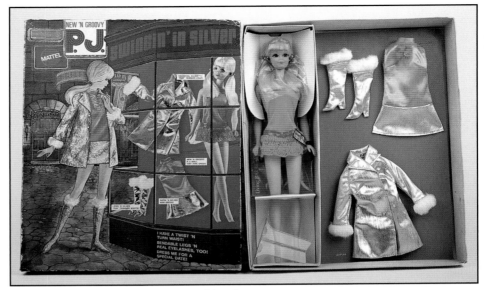

Swingin' In Silver. P. J. Gift Set. Never removed from box.
Author's Collection

Harem-m-m's
#1783
Date 1970-71

NRFB	Mint/Complete
35-85	15-25
	Avg
deep orange jumpsuit	10-15
silver & gold cord belt	20-25

Bright 'n Brocade
#1786
Date 1970-71

NRFB	Mint/Complete
100-150	50-75
	Avg
pink chiffon top w/ embroidery	25-30
pink chiffon pants w/embroidery	20-25
shoes: pink soft bow	10-15

Ruffles 'n Swirls. Blue version mint on card & variation pink with flowers.
Courtesy of Karen Bindelglass

Prima Ballerina
#1787
Date 1970-71

	NRFB	Mint/Complete
	35-85	15-25
		Avg
hot pink satin tutu		10-15
hot pink sheer nylon tights		10-15
shoes: pink ballerina slippers		10-15

Scuba-Do's
#1788
Date 1970-71

	NRFB	Mint/Complete
	35-85	15-25
		Avg
yellow hooded sweatshirt body suit		7-10
orange & yellow swimsuit top		10-15
orange & yellow swimsuit bottom		10-15
orange snorkel		5-7
orange diving mask		5-7
shoes: orange swim fins		5-7

Fiery Felt
#1789
Date 1970-71

	NRFB	Mint/Complete
	35-85	15-25
		Avg
orange felt coat w/ fringe trim		10-15
orange felt hat w/ fringe trim		10-15
shoes: orange rain boots		10-15

The Lace Caper
#1791
Date 1970-71

	NRFB	Mint/Complete
	100-150	50-75
		Avg
ivory lace top w/ pink flowers		20-25
ivory lace pants		20-25
sheer hot pink long vest		15-20
shoes: pink pilgrim		10-15
or pink t-strap		10-15

Mood Matchers
#1792
Date 1970-71

	NRFB	Mint/Complete
	100-150	50-75
		Avg
aqua nylon blouse		10-15
multicolored paisley mini dress		10-15
multicolored paisley wide pants		7-10
aqua vinyl belt		10-15
shoes: aqua pilgrim		10-15
or aqua t-strap		10-15

Scuba-Do's. Never removed from box/card. *Courtesy of Karen Bindelglass*

Fiery Felt.

Mood Matchers.

Skate Mates
#1793
Date 1970-71

	NRFB	Mint/Complete
	100-150	50-75
		Avg
coral suede & white plush skating dress		10-15
coral suede & white plush bonnet		10-15
coral mittens & white plush		10-15
coral sheer nylon tights		15-20
shoes: white skates		10-15

Check The Suit
#1794
Date 1970-71

	NRFB	Mint/Complete
	100-150	50-75
		Avg
yellow cotton shell		15-20
hot pink & yellow jacket		15-20
hot pink & yellow pants		15-20
shoes: yellow pilgrim		10-15
or yellow t-strap		10-15

Fur Sighted
#1796
Date 1970-71
Orange version

	NRFB	Mint/Complete
	175-225	100-125
		Avg
orange & yellow knit sweater		25-30
orange & yellow fur jacket		25-30
orange pants		15-20
orange & yellow fur bonnet		20-25
shoes: yellow pilgrim		10-15

Fur Sighted
#1796
Date 1970-71
Red version

	NRFB	Mint/Complete
	175-225	100-125
		Avg
red & yellow knit sweater		25-30
red & yellow fur jacket		25-30
red pants		15-20
red & yellow fur bonnet		20-25
shoes: yellow pilgrim		10-15

Skate Mates.
Author's Collection

Rainbow Wraps.
Courtesy of Karen Bindelglass

Rainbow
Wraps.

The Ski Scene
#1797
Date 1970-71

	NRFB	Mint/Complete
	175-225	100-125
		Avg
fuschia knit sweater		20-25
orange jacket		10-15
yellow pants		10-15
orange ski bonnet		10-15
orange ski mask		15-20
orange skis		20-25
ski poles w/ orange hand grips		20-25
shoes: orange ski boots		10-15

Rainbow Wraps
#1798
Date 1970-71

	NRFB	Mint/Complete
	175-225	100-125
		Avg
multicolored gown w/ green lamé top		35-40
multicolored shawl w/ coral fringe		35-40
sheer coral petticoat		35-40
shoes: blue pilgrim		10-15
or blue t-strap		10-15

Maxi 'n Mini
#1799
Date 1970-71

	NRFB	Mint/Complete
	250-300	
175-200		
		Avg
blue, pink & gold knit dress w/ braid belt		50-75
blue foil coat w/ blue fur trim		50-75
shoes: blue lamé high boots		50-75

Sharp Shift
Pak
Date 1970

	NRFB	Mint/Complete
	100-350	75-275
		Avg
knit shift dress w/ "Clear Out" fabric		75-100
shoes: red pilgrim		10-15
knit shift dress w/ "Hip Knits" fabric		75-100
shoes: hot pink pilgrim		10-15
knit shift dress w/ "Togetherness" fabric		50-75
shoes: hot pink pilgrim		10-15
knit shift dress w/ "Groovy Get-Ups" fabric		75-100
shoes: white pilgrim		10-15
knit shift dress w/ "Sportin Set" fabric		175-200
shoes: aqua pilgrim		10-15
knit shift dress w/ "Francie bathing suit" fabric		100-125
shoes: white pilgrim		10-15
knit shift dress w/ "The Combo" fabric		100-125
shoes: hot pink pilgrim		10-15
knit shift dress w/ "Twiggy dress" fabric		50-75
shoes: yellow pilgrim		10-15
knit shift dress w/ "The Ski Scene" fabric		75-100
shoes: hot pink pilgrim		10-15

Cool Casuals
Pak
Date 1970-71

	NRFB	Mint/Complete
	100-250	50-175
		Avg
cotton midriff top w/ "Junior Designer" fabric		50-75
cotton hip hugger pants w/ "Junior Designer" fabric		50-75
shoes: blue pilgrim		10-15
cotton midriff top w/ "color magic" fabric		50-75
cotton hip hugger pants w/ "gold" fabric		50-75
shoes: lime green pilgrim		10-15

Maxi 'n Mini

Cool Casuals.
Author's Collection

Cool Casuals.

		Avg
cotton midriff top w/ "Dancing Stripes" fabric		50-75
cotton hip hugger pants w/ "Dancing Stripes" fabric		50-75
shoes: hot pink pilgrim		10-15
cotton midriff top w/ "Weekenders" fabric		50-75
cotton hip hugger pants w/ "Weekenders" fabric		50-75
shoes: hot pink pilgrim		10-15
cotton midriff top w/ "Ruffles 'n Swirls" fabric		50-75
cotton hip hugger pants w/ "Ruffles 'n Swirls" fabric		50-75
shoes: hot pink pilgrim		10-15
cotton midriff top w/ "Bells" fabric		35-40
cotton hip hugger pants w/ "Bells" fabric		35-40
shoes: red pilgrim		10-15

		Avg
cotton midriff top w/ "Sun Spots" fabric		35-40
cotton hip hugger pants w/ "Sun Spots" fabric		35-40
shoes: hot pink pilgrim		10-15
cotton midriff top w/ "Fashion Bouquet" fabric		35-40
cotton hip hugger pants w/ "Fashion Bouquet" fabric		35-40
shoes: lime green pilgrim		10-15
cotton midriff top w/ "Pazam!" fabric		35-40
cotton hip hugger pants w/ "Pazam!" fabric		35-40
shoes: lime green pilgrim		10-15
cotton midriff top w/ "It's A Date" fabric		35-40
cotton hip hugger pants w/ "blue" fabric		35-40
shoes: blue pilgrim		10-15

Perfect Beginnings
Pak
Date 1970

	NRFB	Mint/Complete
	100-350	75-275
		Avg
bra w/ flower detail		
w/ "Color Magic" fabric		50-75
matching panty w/ "Color Magic" fabric		50-75
sheer nylon petticoat w/ ruffle		10-15
powder puff		7-10
gold talc box		7-10
bra w/ flower detail		
w/ "Dreamy Pink" fabric		30-35
matching panty w/ "Dreamy Pink" fabric		30-35
sheer nylon petticoat w/ ruffle		10-15
powder puff		7-10
gold talc box		7-10
bra w/ flower detail w/		
"The Combination" fabric		30-35
matching panty w/		
"The Combination" fabric		30-35
sheer nylon petticoat w/ ruffle		10-15
powder puff		7-10
gold talc box		7-10
bra w/ flower detail w/		
"Twiggy Turnouts" fabric		30-35
matching panty w/"Twiggy Turnouts" fabric		30-35
sheer nylon petticoat w/ ruffle		10-15
powder puff		7-10
gold talc box		7-10
bra w/ flower detail		
w/ "Style Setters" fabric		30-35
matching panty w/ "Style Setters" fabric		30-35
sheer nylon petticoat w/ ruffle		10-15
powder puff		7-10
gold talc box		7-10
bra w/ flower detail		
w/ "Border Line" fabric		30-35
matching panty w/ "Border Line" fabric		30-35
sheer nylon petticoat w/ ruffle		10-15
powder puff		7-10
gold talc box		7-10
bra w/ flower detail w/		
"Floating Gardens" fabric		30-35
matching panty w/		
"Floating Gardens" fabric		30-35
sheer nylon petticoat w/ ruffle		10-15
powder puff		7-10
gold talc box		7-10
bra w/ flower detail		
w/ pale pink nylon fabric		30-35
matching panty w/ pale pink nylon fabric		30-35
sheer nylon petticoat w/ ruffle		10-15
powder puff		7-10
gold talc box		7-10

All The Trimmings
Pak
Date 1970

	NRFB	Mint/Complete
	75-125	50-75
		Avg
Blonde braid w/ pink ribbon		10-15
or brunette braid w/ pink ribbon		10-15
pink & gold satin purse		10-15
pink fishnet hose		15-20
gold lamé gloves		10-15
orange rectangular dangle earrings		35-40
gold belt w/ round accent		10-15

Foot Lights
Pak
Date 1970

	NRFB	Mint/Complete
	75-125	50-75
		Avg
shoes: hot pink pilgrim		10-15
shoes: blue pilgrim		10-15
shoes: white pilgrim		10-15
shoes: yellow pilgrim		10-15
shoes: soft red bow		10-15
shoes: soft light blue bow		10-15
shoes: soft royal blue bow		10-15
shoes: royal blue ankle boots		10-15
shoes: hot pink ankle boots		10-15
shoes: gray ankle boots		10-15

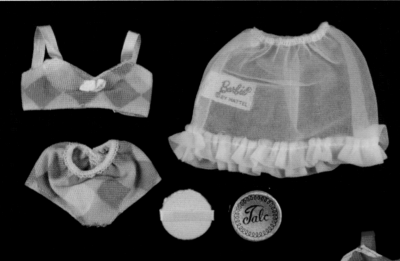

Perfect Beginnings,
"Color Magic."

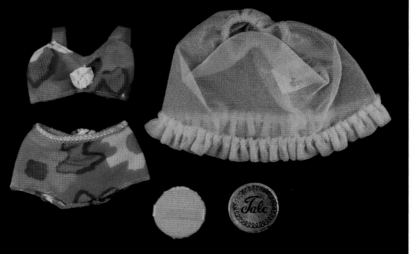

Perfect Beginnings,
"Style Setters."

Country Music
Fashions 'n Style
1055
Date 1971-72

NRFB	Mint/Complete
175-225	100-125
	Avg
red & white blouse	35-40
red & white skirt	35-40
white cotton woven shawl	35-40
45 RPM record "Here In Nashville"	35-40
shoes: white boots w/ red laces	20-25

Country Music.
Author's Collection

Festival Fashion
Fashions 'n Style
1056
Date 1971-72

NRFB	Mint/Complete
250-300	150-175
	Avg
sheer white blouse w/ white cuffs	35-40
coral nylon vest	20-25
multicolored floral nylon skirt	35-40
coral nylon head scarf	35-40
brown suede corset belt	35-40
45 RPM record "Fly Children Fly"	50-75
shoes: brown lace up boots	10-15
or brown suede lace-up boots	75-100

Groovin' Gauchos.
Never removed from box/card.
Courtesy of Karen Bindelglass

Groovin' Gauchos
Fashions 'n Style
1057
Date 1971-72

NRFB	Mint/ Complete
250-300	150-175
	Avg
hot pink blouse	20-25
multicolored velour vest	20-25
multicolored velour gaucho pants	20-25
coral shoulder suede purse	20-25
coral suede neck piece	35-40
45 RPM record "Rapping In Rhythm"	50-75
shoes: hot pink lace up boots	10-15
or green lace up boots	10-15
or coral suede boots	75-100

Perfectly Plaid
Gift Set
Sears Exclusive
1193
Date 1971-72

NRFB	Mint/Complete
1500-1750	275-350
	Avg
red, orange & white plaid knit jumpsuit	50-75
red, orange & white plaid knit jacket w/ white fur trim	50-75
white fur hat	50-75
white vinyl clutch purse	50-75
shoes: red soft pointed flats	20-25

Strollin' In Style
Gift Set
Sears Exclusive
For Jamie
1193
Date 1971

NRFB	Mint/Complete
1750-2100	350-375
	Avg
blue & yellow ribbed sweater coat w/ belt	50-75
blue ribbed pants	50-75
red, blue & yellow knit dress w/ belt	50-75
white scalloped nylon panties	35-40
blue sheer head scarf	50-75
white furry poodle	50-75
blue dog collar	35-40
blue & yellow ball	35-40
shoes: blue pilgrim	10-15
shoes: red boots	35-40

Perfectly Plaid.

Fashion In Motion
Gift Set
Sears Exclusive
For P.J.
1508
Date 1971-72

	NRFB	Mint/Complete
	850-1100	200-250
		Avg
multicolored midriff w/ fringe trimmed sleeves		50-75
multicolored pants w/ orange suede waistband		35-40
multicolored skirt w/ orange suede waistband		50-75
45 RPM record "Hey, Little P.J. Gal"		50-75
shoes: orange suede boots		35-40

Fashion In Motion. P. J. Gift Set.
Never removed from box.
Author's Collection

Fringe Benefits
3401
Date 1971-72

	NRFB	Mint/Complete
	75-100	35-60
		Avg
fuschia knit dress w/ orange suede belt		35-40
shoes: orange suede boots		25-30

Two Way Tiger.

Fringe Benefits.
Never removed from box/card.
Author's Collection

Two Way Tiger
3402
Date 1971-72

	NRFB	Mint/Complete
	75-100	35-60
		Avg
green & orange cotton tunic top		15-20
green & orange cotton pants		15-20
shoes: green pilgrim		10-15
or green t-strap		10-15

Baby Doll Pinks
3403
Date 1971-72

	NRFB	Mint/Complete
	50-75	15-40
		Avg
pink sheer nylon baby doll nighty		15-20
shoes: pink plush slippers		10-15

Baby Doll Pinks.

Glowin' Out
3404
Date 1971-72

	NRFB	Mint/Complete
	75-100	35-60
		Avg
pink satin dress w/ gold & pink skirt		20-25
shoes: hot pink pilgrim		10-15
or hot pink t-strap		10-15

Evening In
3406
Date 1971-72

	NRFB	Mint/Complete
	175-225	75-100
		Avg
pink hostess dress w/ gold medallion		45-50
multicolored floral nylon pants		35-40
gold triangle earrings		15-20
pink bracelet		15-20
shoes: hot pink pilgrim		10-15
or hot pink t-strap		10-15

Midi Mood
3407
Date 1971-72

	NRFB	Mint/Complete
	100-150	50-75
		Avg
yellow cotton blouse		25-30
multicolored floral cotton skirt		20-25
shoes: yellow pilgrim		10-15
or yellow t-strap		10-15

Super Scarf
3408
Date 1971-72

	NRFB	Mint/Complete
	100-150	50-75
		Avg
red knit sweater		15-20
blue & red plaid woven skirt		10-15
red knit scarf		20-25
shoes: red rain boots		10-15

Super Scarf.
Courtesy of Richard Chapman and Glenn Mandeville

Evening In.
Courtesy of Richard Chapman and Glenn Mandeville

Red For Rain.

Poncho Put-On.

Red For Rain
3409
Date 1971-72

	NRFB	Mint/Complete
	100-150	50-75
		Avg
red cotton raincoat w/ belt		20-25
red cotton bonnet		20-25
shoes: white rain boots		10-15

Poncho Put-On
3411
Date 1971-72

	NRFB	Mint/Complete
	125-175	75-100
		Avg
orange, yellow & white jumpsuit w/ gold chain belt		20-25
yellow knit hood w/orange visor		20-25
yellow vinyl poncho w/ orange tabs		20-25
shoes: yellow low boots		10-15

Fun Flakes.

Satin Slumber.

Fun Flakes
3412
Date 1971-72

	NRFB	Mint/Complete
	100-150	50-75
		Avg
pink nylon shell		20-25
pink & white knit top		10-15
pink & white knit pants		15-20
shoes: hot pink pilgrim		10-15
or hot pink t-strap		10-15

Golfing Greats
3413
Date 1971-72

	NRFB	Mint/Complete
	150-200	75-100
		Avg
yellow nylon body blouse		20-25
cotton plaid wrap skirt		10-15
cotton plaid cap w/ aqua visor		15-20
plaid & yellow golf bag		15-20
two golf balls		10-15
wood golf club		10-15
putter golf club		10-15
red round sunglasses		15-20
aqua knit socks		15-20
shoes: aqua sneakers		10-15

Satin Slumber
3414
Date 1971-72

	NRFB	Mint/Complete
	100-150	50-75
		Avg
light blue satin & sheer nylon pajama top		15-20
light blue satin pants		15-20
blue robe trimmed w/ light blue satin		15-20
light blue satin belt w/ sheer nylon trim		15-20
shoes: light blue satin slippers		10-15

Wild 'n Wintery
3416
Date 1971-72

	NRFB	Mint/Complete
	275-325	150-175
		Avg
pink felt hooded jacket		
w/ plush animal print sleeves		15-20
white alligator textured belt		20-25
pink felt mini skirt		15-20
pink knit shell w/ elastic waist		20-25
pink sheer pantyhose		30-35
shoes: white alligator textured tall boots		40-45

Bridal Brocade
3417
Date 1971-72

	NRFB	Mint/Complete
	275-325	150-175
		Avg
white satin brocade gown		
w/ gold detail & white fur trim		40-45
white satin brocade cap w/ tulle veil		40-45
flower & bud bouquet w/ green tulle &		
satin ribbons		35-40
shoes: white t-strap		10-15

Magnificent Midi
3418
Date 1971-72

	NRFB	Mint/Complete
	275-325	150-175
		Avg
red suede & black knit dress w/ black belt		40-45
red suede long coat w/ black fur trim		40-45
red suede hat w/ black fur trim		40-45
shoes: black shiny boots w/ black fur trim		30-35

Wild 'n Wintery. Never removed from box/card.
Courtesy of Karen Bindelglass

Bridal Brocade.

Silver Serenade
3419
Date 1971-72

	NRFB	Mint/Complete
	350-400	175-200
		Avg
silver & aqua knit gown w/ silver straps		40-45
aqua plush fur boa		40-45
aqua sheer pantyhose		50-75
silver lamé gloves		50-75
silver microphone w/ stand		50-75
shoes: aqua t-strap		10-15

Bubbles 'n Boots
3421
Date 1971-72

	NRFB	Mint/Complete
	100-150	50-75
		Avg
multicolored bubbles print dress w/ elastic waist		15-20
purple suede belt w/ gold insert		25-30
shoes: purple suede boots		25-30

The Color Kick
3422
Date 1971-72

	NRFB	Mint/Complete
	225-275	125-150
		Avg
multicolored striped body suit		40-45
yellow plush mini skirt		50-75

Night Lighter
3423
Date 1971-72

	NRFB	Mint/Complete
	100-150	50-75
		Avg
red, purple & green body suit		20-25
purple suede belt w/ gold buckle		40-45
shoes: red low boots		10-15

In Blooms
3424
Date 1971-72

	NRFB	Mint/Complete
	100-150	50-75
		Avg
multicolored grn. & floral caftan		40-45
shoes: blue & blue wedges		20-25

Silver Serenade.

Bubbles 'n Boots.

Night Lighter.
Author's Collection

Turtle 'n Tights
3426
Date 1971-72

	NRFB	Mint/Complete
	225-275	125-150
		Avg
blue ribbed nylon top		25-30
orange suede fringed shirt		25-30
orange suede belt		50-75
blue ribbed nylon pantyhose		25-30
shoes: blue soft pointed flats		10-15

The Dream Team
3427
Date 1971-72

	NRFB	Mint/Complete
	100-150	50-75
		Avg
white nylon nightgown w/ off white lace trim		30-35
off white lace robe w/ light blue satin ties		30-35
shoes: white felt w/ blue satin slippers		20-25

The Dream Team.

The Zig Zag Bag
3428
Date 1971-72

NRFB	Mint/Complete
150-200	75-100
	Avg
multicolored zig-zag nylon shirt	15-20
red & white zig zag pants	15-20
orange terry cloth vest	20-25
shoes: red sneakers	10-15

Cold Snap
3429
Date 1971-72

NRFB	Mint/Complete
50-75	25-40
	Avg
red knit coat w/ fur trim	20-25
shoes: red lace up boots	10-15

Victorian Velvet
3431
Date 1971-72

NRFB	Mint/Complete
100-150	50-75
	Avg
purple cotton velvet dress w/ ivory trim	30-35
shoes: purple t-strap	20-25

Victorian Velvet
3431
Date 1971-72
Rose variation

NRFB	Mint/Complete
250-300	125-150
	Avg
purple cotton velvet dress w/ ivory trim	30-35
shoes: rose t-strap	15-20

In Stitches
3432
Date 1971-72

NRFB	Mint/Complete
250-300	125-150
	Avg
yellow nylon blouse	30-35
multicolored yarn knit vest	30-35
multicolored yarn knit pants	30-35
multicolored yarn knit purse	40-45
shoes: yellow low boots	10-15

In Stitches
3432
Date 1971-72
Variation "Super Scarf" fabric

NRFB	Mint/Complete
450-500	350-375
	Avg
yellow nylon blouse	30-35

multicolored yarn knit "Super Scarf" fabric vest	75-100
multicolored yarn knit "Super Scarf" fabric pants	75-100
multicolored yarn knit "Super Scarf" fabric purse	100-150
shoes: yellow ankle boots	10-15

All About Plaid
3433
Date 1971-72

NRFB	Mint/Complete
200-150	100-125
	Avg
green knit dress w/ orange plaid skirt w/ fringe & orange belt	30-35
orange plaid knit shawl w/ fringe	30-35
orange plaid purse w/ orange trim	30-35
shoes: lime green pilgrim	10-15
or lime green t-strap	10-15

Fun Fur
3434
Date 1971-72

NRFB	Mint/Complete
125-175	75-100
	Avg
beige & white fur coat w/ gold suede trim	20-25
gold suede belt	40-45
beige crocheted tam	35-40
shoes: tan lace up boots	10-15

In Stitches.

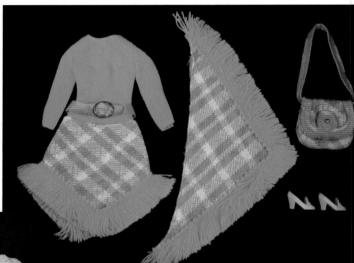

All About Plaid.

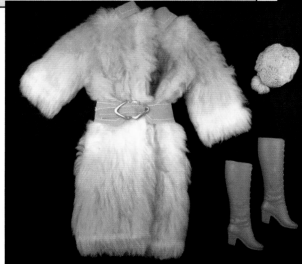

Fun Fur.

Gaucho Gear.

Gaucho Gear
3434
Date 1971-72

NRFB	Mint/Complete
250-300	125-150
	Avg
multicolored floral cotton body suit	10-15
orange gaucho pants w/ gold suede trim	15-20
multicolored floral cotton skirt	10-15
gold suede vest w/ fringe	35-40
gold suede purse w/ fringe	35-40
orange felt hat w/ gold cord trim	35-40
shoes: gold suede boots w/ fringe	35-40

Dancing Lights
3437
Date 1971-72

NRFB	Mint/Complete
375-425	175-225
	Avg
multicolored sheer nylon gown & pink waistband	75-100
pink stole w/ pink nylon lining	50-75
black plastic necklace w/ black butterfly	50-75
shoes: pink t-strap	10-15

Peasant Dressy
3438
Date 1971-72

NRFB	Mint/Complete
375-425	175-225
	Avg
multicolored velour dress w/ purple waistband	50-75
white camisole w/ yellow straps	50-75
white petticoat w/ eyelet ruffles	45-50
shoes: purple t-strap	10-15

Wild Things
3439
Date 1971-72

NRFB	Mint/Complete
775-850	475-525
	Avg
lime green ribbed jumpsuit	50-75
white plush long vest w/ embroidered ribbon	50-75
royal blue textured belt	175-225
shoes: royal blue ankle boots	10-15

Soft 'n Snug
Pak
Date 1971

NRFB	Mint/Complete
100-150	50-75
	Avg
red plush skirt w/ yellow satin waistband	20-25
red plush bonnet w/ yellow ties	20-25
shoes: red pilgrim	10-15
royal blue plush skirt w/ yellow satin waistband	20-25
royal blue plush bonnet w/ yellow ties	20-25
shoes: royal blue pilgrim	10-15
fuschia plush skirt w/ yellow satin waistband	20-25
fuschia plush bonnet w/ yellow ties	20-25
shoes: fuschia pilgrim	10-15

Plush 'n Warm
Pak
Date 1971

NRFB	Mint/Complete
40-45	20-25
	Avg
hot pink hooded body sweatshirt	20-25

Poodle Doodles
1061
Date 1972

NRFB	Mint/Complete
775-850	475-525
	Avg
coral nylon top dress w/ black floral print skirt	75-125
black floral print vest w/ blue suede trim	75-125
black fuzzy poodle	250-300
blue suede & gold chain dog collar	100-150
shoes: black floral print boots	100-150

Kitty Kapers
1062
Date 1972

NRFB	Mint/Complete
775-850	475-525
	Avg
yellow, blue, orange jacket	50-75
yellow, blue, orange skirt	50-75
yellow, blue, orange hot pants	50-75
white fuzzy kitty cat	250-300
yellow bowl w/ food	40-45
shoes: white lace up boots	10-15

Hot Togs
1063
Date 1972

	NRFB	Mint/Complete
	950-1200	775-825
		Avg
olive green, blue, & red plaid jacket		50-75
red ribbed nylon hot pants		50-75
brown suede belt w/ attached bag		150-175
olive green knit thigh-high socks		75-100
olive green knit cap		75-100
olive green sheer pantyhose		75-100
beige fuzzy Afghan dog		225-250
brown suede dog leash		75-100
shoes: dark brown lace-up boots		10-15

Royal Velvet
3215
For Miss America
Date 1972-73

	NRFB	Mint/Complete
	375-425	175-225
		Avg
dark rose velvet gown w/ white fur trim		40-45
white fur muff		40-45
hot pink sheer petticoat		50-75
shoes: rose pilgrim		10-15

Majestic Blue
3216
For Miss America
Date 1972-73

	NRFB	Mint/Complete
	375-425	175-225
		Avg
blue nylon gown w/ sheer overskirt		40-45
white fur short jacketw/ gold trim		50-75
"Miss America" red floral bouquet		20-25
shoes: blue pilgrim		10-15

Regal Red
3217
For Miss America
Date 1972-73

	NRFB	Mint/Complete
	375-425	225-250
		Avg
deep coral satin gown w/ gold lamé top		50-75
deep coral satin cape w/ yellow fur trim		50-75
gold belt		40-45
gold textured clutch purse		50-75
yellow tricot long gloves		100-150
shoes: red low heels		10-15

Hot Togs.

Royal Velvet. For Miss America.
Courtesy of Richard Chapman and Glenn Mandeville

Majestic Blue. For Miss America.
Courtesy of Richard Chapman and Glenn Mandeville

Regal Red.

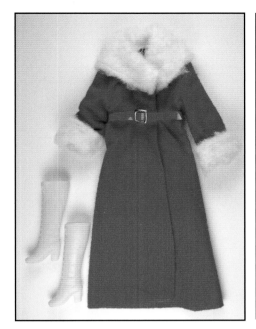

Furry 'n Fun.

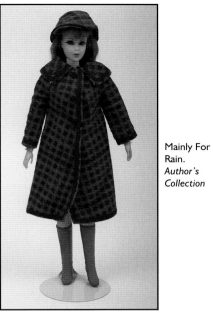

Mainly For Rain.
Author's Collection

Furry 'n Fun
3336
Date 1972

NRFB	Mint/Complete
100-150	50-75
	Avg
red felt coat w/ white fur trim	20-25
long red belt	40-45
shoes: white lace up boots	10-15

All American Girl
3337
Date 1972

NRFB	Mint/Complete
100-150	50-75
	Avg
royal blue nylon top	20-25
orange, blue & white nylon skirt	15-20
royal blue tights	35-40
shoes: red pilgrim	10-15
or orange pilgrim	10-15

Mainly For Rain
3338
Date 1972

NRFB	Mint/Complete
75-125	40-65
	Avg
red houndstooth felt coat	10-15
red houndstooth hat	20-25
shoes: blue lace up boots	10-15

Light 'n Lazy
3338
Date 1972

NRFB	Mint/Complete
75-125	40-65
	Avg
sheer white nylon nighty	10-15
sheer white nylon robe	10-15
white nylon panty	10-15
shoes: white booties w/ lace	10-15

Good Sports.

Golden Glitter
3340
Date 1972

NRFB	Mint/Complete
75-125	40-65
	Avg
gold satin sleeveless dress	10-15
gold satin purse	20-25
sheer yellow pantyhose	35-40
shoes: gold low heels	20-25

Long 'n Fringy
3341
Date 1972

NRFB	Mint/Complete
75-125	40-65
	Avg
yellow nylon body blouse	10-15
red plaid flannel skirt w/ black fringe	10-15
shoes: black pilgrim or	10-15
shoes: black low heels	10-15

Sweet Dreams
3350
Date 1972

NRFB	Mint/Complete
75-125	40-65
	Avg
white w/ pink polka dots cotton pajama top	10-15
white w/ pink polka dots cotton pajama bottom	10-15
pink comb	3-5
pink brush	3-5
pink mirror	3-5
shoes: pink felt slippers	10-15

Good Sports
3351
Date 1972

NRFB	Mint/Complete
75-125	40-65
	Avg
deep red nylon shell	10-15
denim jeans hip-huggers	10-15
purple floral print scarf	10-15
brown belt w/ gold studs	10-15
red round sunglasses	15-20
shoes: white sneakers	10-15

White 'n With It
3352
Date 1972

NRFB	Mint/Complete
75-125	40-65
	Avg
white dress w/ gold belt	10-15
gold lamé duffle purse	15-20
shoes: white pilgrim or	10-15
white low heels	10-15

Sports Star
3353
Date 1972

	NRFB	Mint/Complete
	75-125	40-65
		Avg
red & white cotton body blouse		10-15
denim cotton over-all w/ skirt		10-15
shoes: blue low heels		10-15

Glowin' Gold
3354
Date 1972

	NRFB	Mint/Complete
	75-125	40-65
		Avg
aqua nylon shell		10-15
gold lamé hip-huggers		10-15
shoes: blue low heels		10-15

Picture Me Pretty
3355
Date 1972

	NRFB	Mint/Complete
	75-125	40-65
		Avg
purple floral print mini dress		10-15
white w/ lace half slip		10-15
white w/ lace panty		10-15
shoes: purple pilgrim		10-15

Picture Me
Pretty.
*Courtesy of
Anthony
Alcaide*

Silver Blues
3357
Date 1972

	NRFB	Mint/Complete
	100-150	50-75
		Avg
gold lamé maxi coat w/ brocade skirt		20-25
purple sheer nylon scarf		35-40
shoes: purple pilgrim		10-15
or purple t-strap		10-15

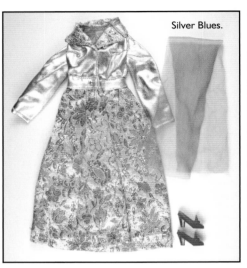

Silver Blues.

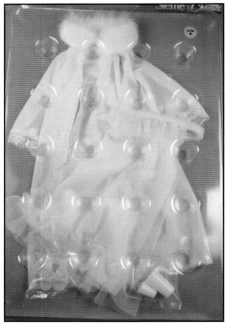

Lovely 'n Lavender
3358
Date 1972

	NRFB	Mint/Complete
	100-150	50-75
		Avg
light pink nylon nightgown		15-20
light pink nylon robe w/ fur trim		15-20
white pitcher		30-35
white tumbler		35-40
shoes: pink open toe		10-15

Pants-Perfect Purple
3359
Date 1972

	NRFB	Mint/Complete
	100-150	50-75
		Avg
red knit sweater		15-20
red knit pants		15-20
gold chain belt		30-35
leopard fur purse w/ black strap		20-25
shoes: black pilgrim		10-15
or black soft bow		10-15

Pants-Perfect
Purple.

Lovely 'n Lavender.

Pleasantly Peasanty
3360
Date 1972

	NRFB	Mint/Complete
	100-150	50-75
		Avg
red floral cotton peasant dress		15-20
white cotton slip		20-25
black velvet corset belt		30-35
shoes: black pilgrim		10-15
or black low heel		10-15

Sweetheart Satin
3360
Date 1972

	NRFB	Mint/Complete
	150-200	100-125
		Avg
ivory satin wedding gown w/ lace trim		20-25
ivory lace cap w/ tulle veil		20-25
ivory lace bouquet w/ pink poms		30-35
shoes: white pilgrim		10-15
or white t-strap		10-15
or white low heel		10-15

Fancy That Purple
3362
Date 1972

NRFB	Mint/Complete
150-200	75-100
	Avg
purple suede shell	20-25
gold brocade wrap skirt	15-20
gold lamé maxi shorts	20-25
purple sheer pantyhose	35-40
shoes: purple pilgrim	10-15
or purple t-strap	10-15

Fun Shine
3480
Date 1972

NRFB	Mint/Complete
150-200	100-125
	Avg
orange sheer nylon blouse	30-35
silver weave skirt w/ orange ties	30-35
orange sheer pantyhose	35-40
shoes: orange pilgrim	10-15
or soft orange bow	10-15

O-Boy Corduroy.

Fun Shine.
Courtesy of Anthony Alcaide

The Short Set
3481
Date 1972

NRFB	Mint/Complete
150-200	75-100
	Avg
white knit sweater w/ multicolored detail	20-25
white knit shorts w/ multicolored detail	20-25
red belt w/ brass closure	15-20
red double pocket belt slide	15-20
shoes: red lace up boots	10-15

Peasant Pleasant
3482
Date 1972

NRFB	Mint/Complete
75-125	40-65
	Avg
orange blouse w/ beige yarn trim	10-15
beige wrap skirt w/ orange trim	10-15
shoes: orange wedges w/ ankle ties	30-35

Purple Pleasers
3483
Date 1972

NRFB	Mint/Complete
75-125	40-65
	Avg
purple nylon blouse	10-15
multicolored paisley nylon skirt	10-15
shoes: white low heel	10-15

Madras Mad
3485
Date 1972

NRFB	Mint/Complete
75-125	40-65
	Avg
red, white & navy plaid maxi-coat	15-20
red, white & navy plaid purse	15-20
shoes: red pilgrim	10-15
or red low heel	10-15

O-Boy Corduroy
3486
Date 1972

NRFB	Mint/Complete
75-125	40-65
	Avg
navy blue nylon top	15-20
red corduroy jumper	15-20
shoes: white lace up boots	10-15

Sleepy Set
3486
Date 1972

NRFB	Mint/Complete
75-125	40-65
	Avg
pink nightgown w/ cotton top & sheer skirt	15-20
pink cotton robe w/ green satin tie	15-20
shoes: white felt slippers w/ pink poufs	10-15

Overall Denim
3488
Date 1972

NRFB	Mint/Complete
150-200	75-100
	Avg
red, blue & pink nylon t-shirt	25-30
denim jean overalls	20-25
red, white & blue backpack	25-30
shoes: white sneakers	10-15

Party Lines
3490
Date 1972

NRFB	Mint/Complete
150-200	75-100
	Avg
black satin dress w/ white lace trim	30-35
white sheer hose	35-40
shoes: black low heels w/ black ties	35-40

Party Lines
3490
Date 1972
Variation orange velvet

	NRFB	Mint/Complete
	250-300	175-225
		Avg
orange velvet dress w/ white lace trim		125-150
white sheer hose		35-40
shoes: black low heels w/ black ties		35-40

Suede 'n Fur
3491
Date 1972

	NRFB	Mint/Complete
	250-300	175-225
		Avg
red nylon full body suit		50-75
tan suede coat w/ fur trim bodice		35-40
tan suede mini skirt		35-40
shoes: brown lace up boots		10-15

Flying Colors
3491
Date 1972

	NRFB	Mint/Complete
	250-300	175-225
		Avg
yellow jersey cardigan top		35-40
orange fur vest w/ pink trim		50-75
yellow, pink & orange jersey skirt		35-40
pink neckband w/ flower		50-75
shoes: hot pink pilgrim		10-15

Satin 'n Shine
3493
Date 1972

	NRFB	Mint/Complete
	250-300	175-225
		Avg
ivory satin wedding gown w/ opalescent trim		50-75
ivory satin headband w/ tulle veil		50-75
white flower bouquet w/ white satin bow		50-75
shoes: white low heel		10-15

SKIPPER FASHIONS

Underpretties
#1900
Date 1964-65

	NRFB	Mint/Complete
	75-125	15-25
		Avg
white petticoat slip		3-5
white tricot panties		5-7
light pink rollers (4)		5-7
light pink comb		3-5
light pink brush		3-5
light pink mirror		3-5

Suede 'n Fur.

Flying Colors.

Underpretties.

Right:
Red Sensation.
Author's Collection

Far Right:
Silk 'n Fancy.
*Courtesy of
Richard Chapman &
Glenn Mandeville*

Red Sensation
#1901
Date 1964-65

	NRFB	Mint/Complete
	75-125	30-45
		Avg
red cotton dress		7-10
straw hat w/ red satin ribbon		10-15
white tricot gloves		10-15
white tricot socks		10-15
shoes: red Japan flats		5-7

Silk 'n Fancy
#1902
Date 1964-65

	NRFB	Mint/Complete
	125-175	45-60
		Avg
satin & red velvet dress		15-20
headband gold elastic		15-20
white tricot socks		10-15
shoes: soft black Japan flats		10-15

Masquerade
#1904
Date 1964-65

	NRFB	Mint/Complete
	125-175	45-60
		Avg
tutu mini dress		5-7
black shorts		7-10
yellow & black hat		7-10
mask		7-10
invitation "come to my party"		7-10
shoes: black Japan flats w/ pompons		15-20

Flower Girl
#1904
Date 1964-65

	NRFB	Mint/Complete
	150-200	45-60
		Avg
yellow dress		10-15
headpiece w/yellow flowers		7-10
floral bouquet small		7-10
white tricot gloves		10-15
white tricot socks		10-15
shoes: white Japan flats		5-7

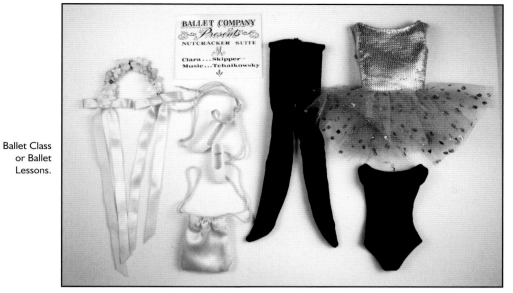

Ballet Class or Ballet Lessons.

Ballet Class or Ballet Lessons
#1905
Date 1964-65

	NRFB	Mint/Complete
	150-200	60-75
		Avg
pink tutu		5-7
headpiece w/flowers		7-10
black leotard		7-10
black tights		7-10
ballet slipper bag		5-7
Skipper ballet program		7-10
shoes: white ballet slippers		5-7

Dress Coat
#1906
Date 1964-64

	NRFB	Mint/Complete
	150-200	45-60
		Avg
red velvet coat		7-10
red velvet hat		7-10
red velvet purse		7-10
white tricot gloves		10-15
shoes: white Japan flats		5-7

School days
#1907
1964-66

	NRFB	Mint/Complete
	150-200	45-60
		Avg
pink knit sweater		10-15
white short sleeve blouse		7-10
pink flannel skirt		7-10
white or pink tricot knee socks		12-15
bowl of matching yarn w/ needles		10-15
shoes: soft black Japan flats		10-15

Flower Girl.
Author's Collection

Dress Coat.
Author's Collection

School Days.
Author's Collection

Skating Fun
#1908
Date 1964-66

	NRFB	Mint/Complete
	125-175	45-60
		Avg
knit body suit		10-15
skirt with straps		7-10
fur hat		7-10
fur muff		7-10
shoes: white skates		10-15

Dreamtime
#1909
Date 1964-66

	NRFB	Mint/Complete
	125-175	45-60
		Avg
pajama top		5-7
pajama pants		5-7
flannel robe		5-7
blue princess phone		5-7
telephone directory		10-15
blue stuffed cat		7-10
shoes: pink scuffs		5-7

Sunny Pastels
#1910
Date 1965-66

	NRFB	Mint/Complete
	100-150	40-55
		Avg
cotton rainbow dress		7-10
rainbow purse tote		7-10
white tricot socks		10-15
shoes: pink Japan flats		5-7

Day At The Fair
#1911
Date 165-66

	NRFB	Mint/Complete
	175-225	100-125
		Avg
Barbie print body suit		15-20
Barbie print head scarf		15-20
red wrap skirt		7-10
miniature Barbie doll		50-75
shoes: red Japan flats		5-7

Cookie Time
#1912
Date 1965-66

	NRFB	Mint/Complete
	100-150	50-65
		Avg
cotton dress w/ red belt		15-20
rolling pin		5-7
cookie mix box		5-7
Easy as Pie cookbook		15-20
metal bowl		7-10
long spoon		5-7
shoes: red Japan flats		5-7

Skating Fun.
Author's Collection

Sunny Pastels.
Courtesy of Lisa Varuolo

Dreamtime.
Courtesy of Lisa Varuolo

Day At
The Fair.

Cookie Time.

Me 'n My Doll.
Author's Collection

Platter Party.
Author's Collection

Outdoor Casuals.
Courtesy of Lisa Varuolo

Rain or Shine.
Author's Collection

Land and Sea.

Me 'n My Doll
#1913
Date 1965-66

	NRFB	Mint/Complete
	175-225	75-125
		Avg
pink gingham dress		15-20
petticoat slip		10-15
miniature Barbie doll		50-75
miniature Barbie doll skirt		20-25
white tricot socks		10-15
shoes: white Japan flats		5-7

Platter Party
#1914
Date 1965

	NRFB	Mint/Complete
	100-150	50-65
		Avg
long dress		10-15
blue record player		10-15
record blue Barbie label		10-15
record red Barbie label		10-15
shoes: red Japan flats		5-7

Outdoor Casuals
#1915
Date 1965-66

	NRFB	Mint/Complete
	125-175	60-75
		Avg
turquoise sweater		10-15
turquoise capri pants		5-7
turquoise dickey		15-20
red wooden yo-yo		7-10
white tricot gloves		10-15
white tricot socks		10-15
shoes: white Japan flats		5-7

Rain or Shine
#1916
Date 1965-66

	NRFB	Mint/Complete
	100-150	35-50
		Avg
yellow raincoat		5-7
yellow belt		7-10
yellow rain hat		5-7
yellow umbrella w/ tassel		5-7
shoes: white knee high boots		7-10
shoes: black Japan flats		5-7

Land and Sea
1917
Date 1965-66

	NRFB	Mint/Complete
	125-175	60-75
		Avg
denim pullover jacket w/ red drawstring		7-10
denim pedal pusher pants		7-10
red and white striped shirt		5-7
denim cap		5-7
red plastic sunglasses		20-25
shoes: white Japan flats		5-7

Ship Ahoy
1918
Date 1965-66

	NRFB	Mint/Complete
	175-225	100-150
		Avg
dress w/ pleated skirt		10-15
blue vest w/ red lining		10-15
Hawaii travel brochure		15-20
Mexico travel brochure		20-25
red toy sailboat		15-20
black camera		15-20
white tricot socks		10-15
shoes: red Japan flats		5-7

Fun Time
#1920
Date 1965-66

	NRFB	Mint/Complete
	175-225	100-150
		Avg
cotton jacket		10-15
blouse		7-10
Capri pants		7-10
embroidered top		10-15
croquet mallet		7-10
croquet ball		7-10
croquet stake		7-10
two wire wickets		10-15
shoes: Japan blue flats		5-7

FunTime.

Happy Birthday.

School Girl.
Courtesy of Lisa Varuolo

Happy Birthday
1919
Date 1965

	NRFB	Mint/Complete
	275-325	175-225
		Avg
blue & white dress		20-25
petticoat slip		5-7
hat w/ blue ribbon trim		25-30
blue satin hair ribbon		25-30
wrapped present		5-7
invitation		10-15
six candles		15-20
paper doily		30-35
plastic cake, brown or yellow icing		12-15
two party favors		15-20
two napkins		10-15
white tricot gloves		10-15
white tricot socks		10-15
shoes: white Japan flats		5-7

School Girl
#1921
Date 1965-66

	NRFB	Mint/Complete
	275-325	175-225
		Avg
red blazer		5-7
red & white skirt		5-7
cotton blouse		10-15
"English" book		5-7
"Geography" book		5-7
"Arithmetic book		5-7
book strap		5-7
red pencil		10-15
yellow pencil		10-15
brown glasses		40-45
apple		7-10
red felt hat w/ feather		15-20
white tricot socks		10-15
shoes: red Japan flats		5-7

Town Togs
1922
Date 1965-66

	NRFB	Mint/Complete
	175-225	75-100
		Avg
felt green jacket w/ belt		15-20
felt green jumper		7-10
yellow turtleneck shirt		10-15
houndstooth stockings		15-20
houndstooth hat		10-15
shoes: black Japan flats		5-7

Can You Play?
1923
Date 1966

	NRFB	Mint/Complete
	125-175	50-75
		Avg
polka dot dress		7-10
red head scarf		15-20
red panties		15-20
jump rope		7-10
ball (not the same as Barbie Tennis Anyone)		15-20
shoes: red Japan flats		5-7

Tea Party
1923
Date 1966

	NRFB	Mint/Complete
	200-275	125-150
		Avg
yellow dress		15-20
silver "B" teapot w/ lid		20-25
two turquoise teacups		10-15
two turquoise saucers		10-15
two spoons		20-25
two cake slices		40-45
two place mats		20-25
turquoise plate		15-20
shoes: yellow Japan flats		10-15

What's New At The Zoo?
1925
Date 1966

	NRFB	Mint/Complete
	100-150	35-50
		Avg
red dress		7-10
sweater jacket		10-15
shoes: red Japan flats		5-7

Chill Chasers
1926
Date 1966

	NRFB	Mint/Complete
	125-175	40-55
		Avg
fur coat		10-15
red hat w/ pompon		15-20
shoes: red Japan flats		5-7

Town Togs.
Courtesy of Richard Chapman and Glenn Mandeville

Can You Play?
Courtesy of Lisa Varuolo

What's New At The Zoo?
Courtesy of Lisa Varuolo

Rainy Day Checkers.

Rainy Day Checkers
1928
Date 1966

	NRFB	Mint/Complete
	200-275	150-175
		Avg
plaid dress		15-20
red felt vest		15-20
red tricot thigh high socks		15-20
checkerboard		10-15
checkers 12 red 12 black		40-45
shoes: black Japan flats		5-7

Dog Show
1929
Date 1966

	NRFB	Mint/Complete
	200-275	125-150
		Avg
cotton top		10-15
pleated skirt		7-10
white dog		40-45
dog leash		20-25
dog food box		10-15
shoes: red Japan flats		5-7

Loungin' Lovelies
1930
Date 1966

	NRFB	Mint/Complete
	100-150	35-50
		Avg
aqua robe		10-15
pajama top		5-7
pajama bottom		7-10
shoes: aqua scuffs		10-15

Let's Play House
1932
Date 1966

	NRFB	Mint/Complete
	200-275	125-150
		Avg
white and turquoise dress		10-15
turquoise pinafore		15-20
handkercheif yellow		7-10
handkercheif pink		7-10
handkercheif green		7-10
nursery rhymes book		15-20
baby cradle		15-20
baby		15-20
shoes: turquoise or blue Japan flats		7-10

Country Picnic
1933
date 1966

	NRFB	Mint/Complete
	475-550	300-350
		Avg
cotton dress		10-15
tote bag		10-15
checked blanket		10-15
checked napkin		15-20
ice cream cone w/ ice cream		15-20
rubber beach ball		25-30
butterfly net		20-25
butterfly		20-25
hamburger		15-20
hot dog		20-25
watermelon		15-20
BBQ fork		15-20
thermos w/ cap		20-25
blue plate		15-20
glass w/ pink drink		15-20
shoes: pink Japan flats		5-7

Dog Show.
Courtesy of Lisa Varuolo

Loungin' Lovelies.
Courtesy of Lisa Varuolo

Let's Play House.

Junior Bridesmaid
1934
Date 1966

	NRFB	Mint/Complete
	475-550	300-350
		Avg
pink dress		40-45
pink hat w/ flowers		40-45
white petticoat		25-30
pink basket w/ flowers		40-45
white tricot gloves		10-15
white tricot socks		10-15
shoes: white Japan flats		5-7

Learning To Ride
1935
Date 1966

	NRFB	Mint/Complete
	200-275	150-175
		Avg
checked jacket		10-15
red knit top		15-20
yellow jodhpurs		10-15
black riding hat		5-7
black riding crop		40-45
black short tricot gloves		40-45
shoes: black knee-high boots		20-25

Sledding Fun
1936
Date 1966

	NRFB	Mint/Complete
	200-275	150-175
		Avg
calico jacket		10-15
red knit top		15-20
blue knit pants		10-15
hood		10-15
mittens		15-20
red sled		40-45
shoes: red galoshes		35-40

Beachy Peachy
1938
Date 1967

	NRFB	Mint/Complete
	200-275	125-150
		Avg
cotton swimsuit top		10-15
cotton swimsuit bottom		10-15
cover-up dress		10-15
pink tote bag		10-15
yellow headband		25-30
shoes: yellow Japan flats		10-15

Note: Variation fabric same as Tea Party #1924

cotton swimsuit top	25-30
cotton swimsuit bottom	25-30
cover-up dress	25-30

Learning To Ride.

Flower Showers.

Rolla Scoot.

Flower Showers
1939
Date 1967

	NRFB	Mint/Complete
	75-125	50-65
		Avg
blue floral raincoat		5-7
blue floral raincoat belt		7-10
blue floral hood		15-20
shoes: hot pink galoshes		15-20

Rolla Scoot
1940
Date 1967

	NRFB	Mint/Complete
	200-275	125-150
		Avg
sweater top		20-25
orange pants		15-20
shoes: pink Japan flats		5-7
shoes: red roller skates w/ clear strap		40-45

All Spruced Up
1941
Date 1967

	NRFB	Mint/Complete
	200-275	125-150
		Avg
tweed dress		15-20
white hat		15-20
white shoulder bag		15-20
white lace thigh-high stockings		25-30
shoes: black Japan flats		5-7

Note: Variation fabric same as Ken Business Appointment # 1424

tweed dress	40-45

Right In Style
1942
Date 1967

	NRFB	Mint/Complete
	200-275	125-150
		Avg
green floral cotton dress		10-15
green jumper		10-15
floral hat		10-15
black granny glasses		35-40
white tricot socks		10-15
shoes: green Japan flats		5-7

Right In Style
1942
Date 1967
Variation turquoise

	NRFB	Mint/Complete
	325-375	200-225
		Avg
turquoise floral cotton dress		60-75
turquoise jumper		60-75
floral hat		10-15
black granny glasses		35-40
white tricot socks		10-15
shoes: turquoise Japan flats		5-7

Popover
1943
Date 1967

	NRFB	Mint/Complete
	200-275	125-150
		Avg
white lace dress		10-15
pink vinyl jumper		30-35
white lace hood		30-35
white lace thigh-high stockings		35-30
shoes: white Japan flats		5-7

Jamas 'n Jaunties
1944
Date 1967

	NRFB	Mint/Complete
	125-175	85-100
		Avg
floral jumpsuit		10-15
floral mob cap		5-7
floral shorts		7-10
floral slip		7-10
white floral pantyhose		30-35
four pink rollers		10-15
shoes: pink scuffs		10-15

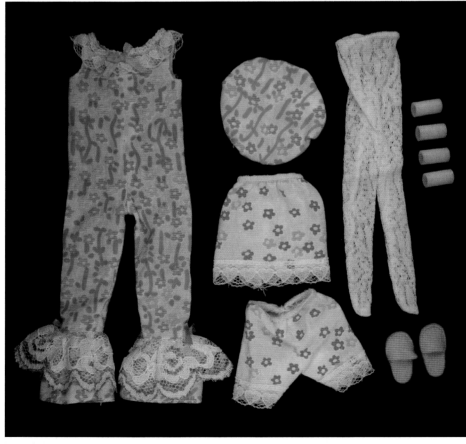

Popover.
Courtesy of Lisa Varuolo

Jamas 'n Jaunties.

Hearts 'n Flowers
1945
Date 1967

	NRFB	Mint/Complete
	200-275	150-175
		Avg
lime green floral blazer		10-15
lime green floral jumper		25-30
lime green floral cap		20-25
black granny glasses		35-40
yellow knit knee-high socks		15-20
yellow shoulder bag		25-30
English book		5-7
Geography book		5-7
Arithmetic book		5-7
book strap		5-7
red pencil		10-15
yellow pencil		10-15
shoes: yellow ankle boots		15-20

Hearts 'n Flowers
1945
Date 1967
Variation blue floral

	NRFB	Mint/Complete
	375-425	200-225
		Avg
blue floral blazer		35-40
blue floral jumper		45-50
blue floral cap		30-35
black granny glasses		35-40
yellow knit knee-high socks		15-20
yellow shoulder bag		25-30
English book		5-7
Geography book		5-7
Arithmetic book		5-7
book strap		5-7
red pencil		10-15
yellow pencil		10-15
shoes: yellow ankle boots		15-20

Hearts 'n Flowers.
Courtesy of Lisa Varuolo

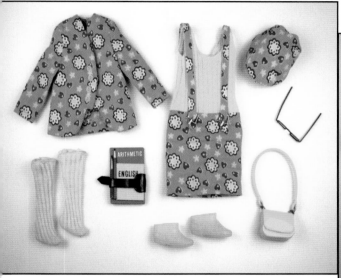

Hearts 'n Flowers.

Hearts 'n Flowers.

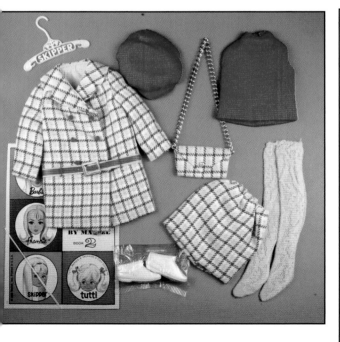

Glad Plaids
1946
Date 1967

	NRFB	Mint/Complete
	200-275	150-175
		Avg
plaid coat		15-20
vinyl belt		15-20
plaid skirt		15-20
fuchsia knit top		15-20
fuchsia knit cap		20-25
plaid purse		20-25
light yellow lace thigh-high stockings		40-45
shoes: white ankle boots		50-75

Left:
Glad Plaids.
Courtesy of Lisa Varuolo

Far Left:
Glad Plaids

Lolapaloozas
1947
Date 1967

	NRFB	Mint/Complete
	200-275	150-175
		Avg
pink & green halter		10-15
pink & green shorts		10-15
pink & green top		10-15
pink & green short jacket		10-15
pink & green pants		10-15
pink & green skirt		10-15
pink & green belt		15-20
shoes: hot pink squishy flats		10-15

Velvet 'n Lace
1948
Date 1967

	NRFB	Mint/Complete
	200-275	90-115
		Avg
red velvet dress		40-45
red velvet coat		10-15
white tricot gloves		10-15
white tricot socks		10-15
shoes: black squishy Japan flats		10-15
or black buckle squishy Japan flats		35-40

All Prettied Up
1949
Date 1967

	NRFB	Mint/Complete
	100-150	50-65
		Avg
dark pink dress		15-20
white lace thigh-high stockings		35-30
shoes: white Japan flats		5-7

Note: variation light pink or embroidered overskirt

light pink dress		15-20
embroidered overskirt pink dress		25-30

Posy Party
1955
Date 1968

	NRFB	Mint/Complete
	200-275	90-115
		Avg
blue floral dress		15-20
pink petti-pants		15-20
white lace thigh-high stockings		35-30
hot fudge sundae		10-15
spoon		15-20
shoes: hot pink squishy flats		10-15

Note: variation light blue floral

light blue floral dress		15-20
pink petti-pants		15-20

Skimmy Stripes
1959
Date 1968

	NRFB	Mint/Complete
	200-275	150-175
		Avg
orange knit dress		10-15
felt orange cap		25-30
lime green granny glasses		40-45
English book		5-7
Arithmetic book		5-7
book strap		5-7
red pencil		10-15
tan pencil		10-15
knit socks		15-20
shoes: orange ankle boots		10-15

Skimmy Stripes.
Courtesy of Richard Chapman and Glenn Mandeville

Velvet 'n Lace.
Courtesy of Lisa Varuolo

Posy Party.
Courtesy of Lisa Varuolo

Baby Dolls
1957
Date 1968

	NRFB	Mint/Complete
	75-125	30-45
		Avg
pink baby doll pajama top		7-10
pink baby doll pajama bottom		10-15
shoes: hot pink scuffs		20-25

Patent 'n Pants
1958
Date 1968

	NRFB	Mint/Complete
	100-150	50-65
		Avg
pantsuit		15-20
red vinyl belt		10-15
red vinyl coat		15-20
shoes: red Japan flats		5-7

Warm 'n Wonderful
1959
Date 1968

	NRFB	Mint/Complete
	200-275	90-115
		Avg
blue & green knit dress		15-20
blue & green coat		15-20
blue vinyl cap		7-10
green fishnet thigh-high stockings		25-30
shoes: blue boots		7-10

Trim Twosome
1960
Date 1968

	NRFB	Mint/Complete
	100-150	50-65
		Avg
striped cotton dress		15-20
white coat		10-15
vinyl belt		10-15
orange purse		15-20
shoes: translucent orange Taiwan flats		7-10

Real Sporty
1961
Date 1968

	NRFB	Mint/Complete
	125-175	60-75
		Avg
yellow romper		7-10
yellow jacket		15-20
hot pink chain belt		15-20
hot pink lace tights		10-15
shoes: hot pink ankle boots		10-15

Patent 'n Pants.

Warm 'n Wonderful.

Trim Twosome.
Author's Collection

Real Sporty.
Courtesy of Lisa Varuolo

Quick Changes!

1962
Date 1968

	NRFB	Mint/Complete
	125-175	75-100
		Avg
light blue shift dress		15-20
light blue & orange skirt		15-20
sweater		15-20
pink knit socks		15-20
shoes: hot pink ankle boots		10-15

Quick Changes!
Courtesy of Lisa Varuolo

Confetti Cutie

Sears Exclusive
Date 1968

	NRFB	Mint/Complete
	575-650	475-525
		Avg
yellow jumper		75-100
knit turtleneck		75-100
knit knee-high socks		75-100
gold chain belt		50-75
blue vinyl cap		7-10
shoes: yellow ankle boots		15-20

Skipper Perfectly Pretty Set

Sears Exclusive
Gift Set
1546
Date 1968

	NRFB	Mint/Complete/ no box/no doll
	825-875	575-650
		Avg
turquoise velvet & white drop waist dress		125-200
turquoise velvet coat w/vinyl belt		125-200
turquoise velvet hat w/ grosgrain ties		125-200
shoes: turquoise Japan flats		7-10

Perfectly Pretty.
Courtesy of Lisa Varuolo

Skipper Bright and Breezy Set

Sears Exclusive
1590
Date 1969

	NRFB	Mint/Complete/ no box/no doll
	700-775	475-525
		Avg
turquoise knit culotte w/ green yarn trim		125-200
green leather look coat w/ green fur trim		75-100
shoes: green Japan flats		7-10

Bright and Breezy.
Courtesy of Lisa Varuolo

Confetti Cutie.

Jeepers Creepers
1966
Date 1969-70

	NRFB	Mint/Complete
	200-275	90-115
		Avg
top		15-20
pedal pusher pants		10-15
sun visor w/ orange ring tie		35-40
rubber ball		35-40
shoes: blue Taiwan flats		7-10

Jazzy Jamys
1967
Date 1969-70

	NRFB	Mint/Complete
	75-125	30-45
		Avg
coral baby doll pajama top		7-10
coral baby doll pajama bottom		7-10
shoes: white scuffs		7-10

Hopscotchins
1968
Date 1969-70

	NRFB	Mint/Complete
	75-125	30-45
		Avg
long sleeve top		7-10
green shorts		7-10
vinyl belt		7-10
shoes: blue Taiwan flats		5-7

Knit Bit
1969
Date 1969-70

	NRFB	Mint/Complete
	125-175	75-100
		Avg
hot pink knit dress		10-15
blue knit belt		10-15
knit headband		5-7
hot pink tricot shorts		7-10
hot pink tricot socks		7-10
jump rope		7-10
hot fudge sundae		10-15
shoes: hot pink ankle boots		10-15

Ice Cream 'n Cake
1970
Date 1969-70

	NRFB	Mint/Complete
	125-175	75-100
		Avg
white blouse		10-15
blue skirt		7-10
blue under-shorts		7-10
pink vinyl belt		10-15
white lace thigh-high stockings		35-30
shoes: white Taiwan squishy flats		10-15

Jeepers Creepers.

Hopscotchins.

Ice Cream 'n Cake.

Pants 'n Pinafore
1971
Date 1969-70

	NRFB	Mint/Complete
	100-150	45-60
		Avg
orange romper		7-10
white apron		10-15
orange head scarf		15-20
shoes: translucent orange Taiwan flats		7-10

Drizzle Sizzle
1972
Date 1969-70

	NRFB	Mint/Complete
	125-175	75-100
		Avg
pink & green dress		10-15
clear vinyl raincoat		10-15
clear vinyl rain hat		15-20
shoes: clear boots w/ orange trim		7-10

Chilly Chums
1973
Date 1969-70

	NRFB	Mint/Complete
	125-175	75-100
		Avg
pink & yellow floral dress		10-15
pink coat		7-10
pink coat belt		7-10
pink cotton hood		15-20
sheer pink nylon pantyhose		25-30
shoes: yellow Taiwan squishy flats		35-40

Eeny Meeny Midi
1974
Date 1969-70

	NRFB	Mint/Complete
	125-175	75-100
		Avg
yellow dress		10-15
yellow tricot petti-pants		10-15
orange present		5-7
cardboard mirror		5-7
shoes: yellow Taiwan flats		5-7

Sunny Suity
#1975
Date 1969-70

	NRFB	Mint/Complete
	100-150	50-75
		Avg
yellow romper		10-15
yellow sun hat		15-20
shoes: yellow sandals		25-30

Pants 'n Pinafore.
Author's Collection

Chilly Chums.
Courtesy of Lisa Varuolo

Eeny Meeny Midi

Schools Cool
1976
Date 1969-70

	NRFB	Mint/Complete
	100-150	50-75
		Avg
floral print dress		10-15
pink princess telephone		7-10
hot pink fishnet tights		25-30
or opaque tights		25-30
shoes: hot pink ankle boots		10-15

Plaid City
1977
Date 1969-70

	NRFB	Mint/Complete
	150-200	75-100
		Avg
plaid coat		10-15
lime green jacket		15-20
lime green skirt		15-20
blue knit dickie		10-15
blue knit tam w/ pompon		25-30
shoes: translucent lime green Taiwan flats		15-20

Lots of Lace
1730
Date 1970

	NRFB	Mint/Complete
	75-125	30-45
		Avg
green & white dress		15-20
shoes: translucent lime green Taiwan flats		15-20

Budding Beauty
1731
Date 1970

	NRFB	Mint/Complete
	75-125	30-45
		Avg
hot pink organdy dress		15-20
shoes: hot pink Taiwan squishy flats		10-15
variation: light pink organdy dress		35-40
variation: hot pink dress w/ bodice fabric from Francie's Pink 'n Pretty # 3369		15-20

Daisy Crazy
1732
Date 1970

	NRFB	Mint/Complete
	75-125	30-45
		Avg
hot pink knit dress		15-20
yellow daisy tricot socks		15-20
or hot pink tricot socks		7-10

Rik Rak Rah
1733
Date 1970

	NRFB	Mint/Complete
	75-125	30-45
		Avg
blue short playsuit		15-20
skirt w/ yellow suspenders		10-15
shoes: blue Taiwan flats		5-7

Plaid City.
Courtesy of Lisa Varuolo

Budding Beauty.
Courtesy of Richard Chapman and Glenn Mandeville

Dramatic New Living Skipper Very Best Velvet Set
Sears Exclusive
1586
Date 1970-71

	NRFB	Mint/Complete/ no box/no doll
	825-875	475-525
		Avg
orange velvet dress w/ yellow organdy flounce		125-200
orange velvet coat w/ vinyl belt		50-75
sheer yellow pantyhose		50-75
shoes: yellow Taiwan flats		7-10

Twice As Nice
1735
Date 1970-71

	NRFB	Mint/Complete
	100-150	50-75
		Avg
blue & pink felt coat		10-15
blue & pink felt dress		10-15
pink felt hat w/ pompon		10-15
shoes: blue Taiwan flats		5-7

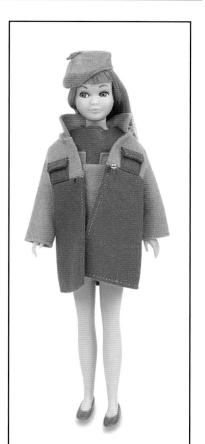

Twice As Nice.
Author's Collection

147

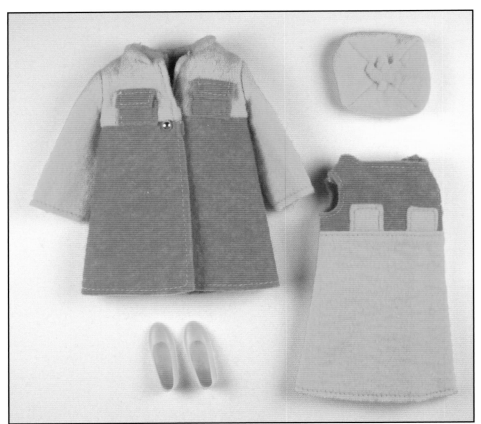

Twice As Nice..

Twice As Nice
1735
Date 1970-71
Variation orange & yellow

	NRFB	Mint/Complete
	175-225	100-150
		Avg
orange & yellow felt coat		25-30
orange & yellow felt dress		25-30
yellow felt hat w/ pompon		35-40
orange Taiwan flats		5-7

Super Slacks
1736
Date 1970-71

	NRFB	Mint/Complete
	100-150	50-75
		Avg
white blouse		7-10
red & white pants w/ red suspenders		10-15
red & white hat		7-10
shoes: red Taiwan flats		7-10

Velvet Blush
1737
Date 1970-71

	NRFB	Mint/Complete
	100-150	50-75
		Avg
red velour dress		15-20
white lace tights		20-25
shoes: white Taiwan flats		5-7

Super Slacks.
Author's Collection

Velvet Blush.
Courtesy of Lisa Varuolo

Fancy Pants
1738
Date 1970-71

	NRFB	Mint/Complete
	100-150	50-75
		Avg
light blue floral tank top		15-20
light blue floral pants		10-15
light blue shorts		15-20
hot pink bag w/ yellow flowers		10-15
shoes: light blue Taiwan flats		5-7

Fancy Pants
1738
Date 1970-71
variation hot pink & orange stripe

	NRFB	Mint/Complete
	425-475	300-350
		Avg
hot pink & orange stripe tank top		75-100
hot pink & orange stripe pants		75-100
orange shorts		75-100
hot pink bag w/ yellow flowers		10-15
shoes: orange Taiwan flats		5-7

Wooly Winner
1746
Date 1970-71

	NRFB	Mint/Complete
	100-150	50-75
		Avg
dress w/ yellow top		10-15
red wool coat		7-10
red wool hat		10-15
dark blue cotton socks		15-20
red shoulder bag		10-15
shoes: dark blue ankle boots		15-20

Pink Princess
1747
Date 1970-71

	NRFB	Mint/Complete
	100-150	50-75
		Avg
pink crepe dress		10-15
light green crepe coat		7-10
pink fur hat		10-15
sheer hot pink nylon pantyhose		25-30
shoes: white Taiwan flats		5-7

Triple Treat
1748
Date 1970-71

	NRFB	Mint/Complete
	175-225	75-100
		Avg
turquoise dress w/ multicolored bodice		7-10
hot pink long sleeved top		15-20
turquoise pants w/ multicolored waist		10-15
turquoise jacket		15-20
multicolored head scarf		15-20
shoes: turquoise Taiwan flats		5-7

Fancy Pants.
Variation hot pink &
orange & blue
version.
*Courtesy of
Lisa Varuolo*

Wooly Winner.
Author's Collection

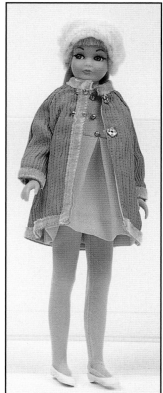

Pink Princess.
Author's Collection

Triple Treat
1748
Date 1970-71
Variation fabric same as black Francie's bathing suit

	NRFB	Mint/Complete
	200-275	75-100
		Avg
turquoise dress w/ multicolored bodice		10-15
hot pink long sleeved knit top		10-15
turquoise pants w/ multicolored waist		15-20
turquoise jacket		10-15
multicolored head scarf		20-25
shoes: turquoise Taiwan flats		5-7

Lemon Fluff
1749
Date 1970-71

	NRFB	Mint/Complete
	75-125	30-45
		Avg
yellow fuzzy robe w/ satin belt		10-15
yellow tricot pajama top		7-10
yellow tricot pajama bottom		7-10
shoes: yellow fuzzy scuffs		7-10

Young Ideas
Sears Exclusive
1513
Date 1970-73
Came in various colors and fabrics, add 20% for harder to find variations

	NRFB	Mint/Complete
	200-275	125-150
		Avg
party dress		10-15
fuzzy coat		10-15
suit jacket		10-15
suit short skirt		10-15
sleeveless knit shell		15-20
playsuit midi top		10-15
playsuit shorts		10-15
sheer pantyhose		25-30
knit knee socks		15-20
wrapped present		5-7
jump rope		7-10
invitation		10-15
shoes: green Taiwan flats		5-7
shoes: blue Taiwan flats		5-7
sometimes found with		
green granny glasses		35-40
green & yellow ball		20-25

Sweet Orange
3465
Date 1971-72

	NRFB	Mint/Complete
	50-75	25-30
		Avg
orange velour dress		10-15
shoes: white Taiwan flats		5-7

Tennis Time
3466
Date 1971-72

	NRFB	Mint/Complete
	75-125	30-45
		Avg
white tennis dress		10-15
tennis racket		3-5
tennis ball		5-7
white tricot socks		7-10
shoes: white Taiwan flats		5-7

Teeter Timers
3467
Date 1971-72

	NRFB	Mint/Complete
	75-125	30-45
		Avg
yellow cotton top		10-15
pink floral pants		10-15
yellow teeter board		20-25

Little Miss Midi
3468
Date 1971-72

	NRFB	Mint/Complete
	75-125	30-45
		Avg
turquoise long sleeved tricot top		10-15
yellow floral midi skirt		15-20
shoes: turquoise boots		7-10
green long sleeved tricot top variation		45-50

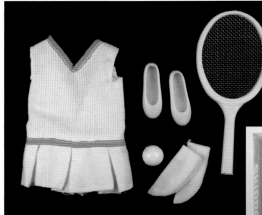

Sweet Orange.

Teeter Timers.
Courtesy of Lisa Varuolo

Tennis Time.

Little Miss Midi.

Ice Skatin'
3470
Date 1971-72

	NRFB	Mint/Complete
	75-125	40-55
		Avg
orange velour skating dress		10-15
white fur hat		10-15
orange tricot tights		15-20
shoes: white ice skates		7-10

Ballerina
3471
Date 1971-72

	NRFB	Mint/Complete
	75-125	40-55
		Avg
turquoise tutu w/ pink tulle		10-15
sheer pink pantyhose		15-20
turquoise ballet bag		5-7
shoes: pale pink ballet slippers		5-7

Double Dashers
3472
Date 1971-72

	NRFB	Mint/Complete
	75-125	40-55
		Avg
navy & orange cotton dress		15-20
navy & orange knit coat		10-15
shoes: orange translucent Taiwan flats		7-10

Lullaby Lime
3473
Date 1971-72

	NRFB	Mint/Complete
	50-75	30-45
		Avg
lime green tricot nightgown		10-15
shoes: hot pink & green scuffs		15-20

Goin' Sleddin'
3475
Date 1971-72

	NRFB	Mint/Complete
	175-225	75-100
		Avg
yellow fur hooded coat		7-10
yellow floral top		15-20
hot pink pants		15-20
hot pink sled		40-45
shoes: hot pink galoshes		15-20

Ice Skatin'.

Double Dashers.
Courtesy of Lisa Varuolo

Lullaby Lime.
Courtesy of Lisa Varuolo

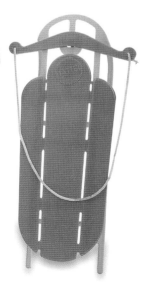

Goin' Sleddin'.
Courtesy of Lisa Varuolo

All Over Felt
3476
Date 1971-72

	NRFB	Mint/Complete
	175-225	75-100
		Avg
light blue & yellow felt coat		15-20
light blue & yellow felt dress		15-20
light blue felt hat		20-25
yellow felt purse		20-25
sheer light blue pantyhose		30-35
shoes: light blue Taiwan flats		5-7

All Over Felt
3476
Date 1971-72
Variation turquoise

	NRFB	Mint/Complete
	225-300	125-200
		Avg
turquoise & yellow felt coat		25-30
turquoise & yellow felt dress		25-30
turquoise felt hat		35-40
yellow felt purse		20-25
sheer blue pantyhose		30-35
shoes: turquoise Taiwan flats		5-7

Dressed In Velvet
3477
Date 1971-72

	NRFB	Mint/Complete
	175-225	75-100
		Avg
white & pink dress		15-20
pink coat w/ white fur trim		15-20
pink hat w/ white fur trim		15-20
sheer pink thigh high stockings		25-30
shoes: white Taiwan flats		5-7

Long 'n Short Of It
3478
Date 1971-72

	NRFB	Mint/Complete
	175-225	75-100
		Avg
long red coat		15-20
red & white sleeveless tricot mini dress		15-20
red & white tricot scarf		15-20
red & white knit tam		10-15
shoes: red boots		7-10

Long 'n Short Of It
3478
Date 1971-72
Variation same as Francie's Buckaroo Blues # 3449

	NRFB	Mint/Complete
	175-225	75-100
		Avg
long red coat		15-20
Buckaroo sleeveless tricot mini dress		20-25
Buckaroo tricot scarf		20-25
red & white knit tam		10-15
shoes: red boots		7-10

Nifty Nickers
3291
Date 1972

	NRFB	Mint/Complete
	75-125	50-75
		Avg
yellow long sleeved tricot top		15-20
blue floral knickers		15-20
red bib style vest		20-25
shoes: red boots		7-10

All Over Felt.
Courtesy of Lisa Varuolo

Dressed In Velvet.
Courtesy of Lisa Varuolo

Long 'n Short
Of It.
*Courtesy of
Lisa Varuolo*

Long 'n Short Of It.

Play Pants.

Party Fair.
Courtesy of Lisa Varuolo

Play Pants
3222
Date 1972

	NRFB	Mint/Complete
	75-125	50-75
		Avg
white floral shirt		10-15
denim short overalls w/ heart applique		15-20
red knit knee socks		10-15
shoes: white tennis		7-10

Dream Ins
3293
Date 1972

	NRFB	Mint/Complete
	50-75	30-45
		Avg
pink & white nightgown		10-15
shoes: hot pink scuffs		15-20

Dream Ins
3293
Date 1972
Variation white w/ yellow trim

	NRFB	Mint/Complete
	75-125	50-75
		Avg
white w/ yellow floral nightgown		25-30
shoes: yellow scuffs		15-20

Turn Abouts
3295
Date 1972

	NRFB	Mint/Complete
	75-125	50-75
		Avg
red & yellow long sleeve knit shirt		10-15
yellow knit shorts		10-15
red & yellow print tank top		10-15
red & yellow print pants		7-10
red & yellow print mini skirt		10-15
red & yellow print hat w/ red pompon		10-15
red shoulder bag		15-20
shoes: red Taiwan flats		5-7

Red White 'n Blues
3296
Date 1972

	NRFB	Mint/Complete
	125-175	75-100
		Avg
red, white & blue long dress w/ blue tie belt		25-30
red long sleeved tricot shirt		15-20
blue cotton shorts		20-25
red tricot knee socks		10-15
shoes: blue Taiwan flats		5-7

Party Fair
3297
Date 1972

	NRFB	Mint/Complete
	75-125	50-75
		Avg
pink velvet dress		10-15
white fur coat		10-15
sheer pink pantyhose		15-20
shoes: pink Taiwan flats		5-7

Super Snoozers
3371
Date 1972

	NRFB	Mint/Complete
	50-75	30-45
		Avg
pink & white pajama top		5-7
pink & white pajama bottoms		5-7
three yellow hair rollers		10-15
yellow mirror		3-5
yellow comb		3-5
yellow brush		3-5
shoes: yellow felt slippers		10-15

Red White 'n Blues.

Fun Runners
3372
Date 1972

NRFB	Mint/Complete
75-125	50-75
	Avg
yellow tricot top	10-15
denim jeans	5-7
red vinyl belt	10-15
red & white calico scarf	7-10
red round sunglasses	10-15
shoes: white tennis	7-10

Flower Power
Best Buy
3373
Date 1972

NRFB	Mint/Complete
50-75	30-45
	Avg
white cotton blouse	5-7
red & white calico long skirt	5-7
pink & white calico short skirt	5-7
red velveteen belt w/ black ties	10-15
shoes: red Taiwan flats	5-7

White, Bright 'n Sparkling
Best Buy
3374
Date 1972

NRFB	Mint/Complete
30-45	10-25
	Avg
white pique maxi coat	5-7
white shoulder bag	5-7
shoes: white Taiwan flats	5-7

Fun Runners.

SKIPPER GIFT SET

Prices reflect NRFB with doll and Mint/Complete prices reflect no doll, just fashion.

Skipper Party Time
1021
Date 1965-66

NRFB	Mint/Complete/ no box/no doll
825-875	575-650
	Avg
red velvet coat	7-10
red velvet hat	7-10
red velvet purse	7-10
satin & red velvet dress	15-20
headband gold elastic	15-20
white tricot gloves	10-15
white tricot socks	10-15
shoes: white Japan flats	5-7

Skipper On Wheels
1032
Date 1965

NRFB	Mint/Complete/ no box
575-650	375-425
	Avg
Barbie print body suit	15-20
Barbie print head scarf	15-20
red wrap skirt	7-10
cotton jacket	10-15
Capri pants	7-10
embroidered top	10-15
red wooden yo-yo	7-10
red plastic sunglasses	20-25
red boating hat	25-30
red scooter	45-50
red skateboard	35-40
shoes: Japan blue flats	5-7
shoes: red Japan flats	5-7
shoes: red roller skates	7-10

Skipper On Wheels. Shown missing skateboard.
Author's Collection

154

SKIPPER PAK

Beauty Bath
Pak
Date 1965-66

NRFB	Mint/Complete
125-175	50-75
	Avg
four pink hair rollers	10-15
pink floral terry cloth towel	5-7
pink floral terry cloth washcloth	10-15
pink scale	5-7
blue shower cap	5-7
gold talc box	5-7
blue powder puff	3-5
Kleenex tissue box	7-10
pink wash stick w/ orange sponge	7-10
pink mirror	3-5
pink comb	3-5
pink brush	3-5

Hat's 'n Hats
Pak
Date 1965-66

NRFB	Mint/Complete
50-75	25-40
	Avg
navy cotton duck hat	10-15
pink cotton hat w/ lace ruffle	10-15
straw hat w/ red satin ribbon	
*same as Red Sensation #1901	10-15
red velvet hat	
*same as Dress Coat #1906	5-7

Just For Fun
Pak
Date 1965-67

NRFB	Mint/Complete
125-175	60-85
	Avg
miniature Barbie doll	50-75
miniature red & white	
checkered Barbie doll skirt	10-15
wooden baseball bat	7-10
white baseball	5-7
jump rope	7-10
red wooden yo-yo	7-10
shoes: red roller skates	7-10
shoes: white skates	10-15

Party Pink
Pak
Date 1965-67

NRFB	Mint/Complete
50-75	25-40
	Avg
pink cotton dress	25-40

Shoe Parade
Pak
Date 1965-66

NRFB	Mint/Complete
50-75	25-40
	Avg
shoes: two pairs red Japan flats	5-7 each pair
shoes: two pairs black Japan flats	5-7 each pair
shoes: two pairs white Japan flats	5-7 each pair
shoes: royal blue Japan flats	5-7
shoes: light blue Japan flats	5-7
shoes: turquoise Japan flats	5-7
shoes: pink Japan flats	5-7
shoes: green Japan flats	5-7
shoes: yellow Japan flats	10-15

Wooly PJ's
Pak
Date 1965-67

NRFB	Mint/Complete
30-55	15-25
	Avg
red & yellow flannel pajama top	5-7
red & yellow flannel pajama bottom	5-7
yellow brush	3-5

Party Pink.

Hat's 'n Hats.
Never removed from box/card.
Author's Collection

Happy Times
Pak
Date 1970

	NRFB	Mint/Complete
	125-175	60-85
		Avg
hot pink record player		10-15
record red Barbie label		10-15
English book		5-7
Geography book		5-7
Arithmetic book		5-7
book strap		5-7
red pencil		10-15
tan pencil		10-15
jump rope		7-10
turquoise vinyl cap		7-10
shoes: turquoise boots		7-10

Nighty Nice
Pak
Date 1970

	NRFB	Mint/Complete
	50-75	25-40
		Avg
turquoise cotton pajama top		5-7
turquoise cotton pajama bottom		7-10
turquoise princess phone		5-7
face mirror		5-7
shoes: yellow scuffs		7-10

Side Lights
Pak

	NRFB	Mint/Complete
	125-175	60-85
		Avg
hot pink bag w/ yellow flowers		10-15
yellow knit tam hat		7-10
hot pink chain belt		15-20
yellow & pink vinyl belt		10-15
yellow vinyl belt		10-15
gold chain belt		15-20

Summer Slacks
Pak
Date 1970
Came in various colors and fabrics; add 20%+ for
harder to find variations

	NRFB	Mint/Complete
	50-75	25-40
		Avg
one-piece jumpsuit		10-15
yellow vinyl belt		10-15

Toe Twinkles
Pak
Date 1970

	NRFB	Mint/Complete
	60-85	30-45
		Avg
shoes: red Taiwan flats		5-7
shoes: royal blue Taiwan flats		5-7
shoes: turquoise Taiwan flats		5-7
shoes: pink Taiwan flats		5-7
shoes: clear boots w/ red trim		7-10
shoes: red ankle boots		10-15
shoes: hot pink ankle boots		10-15
shoes: green ankle boots		10-15

Undertones
Pak
Date 1970

	NRFB	Mint/Complete
	50-75	25-40
		Avg
pink panty		5-7
yellow panty		5-7
white panty		5-7
coral panty		5-7
nylon tights		15-20
pantyhose or stockings		15-20

Action Fashion
Pak
Date 1971

	NRFB	Mint/Complete
	75-100	50-65
		Avg
lavender round sunglasses		7-10
yellow transistor radio		10-15
white baseball		5-7
jump rope		7-10
shoes: white skates		10-15
shoes: red Taiwan flats		5-7
shoes: yellow galoshes		15-20

Check The Slacks
Pak
Date 1971
Came in various colors and fabrics, add 20%+ for
harder to find variations

	NRFB	Mint/Complete
	50-75	25-40
		Avg
bell bottom cotton pants		10-15
shoes: black Taiwan flats		5-7

Action Fashion.

Check The Slacks.

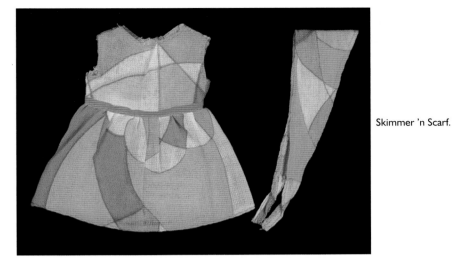

Skimmer 'n Scarf.

Skimmer 'n Scarf
Pak
Date 1971

	NRFB	Mint/Complete
	50-75	25-40
		Avg
multicolored cotton print dress		15-20
multicolored cotton print head scarf		15-20
pink floral cotton dress		15-20
pink floral cotton head scarf		15-20

The Slumber Number
Pak
Date 1971

	NRFB	Mint/Complete
	30-55	15-20
		Avg
flannel robe w/ white cord belt		15-20

Sporty Shorty
Pak
Date 1971

	NRFB	Mint/Complete
	50-75	25-40
		Avg
blue & white polka dot crop top		15-20
blue & white polka dot short skirt		15-20
shoes: orange Taiwan flats		5-7
pink, orange & white striped crop top		15-20
pink, orange & white striped short skirt		15-20
shoes: orange Taiwan flats		5-7

Some Shoes
Pak
Date 1971

	NRFB	Mint/Complete
	50-75	25-40
		Avg
shoes: white Taiwan flats		5-7
shoes: royal blue Taiwan flats		5-7
shoes: yellow Taiwan flats		5-7
shoes: orange Taiwan flats		5-7
shoes: red boots		7-10
shoes: red ankle boots		10-15
shoes: hot pink ankle boots		10-15
shoes: green ankle boots		10-15

Pose 'n Play Skipper And Her Swing-A-Round Gym
1179
Date 1972-73

	NRFB	Mint/Complete
	150-200	50-75
		Avg
slide down around pole		7-10
trapeze		7-10
double glider		7-10
single swing		7-10
base		7-10

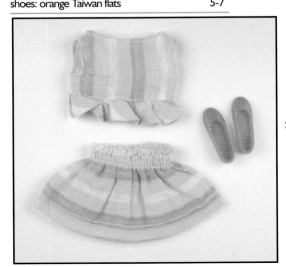

Sporty Shorty.

JAPANESE SKIPPER

Japanese Kimono
S2001
Date 1964

	NRFB	Mint/Complete
	N/A	975-1025 +
		Avg
white brocade w/ redand gold kimono		675 +
red and gold obi		275 +
white brocade w/ red & gold clutch purse		275 +
or red and gold drawstring purse		375 +
shoes: high Japanese sandals w/ socks		375 +

School days
Japanese version
S1907
1964-66

	NRFB	Mint/Complete
	N/A	450 +
		Avg
pink tight cotton knit sweater		275-325 +
* not the same as the American version		
white short sleeve blouse		7-10
pink flannel skirt		7-10
white or pink tricot knee socks		12-15
bowl of matching yarn		10-15
shoes: soft black Japan flats		10-15

SCOOTER GIFT SET

Scooter Cut 'n Button Costumes
1036
Date 1965-67

	NRFB	Mint/Complete/ no box/no doll
	575-650	375-425
		Avg
Sew-Free pink nightgown w/ cap		35-40
shoes: pink scuffs pink		15-20
Sew-Free red & navy coat w/ belt		30-35
shoes: red flats		
5-7		
Sew-Free blue gingham sun dress		35-40

FLUFF GIFT SET

Living Fluff Sunshine Special Set
Sear Exclusive
1249
Date 1971

	NRFB	Mint/Complete/ no box/no doll
	700-775	475-525
		Avg
red velveteen pants w/ red, yellow, blue rick rack		50-75
gold velveteen vest w/ red rick rack		50-75
multicolored full skirt		35-50
multicolored head scarf		50-75
gold opaque tights		50-75
shoes: gold Taiwan flats		35-50

Index

DOLLS

Allan, Bendable Leg, 33
Allan, Dressed Box, 33
Allan, 32
Angie 'n Tangie Pretty Pairs, 51
Barbie #1, 8
Barbie #2, 8
Barbie #3, 8
Barbie #4, 8
Barbie #5, 9
Barbie #6, 9
Barbie Sun Set Malibu, 20
Barbie with Growin' Pretty Hair, 19, 20
Barbie, American Girl High Color, 12
Barbie, American Girl Long Hair, 12
Barbie, American Girl Side Part, 12
Barbie, American Girl, 11, 12, 13
Barbie, Bubble Cut, 9, 10
Barbie, Busy 20
Barbie, Color Magic, 13
Barbie, Dramatic New Living, 18
Barbie, Dressed Box, 21, 22, 23
Barbie, Fashion Queen, 10
Barbie, Forget Me Not Baggy, 21
Barbie, Hair Fair, 14
Barbie, Hair Happenin's, 19
Barbie, Japanese Living, 18
Barbie, Live Action, 18, 19
Barbie, Living , 18
Barbie, Miss Barbie, 11
Barbie, Montgomery Ward, 20
Barbie, Ponytail, 8, 9
Barbie, Quick Curl, 21
Barbie, Standard, 14
Barbie, Swirl Ponytail, 11
Barbie, Talking Busy, 20
Barbie, Talking Nape Curl, 17
Barbie, Talking Side Ponytail, 16, 17
Barbie, Twist 'n Turn Flip, 16
Barbie, Twist 'n Turn, 15, 16
Barbie, Walk Lively, 20
Black Francie, 34
Brad, 43
Brad, Talking, 44
Buffy & Mrs Beasley, 50
Carnation Mail-Away, 10
Casey, Baggy, 39
Casey, 39
Chris, 46
Christie, Live Action, 43
Christie, 42
Christie, Sun Set Malibu, 43
Christie, Talking, 42, 43
Fluff, Living, 38
Francie Sun Set Malibu, 36

Francie with Growin' Pretty Hair, 36
Francie, Bendable Leg, 33, 34
Francie, Black, 34
Francie, Busy, 36
Francie, Hair Happenin's, 35
Francie, Japanese Sun Sun, 36
Francie, Japanese, 33
Francie, Japanese, 33
Francie, No Bangs, 35
Francie, 33
Francie, Quick Curl, 37
Francie, Short Flip, 35
Ginger, Growing Up, 38
Jamie, 46
Julia, Talking, 48
Julia, Twist N' Turn, 48
Kelley, Quick Curl, 47
Kelley, Yellowstone, 48
Ken Sun Set Malibu, 25
Ken, Bendable Leg, 24
Ken, Busy, 25
Ken, Dressed Box, 26
Ken, Flocked Hair, 23
Ken, Live Action, 24, 25
Ken, Mod Hair, 26
Ken, New Good Looking, 24
Ken, Painted Hair, , 23
Ken, Talking, 24
Ken, Walk Lively, 25
Ken,Talking Busy, 25
Lori 'n Rori Pretty Pairs, 50
Midge, Bendable Leg, 27
Midge, Dressed Box, 27, 28
Midge, 27
Midge, Wig Wardrobe, 27
Miss America, Kelloggs, 49
Miss America, Quick Curl, 50
Miss America, Walk Lively, 49
Miss America, Walking, 49
Nan 'n Fran Pretty Pairs, 51
P.J., Live Action, 40, 41
P.J., Sun Set Malibu, 41
P.J.,Talking, 40
P.J.,Twist 'n Turn, 40
Pretty Pairs, Angie 'n Tangie, 51
Pretty Pairs, Lori 'n Rori, 50
Pretty Pairs, Nan 'n Fran, 51
Ricky, 39
Scooter Dressed Box, 37
Scooter, Bendable Leg, 37
Scooter, 37
Short Flip Stacey, 42
Skipper, Bendable Leg, 29
Skipper, Dramatic Living, 30
Skipper, Dramatic New Living, 30
Skipper, Dressed Bog, 32
Skipper, Growing Up, 32

Skipper, Japanese, 28
Skipper, Malibu Sun Set, 31
Skipper, 28
Skipper, Pose 'n Play, 31
Skipper, Quick Curl, 31
Skipper, Re-issue, 30
Skipper, Special Living, 30
Skipper, Twist 'n Turn, 29
Stacey, 41
Stacey, Short Flip, 42
Stacey, Talking, 41
Steffie, Busy Talking, 47
Steffie, Busy, 47
Steffie, Walk Lively, 46
Tiff, Pose 'n Play, 38
Todd, Dressed Box, 45
Todd, 45
Todd, Prototype, 45
Truly Scrumptious, 49
Truly Scrumptious, Talking, 48
Tutti, 44
Twiggy, 39

BARBIE FASHIONS

Aboard Ship, 83
Accessory Pak, 63
Action Accents, 115
Add-Ons, 103
After Five, 62
All About Plaid, 126
All Americam Girl, 129
All that Jazz, 101
All The Trimmings, 120
American Airlines Stewardess, 61
Anti-Freezers, 113
Apple Print Sheath, 54
Apron And Utensils, 66
Baby Doll Pinks, 122
Ballerina, 61
Barbie Arabian Nights, 80
Barbie Baby-Sits (christening), 87
Barbie Baby-Sits, 68
Barbie Doll Accessories, 55
Barbie Hostess Set, 80
Barbie In Hawaii, 79
Barbie In Holland, 79
Barbie In Japan, 78
Barbie In Mexico, 78
Barbie In Switzerland, 78
Barbie Learns To Cook, 83
Barbie Skin Diver, 78
Barbie-Q Outfit, 56
Bathrobe, 72
Beau Time, 89
Beautiful Blues, 98
Beautiful Bride, 95

Belle Dress, 66
Benefit Performance, 91
Bermuda Holidays, 97
Best Bow, 96
Black Magic Ensemble, 77
Bloom Burst, 96
Blue Royalty, 114
Boudoir, 73
Bouncy Flouncy, 97
Bridal Brocade, 124
Bride's Dream, 68
Bright 'n Brocade, 116
Brrr-Furrr, 107
Brunch Time, 83
Bubbles 'n Boots, 125
Busy Gal, 60
Busy Morning, 69
Campus Belle, 74
Campus Sweetheart, 81
Candlelight Capers, 107, 108
Candy Striper Volunteer, 76
Cardigan, 65
Career Girl, 69
Carribean Cruise, 93
Change-Abouts, 103
Check The Suit, 118
Cheerleader, 75
Cinderella, 79
City Sparkler, 112
Close-Ups, 108
Cloud 9, 105
Club Meeting, 92
Coffee's On, 92
Cold Snap, 126
Color Coodinates, 73
Commuter Set, 54
Cook Ups, 96
Cool Casuals, 119
Costume Completers, 73
Cotton Casual, 54
Country Caper, 108
Country Club Dance, 83
Country Fair, 76
Country Music, 121
Crisp 'n Cool, 77
Cruise Stripes, 54
Dancing Doll, 83
Dancing Lights, 127
Dancing Stripes, 101
Debutante Ball, 91
Dinner At Eight, 67
Dinner Dazzle, 99
Disc Date, 83
Disco Dater, 97
Dog 'n Duds, 78
Dream Wrap, 103
Dream-Ins, 109

Dreamland, 92
Dreamy Blues, 112
Dreamy Pink, 102
Dress Up Hats, 73
Dressed-Up, 103
Dressmakers For Barbie, 73
Drizzle Dash!, 97
Drum Majorette, 75
Easter Parade, 58
Enchanted Evening, 60
Evening Enchantment, 95
Evening Gala, 90
Evening In, 123
Evening Splendor, 55
Evening Splendour, 76
Extra Casuals, 103
Extravaganza, 101
Fab City, 110
Fab Fur, 106
Fabulous Fashion, 92
Fabulous Formal, 107
Fancy Dancy, 102
Fancy Free, 67
Fancy That Purple, 131
Fancy Trimmings, 96
Fashion Accents, 115
Fashion Accents, 73
Fashion Bouquet, 114, 115
Fashion Editor, 84
Fashion Feet, 74
Fashion In Motion, 122
Fashion Luncheon, 90
Fashion Shiner, 94
Festival fashion, 121
Fiery Felt, 117
Finishing Touches, 111
Firelights, 104
Flats n' Heels, 103
Flats 'n Heels, 111
Flats 'n Heels, 89
Floating Gardens, 95
Floral Petticoat, 54
Flower Wower, 112
Flying Colors, 132
Foot Lights, 120
For Barbie Dressmakers, 73
For Rink And Court, 73
Formal Occasion, 95
Fraternity Dance, 84
Friday Night Date, 60
Fringe Benefits, 122
Fun At The Fair, 82
Fun Flakes, 124
Fun Fur, 126
Fun 'n Games, 80
Fun Shine, 131
Fur Sighted, 118
Fur stole With Bag, 66
Furry Friends, 115
Furry 'n Fun, 129
Garden Party, 62
Garden Tea Party, 77
Garden Wedding, 90
Gathered Skirt, 65

Gaucho Gear, 127
Gay Parisienne, 57
Glamour Group, 114
Glamour Hats, 88
Glimmer Glamour, 99
Glo Go, 108
Glowin' Gold, 130
Glowin' Out, 123
Going To The Ball, 73
Gold 'n Glamour, 86
Golden Elegance, 69
Golden Evening, 78
Golden Girl, 54
Golden Glitter, 129
Golden Glory, 86
Golden Grove, 106
Goldswinger, 106
Golfing Greats, 124
Good Sports, 129
Goodies Galore, 115
Graduation, 67
Great Coat, 113
Groovin' Gouchos, 121
Guinevere, 79
Gypsy spirit, 113
Happy Go Pink, 109
Harem-m-m's, 116
Have Fun, 88
Helenca Swimsuit, 64
Here Comes The Bride, 93
Holiday Dance, 85
Hot Togs, 128
Hurray For Leather, 103
Icebreaker, 63
Important In-Vestmant, 104
In Blooms, 125
In Stitches, 126
In The Swim, 72
International Fair, 89
Intrigue, 93
Invitation To Tea, 83
It's Cold Outside, 75
Jump Into Lace, 100
Jumpin Jeans, 74
Junior Designer, 82
Junior Prom, 81
Kitchen Magic, 88
Kitty Kapers, 127
Knit Accessories, 72
Knit Dress, 71
Knit Hit, 82
Knit Hit, 99
Knit Separates, 76
Knit Skirt with Glitter, 71
Knit Skirt, 72
Knit Slacks, 71
Knit Top And Shorts, 71
Knit Top, 70
Knitting Pretty, 69
Knitting Pretty, 76
Lamb 'n Leather, 114
Lame' Sheath, 72
Leather Weather, 107
Leisure Hours, 74

Leisure Leopard, 104
Lemon Kick, 113
Let's Dance, 59
Let's Have A ball, 110
Light 'n Lazy, 129
Lingerie Set, 66
Little Bow Pink, 105
Little Red Riding Hood & The
  Wolf, 79
London Tour, 90
Long 'n Fringy, 129
Loop Scoop, 112
Lovely Lingerie, 74
Lovely 'n Lavender, 130
Lovely Sleep-Ins, 113
Lunch Date, 76
Lunch Date, 87
Lunch On The Terrace, 89
Lunchtime, 92
Mad About Plaid, 115
Made For Each Other, 110
Madras Mad, 131
Magnificent Midi, 124
Magnificience, 86
Mainly For Rain, 129
Majestic Blue, 128
Make Mine Midi, 108
Masquerade, 67
Match Mates, 88
Matinee Fashion, 85
Maxi 'n Mini, 119
Midi Mood, 123
Midi-Magic, 109
Midi-Marvelous, 109
Midnight Blue, 81
Mini Prints, 97
Miss Astronaut, 87
Mix 'n Matchers, 96
Modern Art, 82
Mood For Music, 62
Mood Matchers, 117
Movie Date, 62
Movie Groovie, 108
Music Center Matinee, 91
Night Clouds, 101
Night Lighter, 125
Nighty Negligee, 56
Nite Lightning, 106
Now Knit, 112
Now Wow!, 102
O-Boy Corduroy, 131
On The Avenue, 86
On The Go, 73
Open Road, 61
Orange Blossom, 61
Orange Blossom, 67
Outdoor Art Show, 89
Outdoor Life, 84
Overall Denim, 131
Pajama Party, 76
Pajama Pow!, 97
Pan American Airways Stewardess,
  92
Pants-Perfect Purple, 130

Party Date, 69
Party Lines, 131, 132
Patio Party, 94
Peachy Fleecy Coat, 72
Peachy Fleecy, 54
Peasant Dressy, 127
Peasant Pleasant, 131
Pedal Pushers, 103
Perfect Beginnings, 120
Perfectly Plaid, 121
Pert Skirts, 88
Petti-Pinks, 111
Photo Fashion, 87
Picnic Set, 57
Picture Me Pretty, 130
Pink Fantasy, 108
Pink Formal, 87
Pink Moonbeams, 94
Pink Premier, 107
Pink Sparkle, 93
Plain Blouse, 65
Plantation Belle, 57
Pleasently Peasanty, 130
Plush 'n Warm, 127
Plush Pony, 110
Poncho Put-On, 123
Poodle Doodles, 127
Poodle Parade, 85
Pretty As A Picture, 89
Pretty Power, 108
Pretty Wild!, 96
Prima Ballerina, 117
Print Aplenty, 93
Purple Pleasers, 131
Purse Pak, 63
Rain Coat, 66
Rainbow Wraps, 118
Rare Pair, 113
Reception Line, 89
Red Delight, 88
Red Fantastic, 98
Red Flare, 62
Red For Rain, 123
Red, White 'n Warm, 105
Regal Red, 128
Registered Nurse, 61
Resort Set, 56
Riding In The Park, 92
Roman Holiday, 58
Romantic Ruffles, 109
Royal Velvet, 128
Ruffles 'n Lace, 74
Ruffles 'n Swirls, 116
Satin Blouse, 70
Satin Bolero, 70
Satin Coat, 70
Satin 'n Rose, 78
Satin 'n Shine, 132
Satin Skirt, 70
Satin Slacks, 70
Satin Slumber, 124
Satin Wrap Skirt, 70
Saturday Matinee, 81
Scene Stealers, 101

Scoop Neck Playsuit, 65
Scuba-Do's, 117
See-Worthy, 109
Senior Prom, 68
Set 'n Serve, 88
Shape Ups, 116
Sharp Shift, 119
Sheath Sensation, 61
Sheath Skirt And Telephone, 65
Sheath With Gold Buttons, 64
Shift Inti Knit, 104
Shimmering Magic, 91
Shirt Dressy, 105
Shoe Bag, 114
Shoe Pak, 72
Shoe Wardrobe, 73
Shoe Wardrobe, 80
Silk Sheath, 63
Silken Flame, 59
Silver Blues, 130
Silver 'n Satin, 99
Silver Polish, 105
Silver Serenade, 125
Silver Sparkle, 110
Simply Wow, 106
Singing In The Shower, 61
Skate Mates, 118
Skater's Waltz, 83
Ski Queen, 68
Skirt Styles, 96
Slacks, 65
Sleeping Pretty, 84
Sleepy Set, 131
Sleepytime Gal, 92
Slip, Panties, Bra, 63
Slumber Party, 85
Smart Switch, 96
Smasheroo, 103
Snap Dash, 101
Snugg Fuzz, 100
Soft 'n Snug, 127
Solo In The Spotlight, 60
Sophisicated Lady, 70
Sorority Meeting, 62
Sparkle Squares, 100
Special Sparkle, 114
Spectator Sport, 74
Sporting Casuals, 92
Sports Star, 130
Square Neck Sweater, 66
Square Neck Sweater, 72
Stormy weather, 76
Stripes Are Happenings, 99
Stripes Away, 95
Strollin' In Style, 121
Student Teacher, 82
Studio Tour, 94
Suburban Shopper, 58
Suede 'n Fur, 132
Sunday visit, 92
Sunflower, 93
Sun-Shiner, 111
Super Scarf, 123
Sweater Girl, 59
Sweet Dreams (1972), 129

Sweet Dreams (pak), 73
Sweet Dreams, 58
Sweetheart Satin, 130
Swingin' Easy, 69
Swingin' In Silver, 116
Swirly-Cue, 100
Tailored Tops, 88
Tangerine Scene, 111
Team-Ups, 102
Tee Shirt & Shorts, 64
Tennis Anyone?, 63
Tennis Team, 116
Terrific Twosome, 110
The Color Kick, 125
The Dream Team, 125
The Genuine Mink Stole, 80
The Lace Caper, 117
The Short Set, 131
The Ski Scene, 118
The Yellow Go, 98
The Zig Zag Bag, 126
Theatre Date (no hat), 78
Theatre Date, 69
Togetherness, 101
Top Twosome, 96
Tour-Ins, 111
Trailblazers, 101
Travel In Style, 98
Travel Together, 94
Tropicana, 93
Tunic 'n Tights, 102
Turtle 'n Tights, 125
Twinkle Togs, 102
Twinkle Town, 106
Two Piece Pajamas, 64
Two way Tiger, 122
Under Fashions, 89
Undergarments, 54
Underliners, 100
Underprints, 93
Vacation Time, 82
Velvet Venture, 105
Velvet-Teens, 98
Victorian Velvet, 126
Wedding Day Set, 58
Wedding Wonder, 101
Weekenders, 98
What's Cookin?, 75
White Magic, 77
White 'n With It, 129
Wild 'n Wintery, 124
Wild 'n Wonderful, 102
Wild Things, 127
Winter Holiday, 59
Winter Wedding, 110
Winter Wow, 105
Yellow Mellow, 105
Zokko!, 100

SKIPPER FASHIONS

Action Fashion, 156
All Over Felt, 152
All Prettied Up, 142
All Spruced Up, 140

Baby Dolls, 143
Ballerina, 151
Ballet Class, 133
Ballet Lessons, 133
Beachy Peachy, 139
Beauty Bath, 155
Bright and Breezy, 144
Budding Beauty, 147
Can You Play?, 137
Check The Slacks, 156
Chill Chasers, 137
Chilly Chums, 146
Confetti Cutie, 144
Cookie Time, 134
Country Picnic, 138
Cut 'n Buttons Scooter, 157
Daisy Crazy, 147
Day At The Fair, 134
Dog Show, 138
Double Dashers, 151
Dream Ins, 153
Dreamtime, 134
Dress Coat, 133
Dressed In Velvet, 152
Drizzle Sizzle, 146
Eeny Meeny Midi, 146
Fancy pants, 149
Flower Girl, 133
Flower Power, 154
Flower Showers, 139
Fluff, Sunshine Special, 157
Fun Runners, 154
Fun Time, 136
Glad Plaids, 141
Goin' Sleddin', 151
Happy Birthday, 136
Happy Times, 156
Hats 'n Hats, 155
Hearts 'n Flowers, 141
Hopscotchins, 145
Ice Cream 'n Cake, 145
Ice Skatin', 151
Jamas n' Jaunties, 140
Japanese Kimono, 157
Japanese School Days, 157
Jazzy Jamys, 145
Jeepers Creepers, 145
Junior Bridesmaid, 138
Just For Fun, 155
Knit Bit, 145
Land and Sea, 135
Learning To Ride, 139
Lemon Fluff, 150
Let's Play House, 138
Little Miss Midi, 150
Lolapaloozas, 142
Long 'n Short of It, 152
Lots of Lace, 147
Loungin' Lovelies, 138
Lullaby Lime, 151
Masquerade, 133
Me 'n My Doll, 135
Nifty Nickers, 152
Nighty Nice, 156
Outdoor Casuals, 135

Pants 'n Pinafore, 146
Party Fair, 153
Party Pink, 155
Party Time, 154
Patent 'n Pants, 143
Perfectly Pretty, 144
Pink Princess, 149
Plaid City, 147
Platter Party, 135
Play Pants, 153
Popover, 140
Posy Party, 142
Quick Changes, 144
Rain Or shine, 135
Rainy Day Checkers, 137
Real Sporty, 143
Red Sensation, 132
Red, White 'n Blues, 153
Right In Style, 140
Rik Rack Rah, 147
Rolla Scoot, 139
School Days, 133
School Girl, 136
Schools Cool, 147
Scooter, Cut 'n Buttons, 157
Ship Ahoy, 136
Shoe Parade, 155
Side lights, 156
Silk 'n Fancy, 132
Skating Fun, 134
Skimmer 'n Scarf, 157
Skimmy Stripes, 142
Skipper On Wheels, 154
Sledding Fun, 139
Some Shoes, 157
Sporty Shorty, 157
Summer Slacks, 156
Sunny Pastels, 134
Sunny Suity, 146
Sunshine Special Fluff, 157
Super Slacks, 148
Super Snoozers, 153
Sweet Orange, 150
Swing-A-Round Gym, 157
Tea Party, 137
Teeter Timers, 150
Tennis Time, 150
The Slumber Number, 157
Toe Twinkles, 156
Town Togs, 137
Trim Twosome, 143
Triple Treat, 149, 150
Turn Abouts, 153
Twice As Nice, 147, 148
Underpretties, 132
Undetones, 156
Velvet Blush, 148
Velvet 'n Lace, 142
Very Best Velvet, 147
Warm 'n Wonderful, 143
What's New At The Zoo?, 137
White, Bright 'n Sparkling, 154
Wooly PJ's, 155
Wooly Winner, 149
Young Ideas, 150